The State and the Family

The State and the Family

A Comparative Analysis of Family Policies in Industrialized Countries

ANNE HÉLÈNE GAUTHIER

CLARENDON PRESS · OXFORD

Oxford University Press, Great Clarendon Street, Oxford OX2 6DP

Oxford New York

Athens Auckland Bangkok Bogotá Buenos Aires Calcutta
Cape Town Chennai Dar es Salaam Delhi Florence Hong Kong Istanbul
Karachi Kuala Lumpur Madrid Melbourne Mexico City Mumbai
Nairobi Paris São Paulo Singapore Taipei Tokyo Toronto Warsaw
and associated companies in Berlin Ibadan

Oxford is a registered trade mark of Oxford University Press

Published in the United States
by Oxford University Press Inc., New York

First published 1996
First published in paperback 1998

British Library Cataloguing in Publication Data
Data available

Library of Congress Cataloging in Publication Data
Data available

ISBN 0–19–828804–2 (hbk)
ISBN 0–19–829499–9 (pbk)

10 9 8 7 6 5 4 3 2 1

Printed in Great Britain
on acid-free paper by
Bookcraft (Bath) Ltd,
Midsomer Norton, Somerset

PREFACE

The preparation of this book has spanned several years — several years during which I have benefited from the encouragement and support of numerous colleagues and friends. First of all from the ex-Warden and Fellows of Nuffield College (Oxford). Their encouragement during the initial phases of this book has been greatly appreciated and has undoubtedly helped to sustain my motivation. To David Cox, John Goldthorpe, and their colleagues, my sincere gratitude. I am also most grateful to my colleagues at the Department of Applied Social Studies and Social Research in Oxford who have during the last two years repeatedly expressed their interest in this project. A warm thank-you to Stein Ringen whose support has been so appreciated, as well as his comments on an earlier version of this book. Acknowledgements also to Teresa Smith, Mavis McClean and Susan McRae for their very useful comments on a preliminary version, and to Jason Pearce of Oxford University Press.

My most sincere words go however to my family and close friends who have supported me throughout this project. And above all, my deepest thanks to Peter. His patience, support, and computer expertise, have all been faultless. In Alaska, during the long summer nights when the sun was refusing to set early, he spent hours with me improving the presentation of the manuscript. To him, my relatives, colleagues and friends, I am most indebted.

Anne Hélène Gauthier

Haines, July 1995.

EDITORIAL NOTE ABOUT TERMINOLOGY

This cross-national study has drawn on numerous foreign sources. Translations of quotations made by the author are indicated in the text by 'a.t.' (author's translation). In the case of specific legislation, title of commission, or name of interest group, no translation was provided when it was judged not to alter the reader's understanding of the argument. In the case of specialized terms, English equivalents were used — even though this has sometimes meant using expressions which may be unfamiliar to the reader. This is notably the case with the terms 'denatality' (i.e. low fertility, usually below-replacement), 'depopulation' (i.e. population decline), and 'familism' (i.e. quality of being strongly family-oriented) which have been translated directly from French.

Mention should also be made of the expression 'Anglo-Saxon countries', taken here to refer to the English-speaking countries of Australia, Canada, Ireland, New Zealand, United Kingdom, and the United States. Aware that this expression is inadequate for several of these countries, it has nevertheless been used in the absence of a satisfactory alternative. The only distinction made concerns Canada where the province of Quebec has been treated as a separate unit of analysis, in Chapters 8 and 9, in order to reflect its distinct family policy.

CONTENTS

TABLES

FIGURES

1

INTRODUCTION

Since the turn of the century, the family in industrialized countries has undergone major transformations. Family size has declined, marriage has become less popular, unions are increasingly unstable, and women are no longer assuming their traditional role of housewives. At the same time, governments' policies in respect of families have also greatly changed and expanded. Initially limited to mothers' and children's protection, governments' policies have been steadily expanded to cover other aspects of family life and a larger number of families, as well as to provide a higher level of support. As a result, what is often referred to today as family policy encompasses a large number of measures and benefits ranging from measures specifically targeted at working parents, lone-parent families, or low-income families, to those more generally designed to support all families with children. It is the trends over time in these measures and their inter-country variations which are analysed in this book. The task is an ambitious one: a period of study covering a whole century, a comparison between twenty-two countries, and an analysis of the interplay between demographic changes and family policy. The story is however a fascinating one. What is now called family policy has changed considerably over the past 100 years, revealing major similarities in the ways governments have viewed and supported families, as well as revealing major dissimilarities shaped by country-specific events, ideologies, and circumstances.

1.1 Focus of the book

Until recently, the term 'family policy' had been very little used in political and academic circles. Alva Myrdal, in Sweden, talked of 'a programme for family security' in 1939, and a German article published in 1958 used in its title the term 'Familienpolitik' (Wuermeling, *et al.* 1958). During these early years, references to family policy or to governmental programmes for families were however mainly confined to restricted circles. The situation changed substantially from the mid-1960s. For example, the Swedish government set up a Family Policy Committee in 1965, the Austrian government set up a Family Policy Advisory Council in 1967, while suggestions for the adoption of a national family policy were made in the United States during a series of hearings on the family in 1973 (Kamerman and Kahn, 1978). More recently, the setting up of an Observatory on National Family Policies by the Commission of the European Community in 1989, and the declaration of 1994 as the Year of the Family by the United Nations, have denoted an increasing interest for family issues and policies. The adoption of a Governmental Plan on the Family in France in 1990, the setting up of a Commission on the Family in Italy in 1981, and the publication of a report on family policy in Switzerland in 1982, are further examples of the increasing attention devoted by governments to family issues.

What is fascinating here is that this trend is not limited to one country but has instead a clear international dimension. For instance, in both the United States and Norway the family has received considerable attention in recent years despite their very diverging welfare system and political ideology. While President Carter in the United States, in an address before his election in 1977, stressed the role of his government to 'honor, support, and strengthen the American family' (Steiner, 1981: 14), the Norwegian Minister of Consumer and Administration Affairs in 1974 stressed the need to 'conduct an adequate family policy which meets the needs of the family' (Ve Henriksen and Hotter, 1978: 60). The fact that families in both the United States and Norway have undergone major transformations in recent decades may in part explain this common interest in families. The recent emergence of family issues and family policy on the political agenda of governments may be seen as a response to major transformations undergone by the family. These transformations and their resulting welfare needs, have challenged existing systems of state support for families. The decline in fertility, the increase in divorce rate and lone-parenthood, and the entry of women into the labour force, have all reduced the relevance of systems of state support aimed at traditional families. New instruments and policies were needed in order to better support new families.

The changes in family policy over time therefore reflect a strong interplay between demographic changes on the one hand, and government policies and responses on the other. This interplay operates at two levels: (i) at the macro level, by which the decline in fertility and the resultant ageing of the population have put new pressures on the welfare states and led governments to consider policies either to increase fertility or to adjust the existing institutions to the new age structure of the population; and (ii) at the micro level, by which the transformations undergone by the family have called for further state support at the family level. What will be argued here is that demographic changes have been a major driving force in bringing population and family issues to the political agenda and in influencing the development of related policies. Moreover, it will be further argued that the similarities observed across industrialized countries in the transformations undergone by the family in part explain the similarities observed in the responses of governments to these transformations. On the other hand, demographic changes are obviously not the only determinants of policies, and a series of other factors may have shaped the responses of specific governments to demographic changes. For example, although fertility in France and Britain has declined to similar levels in the 1980s, and although the percentage of births outside wedlock has risen to similar levels in both countries, governments in these two countries have reacted differently to the situation. They have both paid attention to the transformations undergone by the family, but their responses to these transformations have widely differed. While the French government has been aiming at increasing its general support for families, especially from a pro-natalist perspective, the British government has been instead concentrating its effort towards families in greater need. And while the British government has viewed the increase in the number of lone-mothers very negatively, in France lone-mothers have been less stigmatized. Undeniably, beyond the common interest in family issues, the specific responses of governments to these issues have varied widely across countries. In addition to the social and demographic transformations undergone by families, other factors such as political ideology and history have obviously influenced the responses of governments.

These two considerations, a cross-national common interest in the family, coupled with cross-national divergences in the responses to the new demographic situation, are the basis of this book. More precisely, the following questions will be driving the analysis:

1. How has family policy developed over time? What have been its main landmarks and trends?
2. How have these trends in family policy varied across countries? And what models of family policy have emerged?

In other words, through an analysis of specific family policy indicators, this book aims at analysing the changes in family policy in different countries and their interplay with demographic changes, assessing the degree of continuity or discontinuity of policies, and emphasizing their inter-country differences or similarities. The book concludes by drawing a typology of models of family policy on the basis of the observed inter-country differences.

1.2   Family policy inputs and outputs

In the following chapters, family policies are analysed from two angles: outputs and inputs. The first approach refers to specific measures, legislation and orientation, which characterized a government's support for families; the second refers to factors which may have influenced the policy-making process and the adoption of specific policies.

Policy outputs

The measures which have been adopted by governments, and which fall under the label of family policy, are numerous. Measures related to health, education, and social security, all include a family dimension and are part of what Kamerman and Kahn (1978) refer to as the cash-benefit package. Adopting a wider definition of family policy, one may even include measures in the fields of environment, consumer policy, and transport which may also affect directly or indirectly the standard of living of families. A narrower perspective is adopted here, and restricts family policy to measures directly targeted at families with dependent children, either as part of social security benefits or other social policy sectors. It includes measures such as direct and indirect cash transfers for families with children (e.g. family allowances, means-tested family benefits, tax relief for dependent children); benefits related to work and granted to workers with family responsibilities (e.g. maternity and paternity leave, child-care leave) ; services to families (e.g. day-care centres, after-school care); other services and benefits for families with children in the field of housing, education, and health; and legislation directly affecting families (e.g. abortion, divorce, child alimony).

On the basis of this definition, two main points need to be stressed. First, it is important to note that, although the term family policy would suggest a comprehensive, explicit, and well co-ordinated policy, in reality what is included under this label encompasses an amalgam of measures, benefits, and legislation, not necessarily part of a coherent political framework. Although in recent years there has been a tendency in several countries to better co-ordinate the different benefits and services to families, in most countries family policy still continues to be a disparate package of measures. None the less, the terms 'family policy' and 'state support for families' will here be used as synonyms, even if the former term would suggest a more comprehensive and co-ordinated package of services and benefits.

The second point to stress is the overlap between family policy and population policy. As will be shown later, the recent decline in fertility has attracted much attention at the governmental level and has led in some cases to the adoption of measures aimed at increasing fertility. Although part of a family policy, these measures — because of their demographic objective — are also part of a population policy, more precisely of a pro-natalist policy. In this book, discussions relating to fertility decline (population issues) are separated for the purpose of the analysis from those related to other transformations undergone by the family (family issues). It should however be borne in mind that measures adopted under the heading of pro-natalist policy or under that of family policy tend to be similar. They often provide similar levels of support, and use similar redistributive instruments. Only their objectives clearly distinguishes them.

Policy inputs

The emergence of family policies will be analysed with reference to two main theories found in the welfare state literature: one emphasizing the role played by social and economic factors, the other emphasizing the role played by key social actors. The first of these theories is referred to as the industrialization thesis, and sees changes in the economic environment (e.g. industrialization, urbanization) as having created new welfare needs, and having led to the development of the welfare state (Wilenski, 1975). When applied to the family policy sphere, this thesis sees changes in the social, economic, and demographic environment of families as major driving forces in the development of the governments' family policy. Decline in fertility, the rediscovery of poverty, and the increase in the participation of women in the labour force have created new welfare needs and led governments to extend and reform their system of state support for families.

The second theory is referred to as the conflict thesis and sees the conflict between different social actors (e.g. labour unions, interest groups, employers) as having been the major driving force behind the development of the welfare state (Korpi, 1978). In the family policy sphere, actors such as family associations, women's groups, and academics may have influenced the development of policies, if not directly at least indirectly, in raising the visibility of family issues, and contributing to their emergence on the governments' agenda. Such indirect influence has been pointed out by Bock and Thane (1991), with references to women's groups, and by King (1973), and McIntosh (1983) with reference to other information diffusers.

1.3 Literature on family policy

Despite the increasing interest in family policy, literature in this field, especially from a comparative perspective, is very sketchy. Studies have either compiled data on specific family benefits at one point in time, or analysed the development in family policy in a specific country, but have rarely done so by combining both a historical and a cross-national perspective. The main studies are reviewed below and have been classified in two groups: those which analyse the orientations, nature, and objectives of family and population policies, and those which have adopted a more quantitative approach in focusing on specific family policy indicators.

Family and population policies

One of the first comparative analyses is David Glass' *Population Policies and Movements in Europe* published in 1940. Written at a time when the decline in fertility was causing concern in several countries, this account of population policies is based on the work the author did as Secretary of the Population Investigation Committee in England. More precisely, it aimed at 'indicating by examples the extent to which governments have in the past been concerned to promote population growth' (Glass, 1940: 86). To do so, Glass examines the cases of England, France, Belgium, Germany, Italy, and the Scandinavian countries. In all cases, evidence clearly suggests that the decline in fertility had captured the attention of governments. Countries however differed greatly in their responses to the situation. While in France and Belgium, as well as Italy and Germany, under the Fascist regime, measures were explicitly taken to promote childbearing, in Scandinavia similar measures were accompanied by a relatively liberal access to family planning (at least in Sweden and Denmark). A sharp contrast, thus, appears between the first group of countries, which aimed at increasing fertility through cash incentives but also through restricted access to contraception, and the second group which adopted a more liberal attitude to family planning. England appears here in a third category of countries which, although concerned with its declining fertility, did not adopt in the 1930s and 1940s any measure that aimed at encouraging fertility. In fact, as will be seen in the following chapters, England has continuously been opposed to any pro-natalist intervention.

Following the Second World War, interest in comparative analysis of family policy seemed to have partly faded. Major developments in the welfare state were taking place, and perhaps surprisingly, there was seemingly less interest in comparisons between countries. It was only in the 1970s that interest for this field of research re-emerged. Berelson's edited book *Population Policies in Developed Countries* published in 1974, and Kamerman and Kahn's edited book *Family Policy; Government and Families in Fourteen Countries* published in 1978, still figure among the classics in this field. Adopting a case by case approach, both provide highly valuable information on the development of population and family policies in several countries. From a methodological and substantive point of view, these two books are also interesting as they identified some key elements to analyse and compare policies across countries. Berelson's analysis extends beyond measures aimed at supporting families to other policies and actions more generally related to population growth and population distribution (e.g. mortality and migration). In each country study, the sections on fertility, assistance programmes to families, and legislation on abortion and contraception, bring together very valuable information. This information is however simply reported country after country, while a genuinely comparative analysis is missing. Reading across the chapters, one nevertheless becomes aware of major inter-country differences, for example between France's explicitly pro-natalist policy and Britain's greater concern about the risk of over-population.

Similar inter-country differences are apparent in Kamerman and Kahn's (1978) study of family policy. Based on an analysis of the general orientation of policies, they present parallel descriptions of the trends in family policy in each of the countries studied. A genuinely comparative analysis appears in a separate chapter in which the authors highlight some of the inter-country similarities and dissimilarities in the nature of policies. Taking into account the goals, objectives, and motives of policies, as well as the related instruments and institutions, they distinguish three categories of countries: (i) those with an explicit and comprehensive family policy (e.g. France, Norway, and Sweden) ; (ii) those with an explicit but more narrowly focused family policy (e.g. Austria, Denmark, Germany, Finland); and (iii) those with an implicit and reluctant family policy (e.g. Canada, United Kingdom, United States). Since this first study, Kamerman and Kahn have published other comparative studies on various aspects of family policies (see Kamerman and Kahn, 1981; 1987; 1991; Kamerman, Kahn, and Kingston, 1983). These studies contain a wealth of information while at the same time highlighting the difficulties involved in carrying cross-national analysis, especially when family policy takes different orientation in different countries.

In recent years, other books based on case-study have also provided valuable information, for example, *Maternity and Gender Policies: Women and the Rise of the European Welfare States 1880s-1950s* edited by Bock and Thane (1991); and *Women and Social Policies in Europe: Work, Family and the State* edited by Lewis (1993). But again, the country by country approach adopted in these volumes suffers from a lack of comparability and makes difficult any genuine cross-national analysis. In contrast, the study of family benefits in eighteen countries by Wennemo (1994) is an unusual attempt to bring together comparable data and to account for the development of family benefits, both cross-nationally and historically.

Family policy indicators

Already in the pre-World War II period, compilations of data on family benefits in a large number of countries were published. The publication on national legislation concerning the employment of women before and after childbirth by the League of Nations in 1919 was one of the first examples of a systematic comparison of family policy indicators in various countries. The International Labour Office then followed with a series of publications which documented and compared cross-nationally family allowances (in 1924), welfare benefits (in 1933), and legislation relative to the protection of pregnant workers (in 1939). A comparison of family allowance schemes also appeared in Britain in Rathbone's book *The Disinherited Family* in 1924. In this book, the author, who would eventually campaign for the introduction of family allowances in Britain, drew her information from various sources including an article on 'The Family Wage System Abroad' published in the British *Labour Gazette* in March 1923. In the United States, comparisons of social security schemes were also published from an early date, starting in 1940 with a publication of the Social Security Administration entitled *An Outline of Foreign Social Insurance and Assistance Laws*. In recent years, these early sources have been complemented by various compilations of social security benefits published by the Commission of the European Community, the Council of Europe, and the United States Social Security Administration.

With regard to more analytical work, a comparison of family benefits was made by Kamerman and Kahn (1982) in their analysis of income transfers in eight countries (Australia, Canada, France, Israel, Sweden, United Kingdom, United States, West Germany). In this study a series of family benefit indicators was analysed for different types of families defined according to their structure (one- or two-parent families), number of children, and income. Although limited in geographical scope, this approach ensured a high level of comparability and was able to highlight major differences across countries in the levels of support for families. A similar methodology has been used by Bradshaw and Piachaud in their 1980 study of *Child Support in The European Community*, and more recently in Bradshaw *et al.* (1993). In the latter study, a comparison of state support for families in fifteen countries (including family allowances, social security contributions and income tax, education, health services, and housing) is carried out for thirty-six different family types. This is by far the most extensive study in terms of the types of benefits considered — although methodologically some of these benefits turned out to be difficult to quantify and compare (e.g. housing and health). Once again, the results show great disparities in the ranking of countries depending on the type of family considered. On the basis of these results the authors conclude their study by ranking countries according to their level of support for families (Bradshaw *et al.* 1993: 265). The following ranking emerges[1], placing:

- Luxembourg, Norway, France, and Belgium among the most generous countries;
- Denmark, Germany, the United Kingdom, Australia, and the Netherlands among countries with middling provision;
- Portugal, Italy, United States, Ireland, Spain, and Greece among countries with the least generous child benefit package.

[1] It is based on average rank orders for all family types, before housing costs. The categories shown here list countries by decreasing rank order (i.e. more generous countries first)

This methodology, which takes account of the structure and income of families, as well as different types of benefits, ensures a high level of comparability across countries. By focusing on the level of provision, and not on the general aim of policies, it however gives only a one-sided image of family policy. For example, it does not highlight the very different types of policy conducted in France and in Norway, despite similar levels of support for families, or the explicit reluctance of the British government to interfere in the social policy sphere, despite middling support for families.

1.4 Methodological approach

The methodological approach adopted here places emphasis on the historical development and the comparative dimension of family policy analysis, rather than on the details of specific policies. In particular, it reflects the dual objective of (i) comparing the development, nature, and objectives of family policies, as well as their actual level of support, and (ii) analysing the social and political context in which these policies were introduced. The methodology consequently represents a trade-off between a study limited in geographical scope and time dimension, but presenting a detailed account of policies, and a study adopting a larger geographical scope and time dimension.

Time perspective and geographical scope

With regard to the time perspective, the analysis starts with the turn of the century, at a time when the first elements of family benefits were introduced, for example, legislation protecting pregnant workers, or setting up the first mother and child welfare centres. As argued, these first measures of state support for families had an influence on subsequent developments, and introduced significant differences across countries. With regard to the geographical scope, the countries studied include all OECD (Organization for the Economic Co-operation and Development) countries with the exception of Turkey and the former Yugoslavia. It includes all western European countries, as well as Australia, Canada, Japan, New Zealand, and the United States. In total, twenty-two countries were included in the analysis. Such a geographical scope undoubtedly represents one of the most extensive studies of family policy published so far. On the other hand, this geographical scope, coupled with the long time perspective, imposed serious limitations.

Interplay between demographic changes and policies

Demographic trends, it is argued in this book, have acted as major catalytic elements in calling for new or reformed policy measures. This interplay between demographic changes and policies operates at different levels and through different processes. There is first the information stage. Publication of data showing a strong decline in fertility or a future decline in population size may reveal trends which were unknown or had been overlooked, and may capture government and public attention. Throughout the book, references will therefore be made to instances when the publication of studies on demographic and social trends have led to widespread discussion. A good example is provided by the publication by Alva and Gunnar Myrdal in the 1930s of *Crisis in the Population Question*, which not only initiated a series of discussions and debates about the nature and consequence of fertility decline, but eventually also led to the setting-up by the government of the first Population Commission. As shown in this book, such an interaction between demographic change, scientific study, and policy response was not unique but was instead found in several countries and at several points in time.

The response of the public and other social actors to these new demographic trends is another channel through which the interplay between demographic changes and policies operates. If a priori one may think that demographic trends, by their nature, may be beyond public preoccupation, the analysis of interest groups' activities and public opinion data reveal that demographic changes have instead in many instances received a high level of attention among the public. This is particularly well illustrated by the case of France where pro-natalist preoccupation was not limited to specialist circles but was widespread among the population. In the pre-World War II period in France, pro-natalist associations attracted a large membership and undeniably exerted pressures on the government for specific action. In the literature on family policy the role of non-governmental actors has often been overlooked. But as revealed in this book they have in several instances contributed greatly in raising the profile of specific population and family issues and directly or indirectly exerted influence on governments.

The response of governments to demographic changes is the last component of this demography–policy interaction. Beyond the family policy legislation itself, the book also examines the attitudes of governments towards population and family issues as revealed through initiatives, such as research commissions, special committees, or conferences, set up or mandated by governments to study specific population or family issues. The weight, mandate, and structure of such governmental initiatives obviously varied enormously. For example, a commission on the family may not have carried the same weight as a departmental conference on the family. Furthermore, a commission on the family in one country may not have carried the same weight as a similar commission in another country. Although aware of this serious limitation, such governmental initiatives are used here as illustrations of a certain interest of governments in family issues. In particular, attention is paid to initiatives launched in relation to family policy, the decline in fertility, and the transformations of the family. Although these initiatives did not necessarily represent a step towards policy formulation, they illustrate the general context in which changes to family policy were introduced. In the analysis, this information is supplemented by statements from politicians which made explicit some of their views concerning either the transformations of the family or the role of the government in supporting families.

Family policy indicators

The analysis of the interplay between demographic changes and policies is complemented by an analysis of the historical trends and country-specific variations in selected key indicators of family policy. The number of measures falling under the label of family policy is wide. For reasons related to data comparability and accessibility, the analysis is restricted to the following key indicators:

- Cash benefits: family allowances, means-tested family benefits, and tax relief for dependent children.
- Work-related benefits: maternity leave, and child-care leave.
- Child-care facilities.
- Legislation on abortion and contraception.

For these key indicators, time-series as well as comparative tables will be presented. This information will be complemented by references to other family policy components, for example in health or housing. The combination of quantitative information on time-series, and more qualitative information on other family policy components, will underline the main themes which dominated the political agenda of governments over time as well as the different phases in the development of family policy.

Sources of data

The studies referred to in Section 1.3 were used to document the landmarks in family policy development and to construct time-series on key family policy indicators. The volumes edited by Flora (1986–7) *Growth to Limits*, as well as the reports produced by the Observatory on National Family Policies of the Commission of the European Community since 1989 were also used. In addition, data on key family policy indicators were obtained from relevant authorities in each country. In view of the very scattered and disparate nature of this information, its compilation in a comprehensive and comparative format has been a considerable task. Within each chapter this information is discussed and summarized in tabular form. It is however obvious that this information is not exhaustive. This will be particularly apparent in the discussion of recent trends in family policies. As a result of increasing interest in family issues, the number of state interventions and initiatives directed at families have been numerous, and only selected ones are reported.

1.5 Outline of the book

For the purpose of the analysis, the book follows a chronological structure and has been divided into three parts.

Pre-World War II period: The first period covers the development in family policy from the turn of the century until the Second World War. It was a period concerned about endemic poverty, and which led to the first measures of support for families, especially in the field of preventive health (e.g. maternity leave, mother and child welfare centres). During this first period, concern was also expressed with regard to the steep fertility decline. In terms of concrete measures, however, very few countries adopted explicit pro-natalist measures. Family allowances were introduced in several countries, but in most cases, they were not seen as being part of any pro-natalist policy.

Post-World War II period until the mid-1970s: The period immediately following the Second World War saw the expansion and consolidation of the welfare state.

Family allowances were extended to all countries, provisions related to maternity leave were strongly upgraded, and several other measures were introduced as part of new social insurance and social assistance programmes. The type of family policy which developed during this period was based on a one-earner family and assumed the presence of the mother at home. This family policy, based on the post-war principles of universality and full employment, was then questioned from the 1960s following a series of changes in the economic, social, and demographic environment of families. While the rediscovery of poverty in the 1960s was to call for a partial abandonment of the principle of universality and the introduction of a series of targeted benefits, women's claims for greater freedom and independence from the 1960s were to challenge both the existing male-breadwinner society, as well as the strict legislation regarding access to family planning. From there on, the new family policy was to gradually liberalize access to family planning, as well as to gradually acknowledge the presence of women and mothers in the labour force. The developments were however slow, and clear divergences appeared between countries during this period. Finally, the onset of deep family transformations from the mid-1960s, including fertility decline, was to bring back population and family issues to the political agenda.

Post-1975 period: The unprecedented low levels of fertility in the 1970s, along with further transformations of the family, gave further visibility to population and family issues. Talk of fertility decline and population ageing became widespread during this period. While acknowledging the potential economic consequences of this new demographic situation, very few countries however adopted an explicit pro-natalist stance. Instead, and in view of the new plurality of families, governments adopted a pro-family attitude, without explicit reference to low fertility. Creating a more supportive environment for families, or a more 'family-friendly' policy, became the order of the day in several countries. Strong inter-country differences were also noticeable during this period.

1.6 Limitations of this study

As a result of the methodological approach adopted in this book, several limitations are apparent. First, although contextual elements are taken into account in this analysis, their effect on the development of family policy is not systematically tested. It is suggested, for example, that the decline in fertility and the increase in the participation of women in the labour force acted as major driving forces behind the development of family policy. But their influence is not assessed through statistical techniques. Neither is the role of governments, and more precisely the whole policy-making process fully accounted in this study. It is instead left as a grey area, a missing link between contextual changes and family policy. To have assessed the role of governments would have required an analysis of a completely different kind.

Second, the heavy reliance on country monographs as a basic source of information obviously underlies the non-exhaustiveness of this study. This will be particularly apparent in the sections on governmental initiatives and those on key social actors. A team of experts from each country under analysis would have been necessary to fill in the missing information. Third, in this analysis of family policy some major components have been omitted. For instance, little acknowledgement is made of the support provided by the governments in the field of health, education, housing, and specific social services. The analysis is also very short with regard to means-tested family benefits, and benefits targeted at specific categories of families (e.g. lone-parent families). Lack of information, and above all space constraints, have prevented a more extensive analysis. Finally, and in contrast to Kamerman and Kahn (1982), Bradshaw and Piachaud (1980), and Bradshaw *et al.* (1993), no analysis is made of the differential support provided by governments according to the type of family (e.g. family structure and income of families). While a 'type of family' methodology would undoubtedly be very interesting, it was impractical considering the time dimension and the geographical scope of this study.

2

EARLY FEARS OF POPULATION AND FAMILY DECLINE

The end of the nineteenth century and beginning of the twentieth witnessed major transformations of the economic and social structure of societies. Industrialization, urbanization, and an increased level of literacy all had a major impact on families. For some families, the new economic era brought prosperity and was synonymous with an improved standard of living. For the large majority, however, the new urban and industrial setting was instead synonymous with dismal living and working conditions. Dwellings were crowded, ill-equipped, and the working environment of most workers was highly hazardous. It is in this context that the issues of poverty and high level of mortality, especially among children, became the subject of major political concern. If the relief of poverty had been so far left to philanthropic organizations, the magnitude of the problem was now calling for governmental interventions. This problem was in fact to lead to the first governmental initiatives directed at the family.

The other topic which attracted attention during this period was the decline in fertility. In several countries, since the 1870s, fertility had been declining and projections were suggesting an eventual decline in population size. At a time when population growth was perceived as a guarantee of military and political power, such a situation did not leave governments indifferent. Conversely, it led to major initiatives related to fertility and population growth. Finally, the third theme which attracted attention during this period was that of birth-control. Promoted by some feminists and Malthusian associations, the issue aroused serious controversies. In most countries, governments were to take a firm stance in making illegal the use of contraception and abortion. Essentially private in essence, the issue was thus aired in public and led to major governmental initiatives.

Three major themes therefore dominated the social agenda of governments in the pre-World War II period: poverty and its links with the well-being of families, fertility and population growth, and birth-control. These three themes are analysed in this chapter and in Chapter 3. They emerged as major political issues in several countries, while at the same time leading to much varied responses from governments.

2.1 Changes in the demographic environment of families

The period ranging from the 1870s to the Second World War witnessed major transformations of the family. Among them, the steep decline in family size was to attract much attention. Fertility, which averaged four or five children per woman in the early 1870s, had declined to levels close or even below two children per woman in the 1930s (see Table 2.1).

Table 2.1 *Total fertility rate in selected countries, 1870–1945*

Country	Average number of children per woman					
	1870	1885	1900	1915	1930	1945
England and Wales	4.94	4.16	3.40^a	2.59	1.95	2.04
France	3.42	2.90	2.89	1.50	2.27	2.28
Germany	—	—	4.77^a	2.89^b	1.88	1.53
Japan	—	—	—	—	4.73	4.63^c
Sweden	4.11	4.34	4.06	3.06	1.96	2.59
United States	—	—	—	—	2.56	2.48

^{a}: 1903 data. ^{b}: Average 1913–18. ^{c}: 1947 data. —: Data not available.

Sources: Festy (1979), Teitelbaum and Winter (1985).

In France, where fertility had already declined to three children per woman by 1870, this situation especially attracted attention. As will be seen in section 2.2, it was accompanied by explicit calls for pro-natalist action. In France, as in other countries, high fertility and rapid population growth were seen as a guarantee of economic growth and military power, and the decline in fertility was thus seen as a threat to nations. This threat was made even more concrete with the publication of projections carried out in the 1930s that suggested an eventual decline in population size. For example, population projections carried out in England in the early 1930s suggested an eventual decline of the population from a maximum of 45 million in 1936 to 41 million in 1956 and 33 million in 1976 (Leybourne, 1934). Such a projection was assuming a continuous decline in fertility until the mid-1940s and a stabilization thereafter at a very low level. As can be seen in Figure 2.1, this projection turned out to be very far from reality. The population never declined, and as a result of the post-war baby-boom, reached 54 million in 1976 instead of the projected 33 million. At the time of the publication of these projections, there was however no sign of fertility reversal and an eventual population decline appeared inevitable. The prospect of population decline was even more worrying when the projection was carried out over a longer time horizon. Assuming a continued decline in fertility until 1985 and of mortality until 1965, the population of England and Wales was projected to decline to 31.5 million by 1975, to 17.7 million by 2000, and to 4.4 million in 2035 (Glass, 1940: 84).

In fact, Britain was of no exception as declining trends were also suggested in projections carried out for Finland, Germany, Norway, and Sweden (Glass, 1940). Similarly, in the United States, six of the ten projection scenarios published in

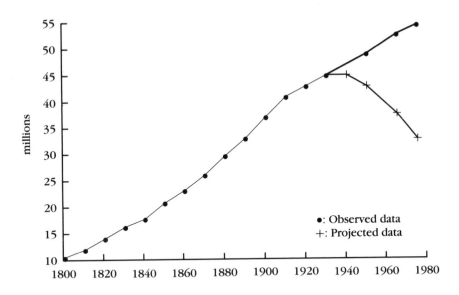

Fig. 2.1 *Population growth, England and Wales, 1800-1976*

1933, as part of a presidential Committee on Social Trends, anticipated that the country's population would begin to decline before 1980 (Spengler, 1978: 47-8). This prospect of depopulation did not leave governments indifferent. For instance, in Finland the government signalled a strong interest in the field of population following the statement, by the chief actuary of the Central Statistical Office in 1934, that the national population would never reach the four million mark (Lindgren, 1978). As will be seen in section 2.2, governments in several countries launched major initiatives in response to this perceived demographic threat.

The prospect of population decline was however only one aspect of the problem, as it was also suggesting some deeper transformations of the family. This was especially apparent from the increasing recourse to means of birth-control as well as from the upward trends in divorce and illegitimate births. For example, estimates for Britain showed a four fold increase in the divorce rate between 1901 and 1930, from 0.5 to 2.1 divorces per 10,000 married people (Glass, 1934). As commented on by Glass, 'the trend does show that by 1914 divorce had established itself as a social phenomenon' (ibid. 293). As an institution, the family was threatened, and much discussion was to take place about its future. The decision by the British Broadcasting Corporation (BBC) to hold a series of radio broadcasts on the recent changes in family life in 1932 illustrated well this widespread concern (Beveridge *et al.*, 1932). These new demographic trends appeared as major issues on the political agenda and were to lead to major governmental initiatives.

2.2   The fear of population decline

The issue of population growth is obviously not a recent one. Already at the end of the eighteenth century, Malthus was advocating the reduction of population growth in order to avoid the evils of over-population. A century later, the sharp reduction in fertility raised however concerns of a completely different nature: that of depopulation. [1]

What prompted concern?

This new fear of population decline was prompted by a series of factors. First, there was the demographic trend itself. In a period particularly disturbed by political and international conflicts, the sharp decline in fertility was seen as particularly harmful to the economic, political, and military power of countries. This was particularly true in France where the early onset of fertility decline was perceived as a real military handicap. While at the turn of the twentieth century, fertility in Germany was still around five children per woman on average, it was already less than three children per woman in France (Festy, 1979). The military consequences of this demographic trend were greatly feared by the French government. As argued by Spengler, the French defeat in the war against Prussia added further to these concerns:

The defeat of France by Prussia in 1870–1871 greatly intensified the alarm of French social scientists and publicists at the low level of natality and population growth in France, in contrast to the levels prevailing in other large European countries ... In France alarmist prophecy and warning became the order of the day, and French writers predicted almost with one voice that France's slow demographic growth relative to that of Germany, Russia and England would give these countries a cumulative military and political preponderance over France. (1979: 121–2)

As a result, pronatalism tended to occupy a major place on the political agenda in France, from a very early stage. This perceived link between high fertility and military power was in fact sustained during both the First and Second World Wars. For example, commenting on France's military situation in 1940, Marshall Pétain stated that the low fertility rate had weakened the military power of the country, and was consequently a real national threat: 'Too few children, too few weapons, too few allies, these are the causes of our defeat' (Ogden and Huss, 1982: 294).

In other countries, the decline of fertility, and especially its decline to unprecedented low levels in the 1930s, also raised serious concern about the future of the population and about the underlying societal malaise. These concerns were exacerbated by the publication in the 1930s of population projections showing the

[1] Although in the 1920s and 1930s pro-natalist ideology represented a major departure from the Malthusian ideology of the nineteenth century, it was not without precedents. Conversely, fears of population decline and populationist ideologies have a very long history. For instance, already at the time of the Roman Empire, the three laws of Augustus had a strong pro-natalist orientation in aiming at 'raising or restoring the prestige of the family by suppressing behaviour which might lead to family disintegration ... and at encouraging the raising of children' (Glass, 1940: 86–7). In the seventeenth and eighteenth centuries, state interventions aiming at encouraging population growth were also introduced in countries such as France, Spain, Prussia, and Italy (Glass, 1940).

future decline of the population if the current trends were to be maintained. Titles such as *The Menace of Underpopulation* by Charles (1934) in England, and *The International Birth Strike* (Der internationale Geburtenstreik) by Kahn (1930) in Germany, further illustrate the alarmist way in which the problem was addressed.

Another event which stimulated much discussion about the consequences of the demographic trends was the publication of *Crisis in the Population Question* (Kris i Befolkningsfragan) in Sweden in 1934. Written by Alva and Gunnar Myrdal, two prominent members of the Swedish Social Democratic party, the book was to have a considerable impact. According to Glass: 'it dropped a bombshell among the thinking public of Sweden ... Discussion of the book was widespread and early in 1935 there were radio broadcasts on the population question' (1940: 317). In fact, the influence of this book was not limited to Sweden but also reached a wider public with the publication of a Danish translation in 1935 and a Norwegian one in 1936. An English version, entitled *Nation and Family* followed in 1947 (Myrdal, 1947). The message conveyed in the book was clearly pro-natalist. However, in many ways, it represented a departure from previous studies. First, like other studies, it stressed the negative consequences of low fertility, but this was seen as a natural and rational response of young people to the problems of poverty, unemployment, and sub-standard housing conditions. Contrary to common belief (coming especially from the Church), the main cause of fertility decline was economic and not moral (Carlson, 1990: 86). Secondly, in addition to the quantitative aspect of population, which was central to previous discussion, the Myrdals also stressed the importance of population quality. More than a third of children, they estimated, were unwanted: a situation which was clearly unacceptable. What they advocated therefore was a policy based on voluntary parenthood. More concretely, they urged the repeal of the 1910 Swedish legislation prohibiting the sale and display of contraceptives, and the dissemination of birth control information. Thus, for the first time, a pro-natalist policy was coupled with free access to birth control. Thirdly, while pro-natalists in France and in other countries were opposed to women joining the labour force, the Myrdals acknowledged the right of women to combine paid employment and child-rearing. In particular, they advocated the implementation of reforms which would allow women to combine work and family more easily and without penalty (ibid. 89). Fourthly, while cash benefits were usually given preference by pro-natalists, as a way of reducing the cost of children and encouraging childbearing, the Myrdals were more in favour of in-kind benefits on the grounds that they best enhanced the quality and well-being of children. Finally, population policy and family policy were not seen as independent and isolated issues, but rather as integrated: 'A population program must work itself into the whole fabric of social life and must interpenetrate and be interpenetrated by all other measures of social change. The population crisis must, if we are to react rationally, make us rethink all social objectives and programs' (Myrdal, 1947: 2).

Public reactions to the population question

The changes in the demographic situation aroused much interest among the public. In particular, this period saw the setting up of several pro-natalist and family orga-

nizations concerned by the question. For example, Glass (1940) in his account of
population policy in Europe refers to several pro-natalist organizations in Belgium,
England, Finland, France, and Germany. The pro-natalist lobby was especially strong
in France, where the issue had already led to the creation of the first pro-natalist
organization in 1896. The Alliance nationale pour l'accroissement de la population
française was particularly influential, especially during the First World War when it
had over 35,000 members, and ran major pro-natalist campaigns (Tomlinson, Huss,
and Ogden, 1985: 25). Messages such as 'More tombstones than cradles! . . . This
is what is waiting for us in the future if we do not adopt immediately a genuine
pro-natalist family policy' (a.t.), and posters showing the declining military force
of France as compared with that of Germany, denoted the alarmist nature of the
Alliance's messages (Tomlinson, Huss, and Ogden, 1985; Ogden and Huss, 1982).
The Alliance's lobby for pro-natalist state intervention was also echoed in the Ligue
pour le relèvement de la natalité française, and in other groups organized around
family associations. The spread of these associations was considerable and by 1922,
in addition to the Alliance, its 8 national associations, and 62 regional associations,
there were also in France 11 Federations of Large Families, and 1 national federation
of single groups of large families (Spengler, 1979: 128). In fact, as will be seen in
later chapters, the family movement is still more active in France than in most other
countries.

Elsewhere in Europe the issue of fertility and population decline also led to
the setting up of pro-natalist associations. In Belgium, the issue was taken up by
the Ligue contre l'infécondité (which later became the Ligue Nationale contre la
dépopulation). Founded in 1911 by medical doctors concerned about low fertility,
this league however never reached the prominence of the French Alliance. Glass
(1940) reports that at the end of 1911, the Ligue had only 544 members, including
92 clerics and 244 doctors. In England, the increasing use of birth-control, and
falling fertility, led also to the foundation of a pro-natalist organization, the League
of National Life, which was described as 'explicitly antagonistic to birth control
and in favour of raising the birth-rate' (ibid. 84).

If academics and policy-makers were alarmed by the decline in fertility, the
existence of these associations and lobbies clearly reflected a wider concern. The
public was however not unanimous, or entirely devoted, to the population question. Pronatalist associations, for example, typically managed to recruit only a limited number of members, France being the exception. Moreover, they were also
confronted with much anti-natalist feeling. In particular, one should not forget that
despite the existence of pro-natalist associations, neo-Malthusianist views were still
strongly prevalent, especially at the turn of the century. Malthusian associations
were widespread and were calling for liberal access to birth-control.

Government reactions to the population question

Prompted by scientific studies which revealed the likely decline of the population,
and influenced by pro-natalist lobbies, governments in several countries responded
to the population question by setting up specific commissions and committees.
Some of these state initiatives for the pre-1945 period are reported in Table 2.2.

Table 2.2 *Population-related governmental initiatives, pre-1945*

Country	Start-up year	Title of initiative
Australia	1903	Commission on Birth Rate and Infant Mortality
Denmark	1935	Royal Commission on Population
Finland	1937	Population Committee
France	1902	First Commission on Depopulation
	1912	Second Commission on Depopulation
	1920	High Council on Births
	1939	Chief Committee on Population
Japan	1927	Commission for the Study of the Problems of Population and Food Supply
	1939	Institute of Population Problems
	1941	Pro-natalist policy
Sweden	1935	First Population Commission
	1941	Second Population Commission
Switzerland	1940	Conference for the Protection of People and the Family
United Kingdom	1944	Royal Commission on Population
United States	1929	Presidential Committee on Social Trends
	1938	Report on Population Trends
International	1927	League of Nations' First Conference on Population
	1939	League of Nations' Population Committee

Again, the French government was to take a major lead by launching two commissions on depopulation, in 1902 and 1912. No concrete results however came out of these commissions, the report of the first one having been published only in private journals, the second having been dismantled by the outbreak of World War I (Bourgeois-Pichat, 1974: 548). But, they were only the beginning of what would be a long history of French pronatalism. With the continuous fears of depopulation, further state initiatives were launched including, in 1920, the foundation of the High Council on Births, and its ninety departmental councils. The mandate of the High Council was clearly pro-natalist: 'to find ways of increasing the birth rate, develop child care, protect and honour families, and in a more general way, prepare such legislative proposals, decrees, and memorandums' (ibid. 549). As will be seen later, the Council was responsible for the adoption of specific measures, including the prohibition of abortion and contraception. Being composed of thirty members at the national level, and thirteen in each departmental council, the Council had however a structure which prevented the adoption of rapid resolutions.

In contrast, its successor, the Chief Committee on Population, set up in 1939, comprised only five members, and was placed directly under the authority of the President. Its flexibility and status meant that the Committee was able to present a proposal after only four months which would become the cornerstone of French pro-natalist policy. The mandate of the Committee was specific: 'to elaborate a global reform, aimed at coordinating and stimulating the action of various ministerial departments to combat depopulation and to provide the country with a family code' (a.t., United Nations, 1989a: 33).

Alongside the French initiative, governments in Scandinavia also initiated concrete actions, especially as a response to the discussions and debates prompted by the Myrdals' book. In fact, Gunnar Myrdal himself played an active role in the first Swedish Commission on Population set up in 1935. Through what was described as his dominating influence, he was able to convince the Commission to endorse most of the measures he advocated. As reported by Carlson: 'Myrdal's energy and intellectual power dominated Wohlin [the chairman] and the commission's work. Despite numerous compromises on language, the commission reports and recommendations closely followed the Myrdal line' (1990: 132). A partial abandonment of these lines however characterized the final report of the Commission. When the Myrdals left the country in 1938 to go to the United States, the Commission felt free to diverge partly from its previous stance. The final report of the Commission in fact included several sections which displeased Gunnar Myrdal, notably the negative connotation it gave to means of birth-control (ibid. 181).

Following the Swedish example, similar population commissions were set up in Denmark and Finland. In Britain, the demographic question led to the launch of the Royal Commission on Population in 1944. Contrary to its French and Swedish counterparts, the British Commission did not take an alarmist stance. Instead, the Commission was careful to point out that despite the low fertility level, the population would continue to grow for some decades. No explicit pro-natalist actions were therefore recommended; the proposals included in the report instead falling under the heading of 'measures to promote family welfare' (Britain, 1949). No concrete political actions followed either as this report was never debated in Parliament, and most of its specific recommendations ignored (Simons, 1974: 620). In fact, over the next decades the British lack of interest in demographic issues was to persist — a situation which contrasts sharply with its French neighbour.

In Switzerland, the population question was raised by the government in 1940 through the holding of a Conference for the Protection of People and the Family. Demographic concerns, eugenic ideologies, and the desire to protect the family, were the main motives behind this initiative (Switzerland, Office Fédérale des assurances sociales, 1982: 21). Concerns about population growth were also at the forefront of the political agenda of the Fascist regimes of Spain, Germany and Italy. The utmost importance of the population factor, along with eugenic principles, was stressed by all leaders. For Mussolini, 'demographic power conditioned the political and thus also the economic and moral power of nations' (Glass, 1940: 220). Such a view was echoed in Spain, with the belief that 'either Spain increases her birth-rate or her ascension to the rank of great powers will be halted' (Nash, 1991: 162). While in Germany, the Minister for Propaganda argued that 'the goal is not children at any cost, but racially worthy, physically and mentally unaffected children of German families' (Bock, 1991: 240). As will be seen later in this chapter, these views led to the adoption of policies which included both positive and coercive measures.

Outside Europe, the fall in fertility also raised concern. In Australia, concerns about this situation led to the setting up, in 1903, of a Royal Commission on Birth Rate and Infant Mortality by the Legislative Assembly of New South Wales — a Commission which was to stand as the first public enquiry of its kind in an English-speaking country (Borrie, 1974: 276). Here also population growth, economic, and political dominance were strongly linked. According to one member of this commission, the demographic problem was of an 'overwhelming importance to the Australian people, and its satisfactory solution will depend whether this country is ever to take its place amongst the great nations of the world' (ibid. 276-7). The increasing immigration to Australia, and the outbreak of the war, meant however that no legislative action followed the findings of the Commission. In the United States, concerns about the declining population growth, and especially its consequences for the economy, were also examined by the government. The Committee on Social Trends, established in 1929, carried out population projections which were to emphasize the likelihood of a future population decline. The population issue was subsequently examined under the auspices of the National Resources Committee. In its demographic report, entitled *Problems of a Changing Population* (1938), the committee took a reassuring stance in concluding that 'transition from an increasing to a stationary or decreasing population may on the whole be beneficial to the life of the Nation' (Westoff, 1973: 740). The similarities of this conclusion with that reached some thirty years later by the Commission on Population Growth and the American Future (see Chapter 7) are striking.

In Japan, the initiatives launched by the government in 1927, 1939, and 1941 reflected an early concern for population issues. It also reflected a major shift from Malthusian considerations to pro-natalist ones. While the 1927 Commission devoted its effort to the problems of rapid population growth and the necessary food supply, the general political atmosphere in the 1930s viewed rapid population no longer as a problem but as being essential for the future of the nation (Muramatsu and Kuroda, 1974: 706). An increase in the country's birth rate was urged, and a target of 100 million inhabitants was set, to be reached by 1960 (from its 72 million in 1945) (United Nations, 1984: 270). In addition, action was taken through the setting up an Institute of Population Problems in 1939, and the adoption of a national pro-natalist policy in 1941.

Finally, at the international level, the population question was also given considerable attention. In the 1920s it was however mainly issues of optimal population, food supply, and rapid population growth which tended to dominate the debate. This was particularly apparent at the First World Population Conference held in 1927.[2] Problems related to a rapidly growing population were also central to members of the Committee on Population Trends, set up by the League of Nations in

---

[2] At the First World Population Conference, the issue of birth control was not raised, despite the wishes of its main initiator, Margaret Sanger (Symonds and Carder, 1973: 12-3).

1939. However, at the first meeting of this committee, references to the problems facing governments with a diminishing population were also made, thus representing a major departure from previous agendas (Symonds and Carder, 1973: 19).

Undeniably, the decline in fertility attracted much attention, not only in pronatalist France, but elsewhere in Europe and abroad. In a wartime context, a strong demography was seen as essential to ensure military and national power. A faltering demography, on the other hand, was perceived as a clear handicap. Against this general trend, there were cases which stood out, especially that of France, with its explicit pro-natalist orientation, and Sweden, with its more socialist one. As will be seen in subsequent chapters, these two distinct orientations tended to be maintained over time, and gave family policy in these countries a distinct flavour.

2.3 The fear of family decline

For many, the decline in fertility was the manifestation of a much deeper problem: that of the crisis of the family. The rise of feminism, the questioning of paternal authority, and the loss of some of the traditional functions of the family, all raised concern in both academic and political circles. Although these concerns were closely linked with those described in the previous section, they tended to concentrate less on the quantitative side of the question, and more on its qualitative side. It was the future of the family as an institution, and not only as a strict reproductive unit, which was perceived as being threatened.

The thesis of family decline

The transformations undergone by the family from the end of the nineteenth century led to much speculation about its future. For one school of thought, these changes reflected the weakening or decline of the family. The family, it was argued, had over time lost some of its main functions (Popenoe, 1988: 195-9). It was no longer fulfilling its functions of:

- Reproduction, as reflected by the decline in fertility.
- Production, owing to the separation of the home and work spheres.
- Co-operation or support, as it was no longer looking after its poor and aged members.
- Socialization, as a result of the introduction of compulsory education.

In other words, the family, as an institution, had been weakened. This was the basis of the family decline thesis, as reflected in the writings of French sociologists Auguste Comte (1798-1857), Frédéric Le Play (1806-82), and Alexis de Tocqueville (1805-59). For them, following the industrial revolution and the French Revolution, the family had grown unstable and weak. This was especially apparent with regard to paternal authority which, it was argued, had been eroded as the result of increasing state intervention into family life. A full restoration of patriarchal authority taken away by the Revolution was consequently advocated (ibid. 12). The family decline thesis was given great prominence in the work of Emile Durkheim (1858-1917) who pictured the family as a 'weakened institution'. The state, he predicted, would be called on to intervene increasingly into family life in view of the decline in the marriage bond and in the weakened solidarity between family members. This increasing state intervention would in turn further reinforce family decline (ibid. 18–20). Considering the contemporary and later influence of these French scholars, it is not surprising to find that major concerns about the family, at the official level, were more forcefully expressed in France at that time than anywhere else.

This pessimistic view came under strong criticism in the United States where the changes in the family were given a different interpretation. As reported by Popenoe, scholars such as William Graham Sumner, Lester Frank Ward, and Franklin Henry Giddings, while acknowledging the fact that the family had lost its traditional functions, expressed a 'common faith in the adaptability of the family as an institution to new social conditions' (1988: 22). This view became central to the thesis of Ernest Burgess (1866–1966), and later on, of Talcott Parsons (1902–79). While agreeing with the loss-of-functions thesis, Burgess saw the family as very strong since it had survived previous economic and political crises. He therefore concluded that: 'it seems safe to predict that the family will survive, both because of its long history of adaptability to changing conditions and because of the importance of its function of affection-giving and receiving in personal satisfaction and in personality development' (Burgess and Locke, 1945: 750).

In other circles, the changes undergone by the family were also a matter of major concern. While in Sweden Myrdal (1947) described the situation as reflecting a 'family crisis', in England Charles (1934) talked about the 'twilight of parenthood'. At least four reasons were suggested to explain these changes. The family had declined as a result of:

1. The rise in feminism, and in particular as a result of the increasing tendency of women to seek independence through employment.
2. A decline in religious faith which had led to family disorganization and individualism.
3. The increase in both the cost of living and the cost of children, themselves caused by factors such as urbanization, legislation against child labour and legislation on compulsory education.
4. The increasingly deliberate use of family limitation encouraged by birth-control propaganda, and a more liberal attitude to the use of such contraceptive means. This factor was explicitly referred to in the Report of the British Commission on Population (Britain, 1949: 40).

Two sets of factors were therefore suggested to account for the new situation: moral (rise in feminism and individualism, loss of religious faith, liberal attitude to contraception), and economic (rise in the cost of children, and poverty). The measures which were adopted to counteract this situation tended to focus on these two aspects (see Chapter 3). On the one hand, they aimed at strengthening the family in its moral sense, and on the other, at further supporting it through financial support. In addition, measures were taken in several countries to curb the use of contraceptives.

Public reactions to family decline

If the issue of population decline had led to the creation of several pressure groups, the fear of family decline also led to the setting up of a specific lobby. This lobby tended however to be less alarmist than the pro-natalist one. Instead of raising the 'family decline' banner, it instead concentrated on the economic and social difficulties which families were experiencing. In particular, it fought for increasing state support for families. Three main camps were active in this field: family associations, welfare associations, and women's ones. An extensive analysis would be needed to do full justice to the role played by these associations in the development of state measures for families. The analysis below is restricted to a review of only some of these associations and their activities. A selected list of associations directly concerned with families and children, and founded in the pre-World War II period, is reported in Table 2.3.

The family associations: In several countries family associations seem to have attracted a large membership, much larger than the pro-natalist ones. For example, the *Ligue des Familles Nombreuses* in Belgium grew from about 3,000 member families at the time of its foundation in 1920, to over 175,000 in 1938 (Glass, 1940: 155). In France, the Fédération des Associations des familles nombreuses comprised more than 100 associations, and had in the 1930s a membership of more than 350,000 families (ibid. 150). These associations were actively involved in campaigns for issues such as higher family allowances and tax rebates for families, in addition to publishing journals, pamphlets, and tracts for their members. In Belgium, the Ligue also ran special funds (housing, education, emergency relief) to further support its members. Through these activities, family associations are acknowledged to have had a considerable influence on governments, especially with regard to the introduction of specific family benefits. For example, Glass (1940) reports that the Belgian Ligue was particularly influential in pressing for the adoption of various measures including family allowances and housing subsidies for families.

The power of these family associations was considerably enhanced in France in 1942 through the Gounot Law which gave regional associations the right and duty to represent families at the public authority level. Under the socialist regimes in Italy and Germany, family organizations became major actors, being used by governments as propaganda organs. For example, the Fascist Union of Large Families was created by the Italian government in 1937, and aimed at: 'increasing the prestige of large families . . . , undertaking propaganda for the pro-natalist policy, helping large families in any way possible, and surveying the application of existing legislation' (ibid. 259). Similarly, in Germany, the Association of children from German families (Bund der Kinderreichen Deutschlands), founded in 1924, was attached to the Race-Policy Department of the government under the socialist regime, and claimed a membership of some 300,000 German families of sound heredity (ibid. 286).

Table 2.3 *Selected family associations, pre-1945*

Country	Start-up year	Association titles
International	1919	Save the Children Fund
	1919	Nordic Child and Youth Welfare Alliance
Belgium	1903	National Childhood Charity*
	1920	League of Large Families*
Finland	1941	Finnish Population and Family Welfare Federation
France	1906	Popular League of Fathers and Mothers of Large Families of France*
	1915	The Largest Family*
	1919	General Confederation of Families*
	1921	National Federation of Association of Large Families*
	1922	National Committee of Childhood*
Germany	1905	League for the Protection of Mothers*
	1919	League of Large Families*
	1924	Association for Children of Germany*
Italy	1937	Fascist Union of Large Families
United Kingdom	1869	Family Welfare Association
	1904	Children's Minimum Campaign Committee
	1911	National Association for Maternity and Child Welfare
	1944	Scottish Council for Single Parents
United States	1911	Family Services America
	1932	Save the Children Federation
	1935	American Mothers Inc.
	1937	National Father's Day Committee
	1938	Christian Children's Fund
	1938	National Council of Family Relations
	1941	National Mother's Day Committee

*: Author's translation.

Welfare associations: In addition to family organizations, which were in most cases either pro-natalist or targeted at large families, there were others which were more concerned with the welfare of families, and more particularly at children and families in need. These associations added to the previous voices in calling for further state intervention. The Oeuvre nationale de l'enfance in Belgium, and the League for the Protection of Mothers in Germany, are examples. It is, however, in the United Kingdom and the United States that this type of association seems to have been particularly prevalent, starting with the Family Welfare Association set up in Britain in 1869. In fact, the welfare and poverty lobby have tended to be systematically more visible in Britain than in most other Western European countries. On the other hand, no French- style family lobby was to ever emerge in Britain.

Women's associations: The other groups to campaign for state support for families were women's groups. Whether or not attached to specific political parties, these women's groups are acknowledged to have played a significant role in the development of social policies directed at families. For example, reviewing the programme of the Social Democratic Party in Sweden, Ohlander found that 'most of the maternity policies were developed by Social Democratic women's groups' (1991: 64). In Britain also, better conditions and material support for working-class mothers were sought by organizations such as the Women's Labour League, the Women's Industrial Council, the Women's Co-operative Guild, and the Fabian Women's Group (Lewis, 1991: 79). Beyond these national initiatives, the international network which existed among women activists also had a significant influence. International organizations, such as the International Council of Women (ICW), founded in the United States in 1888, had a significant influence in allowing women from different countries to share their experiences and set up priority issues and actions. This, in turn, had considerable impact on national organizations, as revealed by the Italian case:

The shape of the assistance programmes set up by the Italian women and the way these were related to their users derived from a careful study of similar feminist and socialist institutions abroad. Italian feminists . . . knew best German and French institutions, but also English and American ones from personal observation, through publications, or especially from direct contact with their promoters. Large number of English, French, German and Scandinavian exponents of women's movements spent long periods in Italy giving lectures and visiting the organizations that had been set up in the main towns and cities, and their works were translated. (Buttafuoco, 1991: 181)

Women's associations and feminist leaders thus acted as disseminators of ideas. Among these leaders, certain names stood out, for example that of Eleanore Rathbone in Britain whose name is associated with the movement for the introduction of family allowances, especially through her 'Family Endowment Committee', and her 'Family Endowment Society'. Rathbone, along with other activists in the campaign for family allowances also founded in 1934 the 'Children's Minimum Council' which fought 'for a range of reforms from the raising of unemployment benefit rates to free milk for school children and nursing mothers and rent rebates as well as family allowances' (Lewis, 1991: 85). In Norway, it is the name of Katti Anker Moller which stood out, especially in view of her involvement on the political scene, and her fight for issues such as greater state involvement for the economic independence of women, liberal access to contraception and abortion, and social recognition of motherhood (Blom, 1991: 23). Moller also collaborated with women's organizations and campaigned for the introduction of a mother's wage (Seip and Ibsen, 1991: 45). Finally, in Italy, Patricia Schiff has been described as the 'initiator and best-known propagandist for maternity funds' (Buttafuoco, 1991: 181). Contrary to Rathbone and Moller, Schiff was opposed to any form of legislative protection, advocating instead the payment of maternity benefits from funds financed by the women workers themselves, the worker's organizations, and only partly by the state (ibid. 183).

In this period marked by deep family transformations, feminists and the family lobby thus played an active role in raising the profile of the family issue, but also in calling for state intervention. The responses of governments to these pressures were in fact to mark the beginning of increasing intervention of the state into family life.

State initiatives towards the family

Obviously, governments were not to stay indifferent to the transformations undergone by the family, and to the active family lobby. At the international level, it is the issue of child protection and welfare which received considerable attention, especially through the adoption by the United Nations of the Declaration of the Rights of Children in 1924. The Declaration, which was also referred to as the Charter of Child Welfare, declared that: 'The child must be given all opportunities for material and spiritual development . . . it is entitled to be fed, clothed, taught to work and protected against exploitation' (League of Nations, 1924: 199).

At the national level, the question of family decline was addressed in most of the population initiatives reviewed in the previous section. For example, the report of the British Royal Commission on Population made a series of recommendations concerning family welfare and the material circumstances of families. According to the authors of the report, better assistance to families, in the form of cash and in-kind benefits, was needed in order to reduce the welfare inequalities between families of different sizes (Britain, 1949: 227). Similarly, the Swedish Population Commission considered measures to improve the well-being of families, including children's clothing allowances, housing benefits, and day-care centres. See Table 2.4. for other family-related initiatives launched during this period.

Despite the widespread concern about the family, countries differed in their approach to the problem. While some countries were concerned with the promotion of the family as an institution, others were more preoccupied with the protection of the well-being of families. For the former, the objective of promoting and reasserting the social value of families was central. For example, the 1919 Constitution of Germany contained several references to the family in which it was emphasized that 'the central and local government authorities have, as their duty, to protect and encourage the family' (Glass, 1940: 273). Similarly, in Spain, 'the restoration of the family as the primary social unit of Spanish society' (Nash, 1991: 160), was a key element of the Francoist ideology, while in Italy, the 'desire to restore the family to its pristine glory' was also supported by Mussolini (Glass, 1940: 22). In the same vein, a Commission on the Family was set up in Italy in 1926 with the objective of 'ensuring that the order of the family system could be maintained against the many menaces of neo-Malthusianism, scientific and empirical' (Livi-Bacci, 1974: 657). Among other things, the Commission was to suggest

Table 2.4 *Family-related governmental initiatives, pre-1945*

Country	Start-up year	Title of initiative
France	1935	Decree for the Protection of Very Young Children
Italy	1926	Commission on the Family
Norway	1934	Commission on Child Allowance
Sweden	1926	Maternity Benefit Commission
Switzerland	1944	Report on Family Policy
United Kingdom	1933	Children and Young Persons Act
United States	1909	White House Conference on Children
	1912	Children's Bureau
	1930	White House Conference on Children
	1940	White House Conference on Children
International	1924	UN Declaration on the Rights of Children

the adoption of several measures including fiscal benefits for large families (ibid.). During this period, a decree adopted in France in 1935 explicitly acknowledged the commitment of the government to protect all children born in its territory, from birth until their third birthday (Norvez, 1990: 16). In Switzerland, the principle of state responsibility in the support for families was stressed in a report on family policy published in 1944. The report still stands today as the most voluminous document on the topic in Switzerland. In particular, it acknowledged the right of the family to state protection: 'The Confederation provides for the survival of the family, which constitutes the basic unit of society and the State, as well as for its maintenance' (a.t. Switzerland, Office Fédérale des assurances sociales, 1982: 22).

On the other hand, other initiatives, in the United States, Norway, and Sweden, focused less on the future of the family as an institution and more on the issue of family welfare. It is under the theme of 'Conference on the Care of Dependent Children', that the first American White House Conference on Children was held under the auspices of President Roosevelt in 1909. Addressing the whole issue of welfare provision, it brought together over 200 child welfare workers. According to Steiner (1976), its impact was considerable especially through its adoption of the principle of public responsibility in the provision of child welfare. In fact, it paved the way for significant measures including the establishment of a federal Children's Bureau (in 1912), and the introduction of the first cash benefit for families, in the form of a mother's pension (see Chapter 3). Two other conferences on children followed in 1930 and 1940, the first one around the theme of child health and protection, the other around the theme of children in a democracy (ibid.). The issue of child protection and welfare was also central to the British government. For example, the adoption of the Children and Young Persons Act 1933, with its emphasis on children in need, was to give a distinct orientation to the British government's policy towards families and children — an orientation which has tended to be maintained over time. Finally, the issue of family welfare was addressed, under a financial support angle, in Norway and Sweden. In Norway, it was addressed by the Commission on Child Allowances in 1934. Following lengthy debates about the issue of mothers' wage, the majority in the report endorsed a public responsibility approach in recommending the introduction of universal allowances to be paid to mothers in families with more than one child (Seip and Ibsen, 1991: 49). A similar issue was addressed in 1926 in Sweden by the Maternity benefit Commission, mandated to suggest a maternity relief scheme (Ohlander, 1991: 67).

The introduction of symbolic measures such as the proclamation of a 'Mother and Child Day' in Italy, and a 'National Mother's Day' in France, also reflected the importance attached to the family issue (Glass, 1940: 243; Tomlinson, Huss, and Ogden, 1985: 28). In addition, awards and medals for parents of large families were given in France and Germany as part of the pro-natalist propaganda, the highest award being given to mothers of eight or more children in Germany, and to mothers of at least five children in France (Glass, 1940: 172, 303). In France, the Alliance Nationale every year still awards the Prix Charles Baron to 'congratulate families which succeed in the difficult challenge of raising a large family' (a.t., Population et Avenir, 1985: 16).

It is therefore apparent from this analysis that, in addition to fertility decline, the broader transformations undergone by the family attracted considerable attention. It was especially the case in countries such as France, Germany, and Italy, where family issues were seen from a pro-natalist angle. On the other hand, in countries such as Britain and the United States, it is more the welfare of families, rather than the pro-natalist question, which seems to have attracted more attention. Again, some of these inter-country divergences will tend to be maintained over time.

2.4   The principle of voluntary parenthood

Alongside fears of population and family decline, attention was also devoted to the question of birth-control from the end of the nineteenth century. At that time, several countries had already modified their penal code to explicitly forbid the use of abortion and contraception. In view of the increasing willingness of women to control their family size, this legislation was further reinforced in the 1920s and 1930s. This was however against a particularly significant movement which was calling for more liberal access to family planning.

The birth-control movement

Already in the eighteenth century, Malthus was advocating family limitation, but not through artificial birth-control, which he was strongly opposed to, but through 'moral restraint', i.e. the postponement of marriage, and abstinence before marriage.[3] It is thus unfortunate that his name eventually became associated with the birth-

[3] Within marriage, Malthus considered that there should be no artificial checks on family size (Glass, 1953: 28).

control movement. The origins of this movement go back to the work of Francis Place in Britain, whose 'diabolic handbills', published in 1823, for the first time, advocated and described the use of birth control to the public (ibid. 31). Although several publications followed this pioneering one, the real launch of the birth-control movement came with the Bradlaugh–Besant court case of 1877. Set around the illegal publication of a pamphlet on contraception, the trial received considerable publicity, and gave a major impetus to the birth-control movement.[4]

Shortly after this trial, the first Malthusian League was founded in Britain; a league which was to have a considerable influence both in Britain and abroad (ibid. 35). Initially, the actions of the League were limited to propaganda in favour of family limitation. Voluntary and responsible parenthood, according to one's means of subsistence, was advocated as a means of reducing poverty. From 1913, however, the League also started to publicize contraceptive methods, and was eventually joined by several other organizations in its campaigns for family planning (ibid. 43–4). The following years saw a steady growth in the number of voluntary birth control clinics. For example, by 1939 the National Birth Control Association in Britain, founded in 1930, was running 66 clinics, while 247 local authorities in England and Wales were providing birth-control advice (ibid. 46). Abroad, the influence of the League was also considerable, leading to the creation of several national leagues, and to the International League in 1900 under the name of Fédération universelle de la régénération humaine (ibid. 39). The International League met regularly and saw a rapid increase in its membership, so that: 'by the time that the fourth conference met [in 1911], there were constituent bodies of the Fédération Universelle in France, Holland, Germany, Spain, Belgium, Switzerland, Bohemia, Portugal, Brazil, Cuba, and North Africa, with Sweden joining a little later, while activity was also being carried on in the United States' (ibid. 40).

The Malthusian leagues were not the only ones to campaign for more liberal access to birth-control. Associations such as the British Society for Constructive Birth Control (founded in 1921), and the German Association for Sexual Reform (founded in 1913), were also actively involved in the campaign for birth-control (ibid. 46, 276). Despite this support, it is important to note that the pro-birth-control movement was able to gain the confidence and support of only a fraction of the population. For the public in general, its academic tone, 'dismal' philosophy, radical ideas about sexuality, and association with atheism, were all unattractive (Lewis, 1980: 196). In Britain, it took the work of Marie Stopes, from the late 1910s, to make the idea of contraception 'acceptable to women, doctors, health officials, and MPs' (ibid. 203). According to Lewis, the message conveyed by Stopes was more successful than that of the Malthusians since 'the working classes were no

---

[4]The accused, who had voluntarily decided to create a test case, had republished a pamphlet by Charles Knowlton entitled *Fruits of Philosophy*. Initially published in 1831 in New York, and in 1832 in London, this pamphlet recommended douching as the most satisfactory method of contraception. It was sold in England for over 40 years without interference from the authorities, before a new edition in 1876 led to the prosecution of its publisher for alleged obscenity. After lengthy hearings, Bradlaugh and Besant were finally exonerated, but the copies of the pamphlet were confiscated (the accused were however fined for refusing to surrender the pamphlet) (Glass, 1940).

longer urged to use birth control because they were considered to be economically or eugenically undesirable, but rather in order to spare them individual hardship and personal suffering' (ibid. 206).

Some groups however remained strongly opposed to the idea of birth-control. Among them, the Catholic Church widely rejected all forms of artificial contraception; a position which was made clear in the 1930 Papal Encyclical (Glass, 1940: 430). On the other hand, the Anglican and Methodist Churches, were vaguer on this question, while the Church of England allowed contraception in certain marital situations from 1931 (ibid.; Anderson and Zinsser, 1988: 417).

Legislation on abortion and contraception

Reflection of their opposition to birth-control, governments in several countries reinforced the prohibition against the use of abortion, and the display, sale, and import of contraceptives. The legislation was complex and was subject to several amendments and changes. Only an overview is provided here. Prohibition was the order of the day, with most countries reinforcing the ban against contraception and/or abortion, and introducing fines and possible imprisonment.

Contraception: With regard to contraception, prohibitive legislation was adopted at a very early stage in Canada and the United States(see Table 2.5).

Table 2.5 *Legislation on contraception, pre-1945*

Prohibitive		Liberal	
Country	Year of introduction	Country	Year of introduction
United States	1873	United Kingdom	1930
Canada	1892	Denmark	1937
Sweden	1910	Sweden	1938
Denmark	1913		
France	1920		
Belgium	1923		
Italy	1926		
Japan	1931		
Ireland	1935		
Germany	1941		
Spain	1941		

In Canada, the prohibition extended to the advertisement, sale, and disposal of contraceptives, and was included in the criminal code in 1892 (Henripin and Gauthier, 1974: 419). Similarly, in the United States the 1873 Comstock Law prohibited the 'importation, transportation in interstate commerce, and mailing of any article whatever for the prevention of contraception' (Westoff, 1974: 736). Legislation relating to contraception was also adopted in Ireland in 1935 making it unlawful to 'sell or expose, offer, advertise or keep for sale, or to import or attempt to import into the State for sale any contraceptive' (Walsh, 1974: 21). Publication and sale of books or periodicals advocating contraception were also prohibited.

Strict legislation forbidding the use and sale of contraceptives was adopted in France, Belgium, Germany, Italy, Japan, and Spain during this period. In France, the prohibition was part of the 1920 law which prescribed 'imprisonment for one to six months, and a fine of 100 to 5,000 francs for any one engaging in birth-control propaganda, or who, for this purpose, divulges or offers to divulge, or who facilitates the use of methods for preventing pregnancy' (Glass, 1940: 159). This strict legislation was mainly driven by pro-natalist motives, as it was seen as 'a real national salvation measure able to increase the birth rate' (a.t., United Nations, 1989a: 32). Similar legislation was adopted in Belgium in 1923 (Glass, 1940: 159). The French and Belgian laws were however more effective in theory than in practice. Their liberal interpretation made possible the use of certain contraceptive devices such as the condom because they were viewed as a protection against venereal disease rather than as means of birth-control (ibid. 160).

Under the Fascist regimes, contraception was also subject to strict prohibitive rules. In Germany, a decree was adopted in 1941 (Schubnell and Rupp, 1975: 307). In Italy, under the heading of public safety, a Royal Decree was adopted in 1931 prohibiting the sale of contraceptives and the publication of birth-control propaganda. It was subsequently confirmed in the revised penal code of 1930 (Glass, 1940: 231–2). In Spain the advertisement and sale of contraceptives was made illegal in 1941 as part of Franco's pro-natalist campaign (Nash, 1991: 168). Finally, in Japan a political atmosphere antagonistic to birth-control prevailed throughout the 1930s. In fact, dissemination of birth-control information was considered to endanger the national interest (Muramatsu and Kuroda, 1974: 706). Rapid population increase was thought to be essential for the future of the nation, and contraception became strictly controlled through the 1931 Regulations for the Control of Harmful Contraceptives Devices (ibid.).

At the other end of the spectrum, the legislation adopted in the United Kingdom was much more liberal, and in 1930 the Ministry of Health gave permission for child welfare centres to give contraceptive advice to married women for whom a further pregnancy would be detrimental to health (Simons, 1974: 635). Liberal access to contraception was also introduced in the 1930s in Denmark and Sweden. In Denmark, the liberalization of legislation followed the recommendation of a Committee appointed in 1932. It still prescribed a fine for the offensive advertising of contraceptives, but allowed their sale in chemists shops and other approved stores (Glass, 1940: 323). Similarly, in Sweden the sale of contraceptives became legal in 1938 (ibid. 325). This liberalization was an endorsement of the Myrdals' principle of voluntary parenthood.

Abortion: With regard to abortion, strict legislation prohibiting it was introduced in several countries in the pre-World War II period (see Table 2.6).

Table 2.6 *Legislation on abortion, pre-1945*

Prohibitive		Liberal	
Country	Year of introduction	Country	Year of introduction
Ireland	1861	Denmark	1937*
Belgium	1867	Sweden	1938*
Netherlands	1881	United Kingdom	1938*
Portugal	1886		
United Kingdom	1893		
France	1920		
Sweden	1921		
Germany	1926		
Italy	1926		
Switzerland	1937		
Japan	1940		
Spain	1941		

*: On restricted grounds (see text).

As in the contraception case, pro-natalist motives, along with eugenic consider-ations, were behind some of these laws. It was for instance the case in France where the law against abortion was strongly reinforced in 1920 (United Nations, 1989a: 32). Before this, abortion had already been made unlawful under the Napoleonic Code of 1810 in which it was treated as a murder (Bourgeois-Pichat, 1974: 558). The law tended however to be applied loosely as revealed by the small number of prosecutions: 'between 1881 and 1910, of the cases brought to trial, sentences were given in fewer than 30 cases per year and under 37 per cent of the per-sons prosecuted between 1881 and 1905 were actually sentenced . . . In practice therefore, the juries generally refused to implement the law' (Glass, 1940: 158).

In Japan, and in the context of a pro-natalist policy, abortion was prohibited through the 1940 National Eugenic Law (Muramatsu and Kuroda, 1974: 707). In Germany, the abortion law of 1926 (and its 1933 and 1935 amendments) was driven by both pro-natalist and eugenic motives in allowing abortion to be performed on eugenic grounds (Glass, 1940: 283–5). It was complemented by a sterilization law of 1926 by which 'biologically inferior material was to be eradicated specifically among the innumerable inferior and hereditarily tainted people who procreate without inhibition' (Bock, 1991: 235).

The situation in Britain was very different. In 1803 an Act had already made abortion a statutory offence and it included various penalties for the offender (Glass, 1940: 427). The Penal Servitude Act 1891 and the Statute Law Revision Act 1893 then superseded the previous legislation in introducing penal servitude for life or not less than three years, or imprisonment for not more than two years for any woman attempting to procure her own abortion or for anyone attempting an abortion on a woman (ibid. 427–8). In 1938, this prohibition was then partially lifted when the Court allowed abortion to be performed on grounds of health (Simons, 1974: 640). Opposition, especially from the Catholic Church, prevented further liberalization of the legislation. It is consequently only in Denmark and Sweden that more liberal legislation on abortion was adopted in the pre-World War II period. In Sweden, abortion on medical grounds was permitted in 1921. Under the 1938 Act, abortion was then allowed for other reasons, including social ones (Jonsson, 1974: 129). Similarly, in Denmark a law, passed in 1937, allowed abortion on medical, therapeutic, and ethical grounds. As Glass commented: 'social grounds have been omitted, but medical grounds are defined more broadly . . . and it will be possible to plead that a further pregnancy would have a serious effect upon the health of a woman who already has a large family and whose income is very small' (1940: 323). With these laws, Denmark and Sweden were the first countries to liberalize abortion.

Concomitant with the fears of population and family decline, most governments took a firm stance against birth-control by adopting legislation prohibiting both contraception and abortion in the pre-World War II period. In the history of family policy, this legislation on abortion and contraception has a special significance as it stood among the first direct interventions of the state into family life. On the other hand, governments in only two countries, Denmark and Sweden, provided women with a more liberal legislation according to a principle of voluntary parenthood. It is only from the 1970s that other countries also liberalized their legislation (see Chapter 7).

2.5 Conclusion

If before the 1920–30 period, population and family issues attracted little attention with the exception of France, the situation was to be rapidly altered as a result of major demographic and economic changes. The decline in fertility, along with the transformations undergone by the family, raised alarm in several circles. The prospects of population decline, along with fears of family decline, led to major state interventions. These first interventions are important as they provided the initial basis for greater involvement of governments in family life, and for their greater role as welfare provider.

Against this general background, there were however substantial inter-country differences in the responses of governments to the new population and family questions. It is in France and Sweden that the issue of low fertility and family decline attracted most attention. In France, it followed an early decline in fertility which tended to be perceived by political leaders as a real military handicap. Pronatalist propaganda, financial incentives, and restricted access to birth-control were therefore to characterize the policy of the French government during the pre-World War II period. In Sweden, on the other hand, the pro-natalist objectives were to be accompanied by an acknowledgement of the principle of voluntary parenthood, and thus, by a more liberal access to contraceptive means and abortion. Concern about low fertility, and pronatalism, were also dominant in Germany, Spain, and

Italy under the fascist regimes. The pro-natalist policy of these governments was however also linked to strong eugenic objectives — a dimension which would eventually be widely condemned by the international community.

Finally, during this pre-World War II period, the actions and attitudes of the British government towards the population and family questions were also distinct. While expressing some concern about the prospects of population and family decline, the British government, contrary to others, eventually opted for a non-alarmist and non-interventionist stance. Strong Malthusian influences, along with a tradition of community-based poverty relief, were to restrict the interventions of the government and to concentrate them on the welfare of families rather than on the strict fertility question.

3

FIRST ELEMENTS OF FAMILY POLICIES

As seen in the previous chapter, concern about the decline in fertility and the transformations undergone by the family led several groups to call for improved state support for families. If, so far, the support provided by governments to families had been very limited, it was to be greatly expanded in this period of major economic and social changes. In particular, three sectors were the target of government intervention: health services for mothers and children, financial support for families, and support for working mothers. Measures introduced under each of these headings constituted the first elements of family policy. These measures were however sketchy, covering only a limited fraction of the population, and not being part of any global policy of support for families. These first elements of family policy were nevertheless important as they marked a precedent in governmental support for families, in addition to providing the basis for the post-World War II welfare state development.

Inter-country differences in this respect were wide. While some governments adopted full responsibility in the support of families from a very early stage, others adopted a more limited approach. In this chapter, some of the first measures adopted by governments to support families are examined. In addition, are detailed the cases of France, Germany, and Sweden which, from this early time, adopted a much more comprehensive policy to support families. These measures were partly prompted by emerging concern about population and family decline. In most cases, they were also prompted by welfare considerations, and were part of the governments' fight against poverty.

3.1 The poverty problem

The economic and social changes which took place at the turn of the century had significant impacts on the quality of life of the population. Infant and child mortality was high, sanitary conditions hazardous, salaries low, and unemployment widespread. Knowledge about the extent and magnitude of the problem was limited however. At that time 'nobody had any clear notion of how extensive poverty was' (Frazer, 1984: 135). The situation changed drastically with the publication of empirical studies revealing the magnitude of the problem. If, so far, relief had been provided mainly through private networks (family, neighbours, Church, charities), poverty was now such that it could no longer be tackled by traditional means. Greater state intervention was obviously needed.

An emerging concern

This 'discovery' of poverty came in the late nineteenth and early twentieth centuries with the disclosure of evidence highlighting widespread poverty, high levels of infant and child mortality, as well as inadequate working and living conditions. In Britain, this evidence was revealed in early publications such as *The Bitter Cry of Outcast London* (Mearns, 1883), *The Life and Labour of the People in London* (Booth, 1902), and *Poverty: A Study of Town Life* (Rowntree, 1901). These studies were very influential. Not only did they raise the visibility of the poverty problem, but they also provided the first empirical estimates of the extent of poverty. The magnitude was enormous. According to Booth and Rowntree, about a third of the population was living in poverty. The findings were alarming, and for the first time it was clear that state relief was essential. In addition to these studies, in Britain, the report of the Interdepartmental Committee of Physical Deterioration in 1904[1] also added to these concerns by revealing the inadequacy of the conditions in which the population was living. The report stressed the 'very shocking conditions [which] existed in certain sections of the population, especially in the poorest parts of the big cities' (Rees, 1985: 32).[2] The consequences of this situation on the health and well-being of families were further highlighted in a series of reports on the levels of infant and child mortality. Newsholme's report in 1889, the Registrar General's first detailed statement of infant mortality in 1905, and Newman's study in 1906, entitled *Infant Mortality: A Social Problem*, all revealed the magnitude of the problem. Many years later, the study of Titmuss, *Birth, Poverty and Wealth* (1943) further revealed the extent of the problem, and its links with poverty.

Governments did not stay indifferent to the issue, and launched significant actions. Slogans such as '3,000 children die unnecessarily every year in Sweden' (Myrdal, 1947: 308), and the American campaign against child mortality in the early 1910s, the Baby-Savings Campaign, reveal the widespread concern about the problem (United States, Children's Bureau, 1913). In France and Germany the problem of infant mortality, as a social issue, also attracted considerable attention. High infant mortality was unacceptable, from an humanitarian point of view, but also since it slowed down population growth. At a time when high population growth and pro-natalist ideologies were highly praised, the issue consequently deserved attention. A member of the French legislature in 1869 argued that 'the slow [population] growth was due to high infant mortality ... [and it] should be reduced' (Spengler, 1979: 119). The objective was therefore clear. A German feminist in 1908 argued that countries had to aim at producing 'the birth of the largest possible number of healthy children' (Stoehr, 1991: 225). The fact that infant mortality was higher in urban areas, among the lower social classes, and

---

[1] This committee was itself responding to claims by military authorities involved in the Boer War that the physical state of the population (and soldiers) had deteriorated.

[2] Other evidence came from the exhibition on sweated industry organized by the *Daily News* in 1906. According to Rees, this exhibition, which revealed to the public the conditions under which workers in the textile industry (mostly women and children) were hired, in terms of earnings, number of hours of work, rooms, and tools, had an 'irresistible' effect (1985: 32-33).

among infants born to unmarried mothers, was also raising particular concern. For example, the 'discovery' of a large difference in infant mortality between high- and low-income groups in Sweden is reported to have aroused considerable public and official concern. In a society which believed in democracy and equality, the disclosure of data showing such social inequalities called for the adoption of immediate relief measures (Myrdal, 1947: 308).

Without over-stating the role played by the discovery of poverty, it can nevertheless be reasonably argued that it contributed to the creation of a momentum about the need for state intervention: 'the combined effect of these discoveries was great enough to change the political atmosphere and to create possibilities for new and more determined actions' (Rees, 1985: 33).

Measures to reduce poverty and infant mortality

If the time was ripe for state intervention, what measures were to be adopted by governments to tackle these problems? Before looking at these measures, it should be mentioned that the family, in itself, was not a prime target group for governments, at least in the early stages of state intervention. Instead, support for the aged, the sick, and the injured seems to have been given a higher priority in dealing with the problem of poverty. Rees refers to the 'awakening interest in old people' and stresses how 'at the turn of the century most countries of the Western world suffered from a guilty conscience about the aged poor' (ibid. 42). Consequently, old-age pensions, worker's compensation schemes, and sickness insurance were the first social security programmes to be introduced in most countries (Schneider, 1982). Only in subsequent periods would governments introduce specific social security programmes for the family.

Children were nevertheless not ignored by the state during this early period. Already the legislation against child labour, and that introducing compulsory education, had reflected the importance attached to the well-being of children. The disclosure of information about high levels of infant and child mortality subsequently reinforced the need for the adoption of further measures, especially in the health sector. The setting-up of a committee by the World Health Organization to investigate maternal welfare and the hygiene of infants and children of pre-school age, in 1932, also reflected the importance given to the issue (Symonds and Carder, 1973: 25). For most political leaders, however, the major cause of infant and child mortality was not solely poverty. Mothers' ignorance about the care of children, along with unhealthy working conditions, were acknowledged to be contributing to the high incidence of mortality. Infant mortality, it was believed, was the result of 'poor perinatal care and short confinements of mothers, artificial feeding and inadequate care of infants, overwork and under-nutrition of pregnant mothers' (Stoehr, 1991: 225). Women were consequently 'morally responsible for child mortality . . . and were held responsible for the well-being of their children' (Ohlander, 1991: 60-1). As a result, the first measures of state support for families would give priority to four key aspects:

1. Increasing the education of mothers concerning the care of their children.

2. Providing them with medical and maternity assistance.
3. Providing families with emergency cash support.
4. Improving the working conditions of mothers.

It is not an easy task to give a comprehensive account of the measures which were introduced during this period under these four headings, especially in view of their temporary or local nature. Moreover, it is important to stress that, despite the increase in state support, charities and women's groups continued to play a major role as welfare providers during the whole of the pre-World War II period.

Educational services: In order to combat mothers' ignorance, schools and institutions were founded in several countries to 'educate young women for their obligations as mothers and homemakers' (Cova, 1991: 123). Examples of such initiatives included a school for mothers at Bordeaux in France (founded in 1897), and cooking and housewifery schools set up by the German women's movement in the 1890s (ibid.; Stoehr, 1991: 220). Similarly, in Italy, the Pro Maternitate, set up by women activists and workers in 1898, provided educational services. It was described as 'a financial and educational organization that assisted mothers by providing lessons on hygiene and the correct rearing of newborn children' (Buttafuoco, 1991: 184). The objective of educating women was also taken up by birth-control activists, for example by Marie Stopes in Britain through her pamphlet entitled: *A Letter to Working Mothers on How to have Healthy Children and Avoid Weakening Pregnancies* published in 1919. In fact, as reported by Cova, the turn of the century saw a major increase in educational services aimed at women, and in most cases, provided by women's groups: 'maternal and infant health courses and maternity guides multiplied; the feminist journals were eager to advertise them in order to combat "maternal ignorance", to organize high-quality material instruction and to claim women's right to education in general ' (1991: 123). Charities and women's groups consequently played a major role as providers of educational services. Only much later was the state going to take a more active role in the provision of such services.

Medical and maternity assistance: In addition to these educational services, assistance in the field of health and maternity also experienced a rapid development from the 1900s. For example, Thane reports that by 1914 at least 400 maternity and child welfare centres were in place in Britain 'providing advice to mothers about child care, plus a variable range of additional services including medical treatment, free or subsidized meals for mothers and young children and sometimes pregnant women, and lessons in cookery, sewing and housewifery' (Thane, 1991: 102). Advice to mothers was also provided by local authorities through the services of health visitors. In Norway, mothers' health services were mainly provided by the Norwegian Women's Public Health Association, (founded in 1896) through their clinics which provided assistance and advice on breast-feeding and other infant-care problems (Blom, 1991: 31).

Stemming from private initiatives, these services covered only a small fraction of the population. Their coverage was eventually expanded when governments enacted legislation on maternity and child welfare, comprising both in-cash and in-kind benefits. The listing in Table 3.1 is very disparate but captures some of the main legislation enacted by governments during the pre-1945 period.

In several cases, the new legislation or programme applied only to poor families, while in others it covered all mothers with young children. Once again, these measures were important as they introduced some of the first elements of state support for families. In Britain, state assistance to mothers was first provided through the 1918 Maternity and Child Welfare Act which enabled local authorities to establish Maternity and Child Welfare Committees. According to Thane, their activities were wide-ranging:

The services they might provide were: provision of hospital services for children under five, maternity hospitals, 'home helps' (i.e. domestic workers to take over the housework of the mother after childbirth, free of charge for necessitous women), food for expectant and nursing mothers and for children under five, crêches and day nurseries, homes for the children of widowed and deserted mothers and for illegitimate children. (1991: 106).

In Denmark, Finland, Germany, Luxembourg, the Netherlands, Norway, and Switzerland, similar services were provided but were in most cases restricted to women without resources, or to those not covered by a private insurance. Significant actions were also taken under the socialist regimes to protect mothers and children. For example, in Italy, the ONMI (National Foundation for Maternity and Child Welfare), founded in 1925, provided women and children without adequate resources with health and hygiene advice, food supplements, crêches, and day nursery facilities (Saraceno, 1991: 205–8). In Germany, maternity homes were also set up, but under the initiative of the fascist government and to serve its ideology. The *Lebensborn* were indeed aimed at 'assisting mothers who bore children by men who were thought to belong to the racial élite' (Bock, 1991: 244). The *Lebensborn* were in existence nine years and counted six well-furnished maternity hospitals in Germany, as well as nine in Norway, one in Belgium, and one in France (ibid.). In Spain, the Maternity and Child Welfare Scheme (Sanidad Maternal e Infantil) was created as an administrative service of the Health Service, and aimed at protecting pregnant women, mothers, and young children (Nash, 1991: 173). In the United States, the adoption in 1921 of the Sheppard- Towner Act constituted a landmark in American social policy history. This Act, which provided states with matching federal funds for prenatal and child health centres, was however defeated in 1929 following pressure by the Medical Association who fought to take over control of the services that these clinics provided (Frank and Lipner, 1988: 12).

In addition to these services, there were other measures aimed at improving the health of mothers and children. For example, in several countries measures were taken to encourage breast-feeding and to regulate the nursing industry. In France, the Roussel Law of 1874 was aimed specifically at regulating the 'nursing industry' by 'providing for governmental registration of, and surveillance over, children under two placed with mercenary nurses' (Spengler, 1979: 230). The practice was however strongly disapproved of and suckling bonuses were subsequently introduced in 1916 in order to discourage it (ibid. 233–4). Nursing benefits were also

Table 3.1 *Mothers and children assistance programmes, pre-1945*

Country	Start-up year	Title of programme
Australia	1907	Child Welfare Act
Austria	1920	Poor relief scheme
Denmark	1933	Public assistance scheme
Finland	1937	Maternity assistance scheme
France	1904	Assistance for destitute children
	1919	Assistance to nursing mothers
Germany	1924	Social relief scheme
Ireland	1915	Maternity and child welfare service
Italy	1925	Foundation for National Maternity and Child Welfare (ONMI)
Japan	1929	Poor relief scheme
Luxembourg	1907	Assistance for Children and Young Persons
Netherlands	1912	Poor relief scheme
New Zealand	1927	Child Welfare Act
Norway	1915	Child welfare scheme
Portugal	1935	National Foundation for the Welfare of the Family
Spain	1923	Maternity assistance
Sweden	1924	Child Welfare Act
Switzerland	1912	Public relief scheme
United Kingdom	1918	Maternity and Child Welfare Act
United States	1921	Sheppard-Towner Act (repealed in 1929)

Notes: Australia: State of Western Australia only. Provided cash benefits to handicapped children or children in care. Related schemes were adopted subsequently in other states. Austria: As part of the State Constitution. Provided medical assistance to indigent persons, and education assistance for indigent children. Denmark: Provided medical care and cash benefits to necessitous women and women not covered by a recognized sickness insurance funds. Finland: Provided cash benefits to women with small resources. France: Included monthly nursing allowances. Germany: Provided medical assistance and cash benefits to indigent women not entitled to insurance benefit. Ireland: Provided maternity and child welfare service, including medical assistance and day nurseries, to expectant mothers, nursing mothers, and children under the age of 5. Italy: Provided medical assistance, food supplements, and day care facilities to women and children without adequate resources. Japan: Provided food and medical assistance to pregnant mothers and children under the age of 13. Luxembourg: Provided medical assistance to indigent women and those not fully solvent. Netherlands: Provided care to indigent women, including free assistance at childbirth. New Zealand: Provided care to children in need. Norway: Provided cash benefits to pregnant women not covered by insurance or, if covered, unable to provide for their own maintenance and medical assistance. Portugal: Provided assistance to pregnant women at the time of confinement. Spain: Provided cash benefits and medical assistance to insured women under the old-age insurance scheme. Sweden: Provided public assistance for boarded children. Switzerland: Provided care for indigent women including assistance at confinement. United Kingdom: Provided medical assistance, food, and maternity and child welfare services to expectant and nursing mothers, as well as children under the age of 5. United States: Provided the states with matching federal funds for prenatal and child health centres.

introduced in several other countries as part of the benefits to working mothers. By 1939, such benefits were available in Austria, France, Germany, Greece, Luxembourg, Spain, and Switzerland (ILO, 1939). In Italy, the importance of breast-feeding was acknowledged through the regulations and services provided by the ONMI, which placed an obligation 'to breast-feed on mothers who keep their children' (Saraceno, 1991: 207).

With regard to schoolchildren, several measures were adopted during this period, including school meals and free medical examinations. Coverage was limited, as the measures were mainly intended for the most needy children. These measures had nevertheless a significant impact. For instance, it is estimated that in Oslo, about 46 per cent of the schoolchildren received what came to be known as the 'Oslo breakfasts', introduced in 1931 (Glass, 1940: 341). During this period, meals for schoolchildren were also introduced in Great Britain (in 1906) and Ireland (in 1911), while medical inspection of schoolchildren shortly followed (1919 in Ireland, 1921 in Great Britain). During the Second World War these measures were complemented by further schemes. The health of children and the question of nutrition were seen as a matter of major political importance, and led to significant action. For example, in Britain, this concern led to the adoption of a National Milk Scheme in June 1940, which 'provided every pregnant or nursing mother, and every child under 5, with a daily pint of milk, as well as vitamin supplements in the form of fruit juice, cod-liver oil, "national rosehip syrup", and pills' (Lewis, 1980: 187).

These early benefits for mothers and children thus marked the beginning of increasing state support for families. The coverage in these early decades of the century was however patchy, and a large role was still played by philanthropic organizations. Furthermore, apart from the nursing benefits, these measures were mostly provided in-kind. The gradual introduction of cash benefits marked another major development in this field.

3.2   Cost of living bonus and family allowances

If the discovery of poverty had created enough momentum for the implementation of maternity and infant welfare services, consensus concerning the provision of state-administered cash benefits was still missing. The pre-World War II period witnessed major experiments and discussions concerning cost-of-living bonuses, family allowances, and living wages. These developments were to pave the way for the post-war universal family allowances.

First experiments

It is in France that the precursor of family allowances was first developed. This early form of cash benefit was initiated by private employers, and consisted of a supplement to wages which were given to married workers with children. Such a scheme was first instituted in 1891 by the engineering firm Joya in Grenoble.[3] The

---

[3]It should be noted that the Michelin factory, in Clermont-Ferrand, instigated a family allowance scheme in 1876 (Glass, 1940: 179). Family allowance schemes for public employees were introduced

reasons motivating the adoption of such a scheme were numerous, including the aim of protecting families from a steep degradation of living standards. But above all, in this context of high inflation, the introduction of such a measure was mainly motivated by economic considerations. The introduction of family allowances was seen, from an employer's point of view, as a more efficient solution than a general increase in wages, which would not only reinforce the inflationary movement, but would also be more expensive.[4] In addition, the introduction of family allowances was thought to diminish the risk of workers joining trade unions; a risk which was highly feared by employers. Finally, the introduction of family allowances was seen by employers as a way of making their companies more attractive, and thus, of reducing labour turnover. Economic considerations over welfare ones seem therefore to have driven the introduction of the first forms of family allowances.

The administration of such schemes was however problematic because it could eventually lead to discrimination against workers with family responsibilities since they would be more expensive than childless workers. This problem was solved through the creation of equalization funds (Caisse de compensation) which grouped together several employers and which administered the payment and financing of family allowances. The principle was that the employers' contribution to the fund would be proportional to the total number of workers, and not to the number of workers supporting a family, thus eliminating the potential risk of discrimination against married men (Glass, 1940: 102). These equalization funds experienced rapidly growing popularity, either as regional funds or professional ones. By 1923, Rathbone reports that there were 120 funds in operation in France, covering 7,600 firms and distributing family allowances to 880,000 wage-earners (Rathbone, 1924). Their popularity extended also to other countries, and, following the French initiative, similar employers' schemes were set up in Belgium, Germany, Holland, and Switzerland. In fact, the setting-up of the first equalization fund in Belgium in 1921, at Verviers, was meant to avoid the exodus of workers to the northern parts of France where family allowances schemes were already in place (Glass, 1940: 126).

Opinion on family allowances

In France, family allowances gained strong support from employers. They were seen as a measure particularly well-suited to the existing economic context, but only if they remained a private initiative exempt from any state intervention. In particular, it was argued that: 'to be effective the family allowance system must be free to adapt itself to the special conditions of different industries and districts. State intervention would impose a heavy burden, and would involve the establishment of a complicated system of management and control' (ILO, 1924: 80).

Outside France, employers were divided about the value of family allowances. In several countries, including Germany, the view was that family allowances should

---

from 1890 (for railways workers), and in 1917 for civil servants (ibid. 101).

[4] Family allowances were paid only to married employees with children, while a general wage increase would apply to all employees, including childless and unmarried workers.

be seen as an exceptional relief measure in times of economic hardship, and that at other times the principle of equal pay for equal work should prevail (ibid. 110). Workers' organizations, on the other hand, were opposed to the family allowance scheme as it stood, that is, under the responsibility and initiative of employers. They felt that it was unacceptable that only workers belonging to selected firms benefited from these allowances, and that different rates of family allowances applied across different equalization funds. Moreover, they saw these employers' schemes as a means of keeping wages down, and of increasing the employers' dominance since they could suppress the allowances at any time. They argued that it was unacceptable that, because of their link with employment, family allowances would not be paid if a worker suddenly became sick or unemployed, or in cases of strikes or lock-outs. They consequently called for the adoption of family allowance schemes which would be administered by the state, in the same way as the provision for other categories of beneficiaries (i.e. the sick, unemployed, disabled or aged), and which would not be linked with employment. Pro-natalist groups and family associations also rallied workers in calling for state-administered allowances. Family allowances, they argued, should be independent from wages, and should moreover be independent from assistance to necessitous families (ibid. 85). Family allowances also received the support of the Catholic Church, although the 1891 Papal Encyclical gave preference to the idea of a living wage, that is, a wage which would be sufficient to cover the needs of the worker and his family (MacNicol, 1992: 247; Glass, 1940: 100). In fact, the only groups strongly opposed to family allowances were some feminists who argued that such an allowance, tied as it was to employment and given to fathers, increased the dependency of women (ILO, 1924: 93). Instead, many feminists rallied around the idea of a mother's wage.

Living wage and cost-of-living bonus

Outside Europe, the question of wages and family needs was also given some attention. In Australia, which had a long tradition of state intervention in many aspects of economic life, there was strong support among employers and unions for the introduction of a minimum wage (MacNicol, 1992: 254). In this respect, a major test case took place when the Court was asked in 1907 to pronounce judgment on the acceptability of the wages paid by the Sunshine Harvester Company. The case, which led the Court to fix a level which should be sufficient to provide a family of five with a minimum acceptable standard of living, created a precedent in wage-fixing negotiation (ibid. 255–6). The judgment was never formally implemented however, and in 1919, the question of a family wage was again raised, this time through the Royal Commission on the Basic Wage. After having reviewed family needs in terms of food, clothing, housing, transport, and so on, the Commission finally established a basic minimum income to provide for the needs of a family composed of a man, his wife, and three children. Considered as being too high by the government, the Commission eventually suggested a lower minimum wage, plus a complementary family allowance. This recommendation was never implemented, mainly for economic reasons.

Formal opposition to family allowances was subsequently expressed by the 1927 Royal Commission on Family Endowment on the grounds that: 'basic wage schemes then in operation already contained an element of family needs adjustment, sufficient, if directly applied, to provide for all existing children' (ibid. 259). Furthermore, the Commission argued that the cost of family allowances would be prohibitive and would weaken parental responsibility. As a result, family allowances were not introduced on a national level, but only in New South Wales, in 1927, and on a means-tested basis. The previous year, a similar means-tested scheme had been adopted in New Zealand, but only for the third and subsequent children. This scheme, which followed lengthy debates about the notion of a minimum wage, constituted the first nation-wide family allowance system in the world. Its scope was eventually considerably extended in 1939 to cover all children.

In most other industrialized countries, neither the concept of equalization funds nor that of living wages were seriously considered. But, in the context of the economic hardship of the 1920s and 1930s some measures were nevertheless implemented in order to provide families with some relief. Cost-of-living bonuses were introduced by some employers in Denmark, Finland, Norway, and Sweden after the First World War, but were considered to be strictly temporary. As soon as economic conditions were improved, these schemes were abolished (ILO, 1924). In Austria, a temporary relief system was also adopted in 1921 following the model of the French equalization fund, but was eventually dismantled (ibid.).

Widows' allowances and family allowances

The breakthrough came in several countries through the introduction of cash benefits targeted not at all families, but at an acknowledged deserving group: widows and orphans. Despite their selective nature, widows' and orphans' benefits constituted a precedent as they were the first form of cash benefits for families administered and provided by the state (see Table 3.2). In Britain, this early form of cash benefit was provided in the form of the separation allowance, introduced in 1914 for the wives and children of soldiers. This allowance was transformed in 1925 into a widows' and orphans' pension as part of the Contributory Pensions Act. For family allowance activists, this intervention raised some hopes that the government might eventually extend this measure to all mothers and maintain it in peace time (Fleming, 1986: 48). In Canada, Denmark, Germany, and Australia, widows' and orphans' pensions were introduced immediately before or just after the First World War. In the United States, widows' allowances were introduced in 1911, and aimed at providing widows with money in order to allow them to keep their children at home rather than send them to orphanages. By 1919, the scheme had been adopted by thirty-nine states (Patterson, 1981). This initial state intervention into family life created a major precedent. In particular, it provided the basis for a new benefit in 1935 (as part of Roosevelt's New Deal) which extended the widow's benefit to divorced and deserted mothers (ibid. 68).

Table 3.2 *First cash benefit schemes for families, pre-1945*

Country	Year of introduction	Title of scheme
A: Widows' and orphans' allowances		
Australia	1925	Widows' pension*
Austria	1926	Orphans' pensions*
Belgium	1924	Widows'/orphans' insurance*
Canada	1916	Mothers' allowance**
Denmark	1913	Orphans' assistance**
Finland	1897	Widows'/orphans' insurance*
France	1928	Widows'/orphans' insurance*
Germany	1911	Widows'/orphans' pensions*
Luxembourg	1911	Widows'/orphans' pensions*
Netherlands	1913	Widows'/orphans' pensions*
New Zealand	1926	Widows'/orphans' pensions**
Switzerland	1925	Widows'/orphans' insurance*
United Kingdom	1914	Separation allowances
	1925	Widows'/orphans' pensions*
United States	1911	Mothers' pensions**
B: Other cash benefits for families		
Australia	1927	Child allowance
Belgium	1930	Family allowances
France	1913	Assistance for large families
	1918	Birth premiums
	1923	Benefits for large families
	1932	Family allowances
Germany	1936	Family allowances
Italy	1937	Family allowances
	1939	Fertility premiums
Luxembourg	1924	Assistance for large families
Netherlands	1925	Cost-of-living bonus
	1939	Family allowances
New Zealand	1926	Family allowances
Spain	1926	Assistance for large families
	1938	Family allowances
United Kingdom	1944	Family allowances
United States	1935	Aid to dependent children

Key: *: Contributory scheme (as part of social insurance). **: Non-contributory scheme (as part of social assistance). Notes for part A: Australia: New South Wales only. Provided weekly cash benefits. Austria: Provided orphans' pension to children of salaried employees. Belgium: Provided benefits to workers (extended to salaried employed in 1930).

Table 3.2:*(cont.)*

Canada: First adopted in Manitoba. Extended to other provinces as follows: Saskatchewan (1917), Alberta (1919), Ontario and British Columbia (1920), New Brunswick and Nova Scotia (1930). Denmark: Provided means-tested assistance to orphans. Finland: Provided assistance to members of the Fund (Mutual Aid Fund). A State Official Fund for widows and orphans also provided assistance to members. France: Provided pensions to insured members. Restricted to widows with at least three children under the age of 13. Germany: Provided pensions to insured workers (extended to salaried in 1913). Luxembourg: Provided pensions to insured members. Netherlands: Provided pensions to insured members. New Zealand: Provided pensions on a non-contributory basis (means-tested). Switzerland: Provided pensions to insured members. The Fund for Old Age and Widows and Orphans was set up in 1926. United Kingdom: Provided pensions to insured members. United States: First adopted in Illinois. By the end of 1919, similar schemes had been adopted in 39 States. Notes for part B: Australia: New South Wales only. Restricted to second and subsequent children (means-tested). Belgium: General scheme. France: (1913) Restricted to families with more than three children. Subject to a means-test. (1923) Restricted to families with three and more children. (1932) General family allowance scheme. Germany: Restricted to fifth and subsequent children (of sound German origin). Italy: (1937) Provided to workers in industry, commerce, and agriculture (means-tested). Luxembourg: Restricted to large families with more than three children. Subject to a means-test. Netherlands: (1925) Paid in respect of every child below the age of 18, equal to 3% of wages. (1939) Restricted to employees. Paid for third and subsequent children. New Zealand: Restricted to third and subsequent children. Subject to a means-test. Spain: (1926) Restricted to families with eight and more children. Subject to a means-test. (1938) Restricted to employees. United States: Restricted to lone-parents. Subject to a means-test.

Contrary to other countries, however, this new ADC (Aid to Dependent Children) benefit was never generalized into a comprehensive family allowance system.

Meanwhile, in France and Belgium, governments eventually yielded to public pressure and transformed the equalization funds into national family allowance schemes. In both countries, pro-natalist and economic considerations were the main motives behind this state intervention. In particular, referring to the Family Allowance Bill, the Belgian Minister of Labour stated that: 'Above all, the Bill aims at encouraging births and large families' (Glass, 1940: 128). But, as argued by Glass, family allowances were also introduced for other reasons:

It would, however, be quite incorrect to deduce that the Act was passed largely because of its possible demographic results. Much support was given to it for entirely different reasons. Many people simply wanted to remove the inequality created by the 1928 Act, which left over half the employed population out of the scheme. Others were afraid that, unless the State took over the system, it might gradually break up as it had in so many other countries. And certainly the workers' organizations welcomed a measure which removed family allowances from the dependence upon the generosity of the employers. The combination of these motives made the passage of the Act an easy matter, and the family allowance system, though of later growth than in France, was made compulsory two years earlier. (ibid. 128–9)

Under National Socialist regimes, actions were also taken to introduce a general system of family allowances. For instance, in Germany, a system of grants was adopted in 1936. Of a pro-natalist nature, the grants were available only from the fifth child (from the third in 1939), and were subject to strict eugenic eligibility conditions (ibid. 295–6; Bock, 1991: 242–3). In Italy, a general system of family allowances was introduced by the government in 1937 making it 'obligatory to pay family allowances in respect of dependent children to every family breadwinner, of whatever nationality, employed by other persons' (Glass, 1940: 252). There also, this state initiative was driven by pro-natalist, economic, and welfare considerations. In 1939, the pro-natalist objective was given further weight through the introduction of fertility bonuses to be given as a lump sum at the birth of a child (Saraceno, 1991: 203). In a similar way, family allowances and family bonuses were introduced in Spain, in 1938 and 1945 respectively. Both were conditional on employment and were paid directly to the father. Only under exceptional conditions were the allowances paid to the mother (Nash, 1991: 172).

If at the turn of the century the role of governments as providers of cash benefit for families was nearly absent, the above examples are illustrative of major changes. On the eve of the war, more than a dozen countries had introduced nation-wide schemes, either in the form of widows' and orphans' pensions, family allowances, or lone-parent benefits. These early forms of cash benefits constituted a major development in the history of state support for families.

3.3 Motherhood and employment

The other major development in state support for families was in the field of maternity policies. Since high levels of infant and child mortality were partly seen to be the result of unfavourable working conditions, several measures were directed at working mothers in order to improve their conditions immediately before and after childbirth. Before analysing these measures, it is important to review the prevailing attitudes concerning working mothers as they strongly influenced the subsequent legislation.

Opinion on working mothers

Among women's groups, three main ideologies prevailed: one which valued motherhood as a profession, and saw it as a social function; one which sought recognition of women's right to work and demanded equality between men and women; and a middle position, which asked for the recognition of the woman's right to choose between paid employment and housework. The first position was clearly expressed by the German Verband Fortschrittlicher Frauenvereine (League of Progressive Women's Associations) in its demand for housework, or mother-work, to be recognized as a 'productive occupation' and as 'professional work' (Stoehr, 1991: 214). This position was also emphasized in Germany by feminists, such as Marianne Weber, who stressed the value of housewives' work (ibid. 218). In Norway, the principle of 'motherhood as women's main profession' was endorsed by Katti Anker Moller, while in France, discussions centred around the concept of 'maternity as a social function' (Blom, 1991: 24; Cova, 1991: 122). The second position is entirely opposed to the previous one in calling for the recognition of women's work and equality with men. This position found support, for example, among the feminist middle-class movement for women's rights in Norway, and in the person of Kathe Schirmacher in Germany (Seip and Ibsen, 1991: 48; Stoehr, 1991: 216). The third position was one of compromise in calling for the acknowledgement of a woman's right to choose between motherhood and employment (and to combine both). For instance, in Britain, Labour Women 'sought a feminism which valued rather than devalued the home and maternal experience of women without simultaneously devaluing women's paid labour' (Thane, 1991: 96). The right of women to employment and motherhood was also claimed by the leader of the Norwegian Association for Women's Rights, Margarete Bonnevie, who argued that child allowances 'might be used to procure help from maids or nurses to take care of children so that mothers who wanted to pursue their professional careers or political activities might be free to do so' (Blom, 1991: 33-4).

Despite these diverging opinions, there was a common point. All these groups called for state intervention in order to reduce women's financial dependence on their husbands. For supporters of full-time motherhood, this meant providing women with a mothers' wage, while for others, state intervention was meant to provide women with facilities so as to enable them to combine paid employment and motherhood. In particular, Eleanore Rathbone in Britain, and the Ligue de la Mère au Foyer in France, actively campaigned for the introduction of a mother's wage. This call however did not receive much support from governments. If the concept of family allowances had already faced considerable opposition in several countries, that of a mother's wage was even more controversial.

Governments' views about women's employment also diverged. There was first the view that full-time motherhood was preferable for the well-being of children, and for that of the whole family. Only if money was desperately needed, for instance among the working classes, was it acknowledged that a woman might need to take up paid employment. This view was prevalent in several countries, and was even accompanied by measures to forbid female employment. For example, in Britain as in several other European countries, 'marriage bars' were aimed at excluding women from a whole range of occupations (Thane, 1991: 98; Offen, 1991: 144). In a similar vein, the Fuero del Trabajo in Spain was aimed explicitly at excluding married women from employment (Nash, 1991: 171). In Germany, the marriage loans produced the same effect by being granted only to couples in which the wife gave up employment after getting married (Glass, 1940: 287-9). The only period when this view was altered was during the war when serious labour-force shortages led governments and employers to seek women's participation. This was however viewed as an essentially temporary measure.

In contrast, in countries such as Sweden and France, the right of women to paid employment was more accepted. For instance, Jenson reports that while in Britain the belief was that 'the mother's place was at home', in France, the state was generally supportive of women's work (Jenson, 1980: 21). Similarly, in 1939 the Swedish government expressed its support of women's employment by making it unlawful for employers to dismiss women because of marriage, pregnancy, or childbirth (Sundstrom, 1991: 188).

Despite these divergences, there was none the less a consensus: in view of the high levels of infant mortality, governments should regulate the working conditions of pregnant women who needed to work for financial reasons.

Maternity leave benefits

Concern about the health of mothers and children was one of the main motives behind the adoption of the first legislation allowing women (or making it compulsory) to take time off from work immediately before and after confinement. For most countries, the first legislation concerning time off for childbirth was adopted between 1900 and 1915. The measure, which was restricted to unpaid leave, was mainly preventive, and was seen as a means of avoiding adverse effects on children's health. It was a relatively complex legislation covering in most cases only specific categories of workers, for example, wage-earners or factory workers. A summary of this legislation appears in Table 3.3.

Switzerland, Germany, and Austria took the lead before 1885 by introducing leave of three to eight weeks. Other countries followed shortly: Portugal (1891), the United Kingdom (1895); Belgium (1899); Spain (1900), Sweden (1900); and Ireland (1901). While the appearance of leading industrialized countries in this list is not surprising, the particularly early adoption of legislation in Portugal, Spain, and Italy should be underlined.

This was the first step. The next one came through the introduction of cash benefits to be paid during the period of maternity leave. Again, it was relatively complex legislation covering specific categories of workers, in addition to imposing in several cases maximum salaries above which workers became ineligible to the scheme. A summary of this legislation appears in Table 3.4.

This time the lead was taken by Germany with the introduction, in 1883, of benefits representing 50 per cent of the women's regular pay. This innovative measure was part of Bismarck's social security system, which acknowledged state and employers' responsibility for the compensation of social risks (sickness, accident, disability). The coverage of the initial scheme was limited, and was eventually significantly improved with the adoption of the Federal Insurance Code in 1926. Again, other countries gradually followed, but with less comprehensive schemes, most of which were voluntary rather than compulsory, and provided lump-sum or flat rate benefits instead of benefits proportional to wages.

The developments in this field were nevertheless significant. On the eve of the Second World War, all countries, with the exception of Canada and the United States, had adopted some form of paid maternity leave. In Italy, cash benefits were first introduced in 1910 and were administered by the National Maternity Fund. The Fund was a national version of local funds initiated earlier by women and financed by female workers themselves, along with donations from benefactors (Buttafuoco, 1991: 183-7). The National Fund performed the same function but was financed through both state and employers' contributions. However, the unwillingness of employers to contribute to it, in addition to the few safeguards that it provided to women, aroused severe dissatisfaction (ibid. 189-191). Only in 1925 were more satisfactory conditions introduced through the creation of the ONMI (National Foundation for Maternity and Child Welfare) which placed the maternity funds

Table 3.3 *First maternity leave legislation (unpaid scheme), pre-1945*

Period	Country	Year of introduction	Duration of leave
Pre-1905	Switzerland	1877	8 weeks
	Germany	1878	3 weeks
	Austria	1884	6 weeks
	Portugal	1891	4 weeks
	United Kingdom	1895	4 weeks
	Belgium	1899	4 weeks
	Spain	1900	4 weeks
	Sweden	1900	4 weeks
	Ireland	1901	4 weeks
1905–1918	Italy	1907	4 weeks
	New Zealand	1908	4 weeks
	France	1909	8 weeks
	Netherlands	1910	4 weeks
	Japan	1911	5 weeks
	Australia	1912	4 weeks
	United States	1912	4 weeks
	Greece	1912	8 weeks
	Denmark	1913	4 weeks
	Norway	1915	4 weeks
	Finland	1917	4 weeks
1919–1944	Canada	1921	12 weeks
	Luxembourg	1925	8 weeks

Canada: No national scheme, only provincial legislation. Data refers here to British Columbia (i.e. first province to introduce such legislation). France: The scheme was voluntary. In 1913 a 6-week compulsory scheme was introduced. Luxembourg: The scheme was introduced through the Social Insurance Code and included cash benefits. Norway: An earlier scheme introduced in 1909 included leave for 6 weeks with cash benefits, but was voluntary. The 1915 Workers Protection Act was compulsory and included 6 weeks of unpaid leave. United States: No national scheme, only state legislation. Data refers here to Massachusetts (i.e. first state to introduce such legislation). Note that the coverage of the schemes was restricted to the following groups of workers (i) Workers in industry: Germany, Portugal, Sweden, Switzerland; (ii) Workers in factories: Japan (wage-earner only), Ireland, Netherlands, New Zealand, United Kingdom, United States (Massachusetts); (iii) Workers in factories and industry: Finland; (iv) Workers in industry and commerce: Canada (wage-earner only), Greece (wage-earner only); (v) Wage-earners in general: Denmark, Luxembourg, Spain; (vi) Wage-earners and employees: Norway.

Table 3.4 *Maternity leave benefits (paid schemes), pre-1945*

Period	Country	Year of introduction	Duration of leave	Type of benefit
Pre-1900	Germany	1883	6 weeks	c/50%
	Belgium	1894	6 weeks	v/FR
1900-15	Italy	1910	4 weeks	c/LS
	Austria	1911	4 weeks	c/60%
	Switzerland	1911	6 weeks	v/FR
	United Kingdom	1911	4 weeks	c/LS
	Australia	1912	4 weeks	m/LS
	France	1913	8 weeks	c/FR
	Ireland	1913	4 weeks	c/LS
	Netherlands	1913	12 weeks	c/100%
	Denmark	1915	2 weeks	v/FR
	Norway	1915	8 weeks	v/FR
1916-44	Japan	1922	10 weeks	c/60%
	Portugal	1922	10 weeks	c/100%
	Luxembourg	1925	8 weeks	c/50%
	New Zealand	1926	4 weeks	v/LS
	Spain	1929	10 weeks	c/FR
	Sweden	1931	8 weeks	v/LS
	Greece	1934	12 weeks	c/33%
	Finland	1937	6 weeks	m/LS

Key: c: compulsory; v: voluntary (optional); m: means-tested benefits; LS: lump sum benefit; FR: flat rate benefit; x%: benefits proportional to earnings (indicated percentage of earnings). Finland: Cash benefits provided under the Maternity Assistance Law 1937. Duration of leave regulated by the Work Order 1934. Germany: The 1883 legislation introduced sickness insurance for blue-collar and (a small number of) white-collar workers below a certain income level. The maternity benefits, equal to 50% of wages, were paid for a maximum of 6 weeks. The laws of 1885 and 1886 extended the coverage of the scheme to workers in trade and agriculture. New Zealand: Cash benefits provided under the National Provident Act 1926. Duration of leave regulated by the Factories Act 1908. Portugal: Under the Hours of Work Regulation 1922 the employer must pay the full wages during the statutory absence of women emplyed in commercial and industrial establishment. The Corporative Social Insurance Decree 1933 included variable provisions according to the insurance funds. Sweden: Cash benefits provided by the Royal Order: Sickness Insurance Funds 1931. Duration of leave regulated by the Workers' Protection Act 1931. Note that the following restrictions applied with regard to the coverage of scheme: (i) Members only: Belgium (Members of the Mutual Benefit Societies), New Zealand (Members of National Provident Fund), Sweden (Members of Sickness Insurance Funds); (ii) Insured workers only: Switzerland (under the Sickness Insurance Act); (iii) Wage-earners only : Greece, Japan (high-earners excluded), Luxembourg (high-earners excluded), Netherlands (high-earners excluded); (iv) Wage-earners and employees: Norway, Spain; (v) Workers in industry and commerce: Portugal.

under a single umbrella.

In addition to these early initiatives, an important impetus came in 1919 with the adoption by the ILO (International Labour Office) of the Maternity Protection Convention. This Convention, which included provision for six weeks leave before childbirth and six weeks after childbirth, also included specifications on cash benefits 'sufficient for the full and healthy maintenance of the mother and child' (ILO, 1939: 51). This Convention was followed by significant upgrading in maternity leave schemes in several countries. In particular, a certain convergence towards a 12-week leave with flat rate benefits was observed, but still with major inter-country differences. The situation, as of 1945, was very disparate, with Australia, Denmark, Finland, New Zealand, and Sweden providing only voluntary or means-tested maternity benefits, and Canada and the United States not providing any form of maternity pay. The appearance of Finland and Sweden among the former group is interesting. Despite the support for working women, on the eve of the Second World War, the Finnish and Swedish governments had still not implemented a national compulsory scheme. In contrast to this lagging position, these two countries will emerge as definite leaders with regard to the provision of maternity benefits from the 1960s. These inter-country dissimilarities are clearly noticeable from Figure 3.1.

By 1945, eleven countries still offered maternity leave of a duration below the 12-week period specified in the ILO convention. Moreover, more than half the countries provided women with only limited cash benefits, either in the form of flat rate benefits or lump sum payment. Only in Belgium, Germany, Greece, Japan, Luxembourg, and the Netherlands were wage-related benefits provided.

Child care facilities

If concern about the health and well-being of children justified maternity leave legislation, fewer efforts were devoted to the development of child-care facilities. Provision in this field came mainly from the informal sector. Already in the nineteenth century several day-care centres had been set up by religious and other philanthropic groups in countries such as Belgium, Canada, Germany, Finland, Portugal, Spain, and the United States (Olmstead and Weikart, 1989). Welfare considerations were dominant as these centres were targeted at families from poor or modest backgrounds whose mothers were forced to work for financial reasons. Children from lone-parent families and from working class parents were the main clients of these centres. But, these early nurseries had also another vocation: that of providing children with a better environment, and of protecting them from 'accidents and vagrancy' (Delhaxhe, 1989: 24). Influenced by Froebel's (1782–1852) theory, early education was given much importance. Government intervention in this field was minimal, and in most cases restricted to the adoption of adequate child-care standards (see Table 3.5).

In Belgium, for example, the government published in 1880 the first regulation concerning the standards for institutions taking care of children aged 3 to 6 years old (ibid. 24–5). In the same vein, the German government adopted in 1922 the Youth Welfare Act which acknowledged the right of every child to an education,

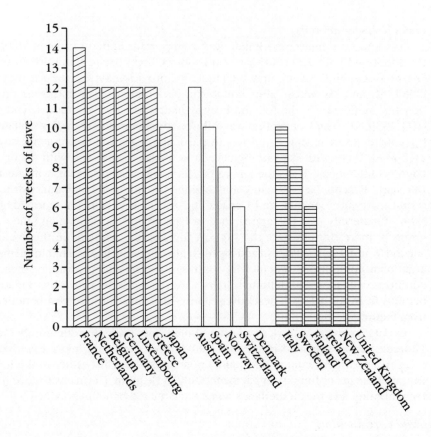

Fig. 3.1 *Maternity leave schemes, 1945*

Type of benefits: ⬚ Wage-related   ⬚ Flat rate   ⬚ Lump sum

Note: Benefits equal to the following percentage of wage were paid: France (50%), Netherlands (100%), Belgium (60%), Germany (50%), Luxembourg (50%), Greece (33%), Japan (60%). Portugal is excluded in view of its variable maternity provision (see Table 3.4).

and obliged public authorities to provide, directly or indirectly, such provision. The law still minimized public intervention in giving priority to welfare organizations in the running and founding of kindergartens (Tietze, Rossbach, and Ufermann, 1989: 44). On the other hand, publicly funded institutions were set up in Finland from 1888, and in Portugal from 1882. In the United States, childhood care and education programmes received the support of the federal government from the 1930s as a way of providing jobs for unemployed professionals. Olmstead (1989) reports that through the federally sponsored Work Projects Administration scheme, 1,900 programmes were established, covering nearly 40,000 children (by 1937).

Table 3.5 *Child-care related legislation and programmes, pre-1945*

Country	Start-up year	Title of programmes
Belgium	1880	First regulations for the institutions taking care of children aged 3 to 6
Finland	1888	First public kindergartens for children of poor families
Germany	1922	Youth Welfare Act
Portugal	1882	First official kindergarten in Lisbon
United States	1935	Early Childhood Care and Education Programme
	1941	Lanham Act

But, as in other countries, the coverage of these programmes was still limited, and their financing mainly reliant on private donations.

The situation changed considerably during the war when the participation of women in the labour market was strongly encouraged. For example, in the United States stronger state support for child-care was given through the 1941 Lanham Act which provided matching funds for states to establish day care centres and nursery schools. The results were impressive: between 105,000 and 130,000 children were enrolled in Lanham centres by 1945 (ibid. 371). Following the end of the war, however, these centres and other wartime child-care programmes were dismantled everywhere, with the exception of California and New York City. The return to peace had a similar effect in Britain where the wartime nurseries were rapidly closed in 1945 (Lewis, 1991: 29).

In contrast to these minimal state interventions, the public provision of day care was given considerable attention in Sweden where it appeared among the main items considered by the 1935 Population Commission (Carlson, 1990: 131). At the time of the Commission, day nurseries, kindergartens, and nursery schools were already in place, but covered only a fraction of the children's population. The Commission consequently saw a need for both expanding and subsidizing these activities (Myrdal, 1947: 392). Parliament however took no substantive action in this field in view of the additional funds needed in the military sector on the eve of the Second World War (Carlson, 1990: 176).

In this early period, much opposition was thus expressed by governments towards women's participation in the labour force, and was reflected by the existence of explicit employment bars, or by implicit lack of support for working mothers. Despite this situation, significant measures were taken to protect pregnant workers. The introduction of maternity leave, however, was not driven by considerations related to women's equality, but instead by considerations related to the health of mothers and children. If women had to work for financial reasons, governments acknowledged that they and their children had to be protected. Measures taken in the field of day care were also driven by similar motives, that is to protect children of working mothers, but not to encourage women's employment. Such an ideology was prevalent, for example, in Britain where a clear opposition to women's employment was accompanied by no public provision for child care (excepted during the war). In contrast, the situation in France and Sweden denoted a much greater support for working mothers.

3.4   From piecemeal intervention to comprehensive programmes

Although the pre-World War II period experienced a significant increase in state interest in and support for families, the concrete measures which were implemented were isolated rather than part of a comprehensive package of cash benefits and services. Furthermore, they had only limited coverage, being mainly targeted at the most needy families. There were some exceptions however as in the cases of France, Sweden, and Germany.

In France, a major development came in 1939 with the adoption of the Code de la Famille. The Code, which was to form the cornerstone of French family policy, had been prepared by the Chief Committee on Population referred to in Chapter 2. Through the Code, the government was to provide families with a comprehensive package of benefits, in addition to strengthening the pro-natalist orientation of its policy. The Code included two main components. The first comprised a series of cash benefits including family allowances. These allowances had been introduced at an earlier stage, but were substantially reformed under the Code, by being eliminated for the first child, and strongly increased for the third and subsequent children. A birth premium for the first child was also introduced, provided that it was born within two years following marriage. In addition, the Code generalized to all urban agglomerations the cash benefit for the housewife (*allocation pour la mère au foyer*). The allowance was fixed to 10 per cent of the basic wage (Glass, 1940: 213). Finally, as part of the new Code, the tax system was reformed to make it more favourable for families. In particular, the tax rebate for children was strongly increased, as well as the tax penalties for childless individuals (ibid. 169, 215-6).

The second component of the Code comprised measures which fell under the heading of protection of maternity and childhood, and the protection of people. They included a strengthening of the ban against abortion, the development of perinatal health services, the enactment of legislation concerning adoption, and the development of programmes against substance abuse and alcoholism. In addition, a section was devoted to 'family and education' which made compulsory the teaching in schools of demographic problems (Chauvière, 1992: 1447-8). With this Code, the government was consequently grouping in a single package a series of measures targeted at families, and in this respect, brought a major development in the field of family policy. The mere fact that the responsibility for implementing this Code was given to eighteen distinct ministries, meant however that the new policy was still disparate and deficient (ibid. 1448). It nevertheless constituted a formidable step compared to the actions taken by governments in most other countries, which were more piecemeal.

In Sweden, under the influence of the Myrdals, the notion of family policy was given considerable attention. As mentioned in Chapter 2, pro-natalist considerations also stimulated this discussion. However, and conversely to France, the principle of voluntary parenthood was clearly acknowledged in the policy package suggested by the Myrdals. Population quality, as well as population quantity, had to be supported. In their blueprint for a population/family policy, the Myrdals consequently suggested liberal access to contraception, and measures related to free health services, housing benefits, food subsidies, free education, free nursery education, clothing subsidies, subsidized and improved recreational facilities for families, increased employment security for fathers and mothers, and social responsibility for children of broken families or handicapped families (Myrdal, 1947: 131–2).

Most of these measures received the backing of the first Commission on Population, which was strongly dominated by Gunnar Myrdal. In particular, the Commission endorsed Myrdal's view in giving preference to in-kind rather than in-cash benefits. Some of these measures, including the tax exemption for children, and rent rebates for families with children, were implemented at an early stage. In addition, measures in the form of home-furnishing loans, means-tested cash benefits for orphans and certain categories of children, and advance maintenance payment for divorced women were also adopted in 1937–38 (Glass, 1940). Moreover, in support of the principle of voluntary parenthood, legislation on abortion and contraception was liberalized in 1938. Further developments in this field were however prevented by the wartime preparation. Although the measures adopted by the Swedish government in the pre-World War II period did not constitute a policy package in the same sense as that adopted in France, they nevertheless clearly reflected the acknowledgement of state responsibility in the support of families.

The last case considered here is that of Germany under the national socialist regime. Again, the series of measures which was adopted by the Fascist government comprised both in-kind and in-cash benefits, and as in France and Sweden, carried strong pro-natalist orientations. But contrarily to these two other countries, the population policy adopted in Germany also included explicit eugenic objectives which banned certain families from state support, and which imposed sterilization for 'hereditary inferior individuals' (Bock, 1991: 235). Among the other measures adopted, a marriage loan was introduced in 1933. The loan, which was also subject to eugenic criteria, was interest-free and partly cancelled out on the birth of each child. In addition, it was only granted if the future wife agreed to give up employment upon marriage (Glass, 1940: 287). Tax exemption for children and tax penalties for childless couples were also increased between 1934 and 1939 in an effort to stimulate fertility (ibid. 299–301). Finally, a child allowance scheme was introduced in 1936, but once again under strict eugenic considerations. This series of measures thus formed a significant package for families, and marked a significant involvement of the state towards families. This policy constituted a precedent in the field of family policy, even though its eugenic orientation and coercive components would eventually be strongly disapproved of by the international community.

3.5 Conclusion

Although state support for families is mainly the product of the post-World War II era, the measures which were adopted in the pre-war period undeniably marked a major departure from the earlier time in reflecting a major increase in the degree of state intervention into family life. The newly implemented in-kind and in-cash benefits for families contrasted considerably from earlier measures of relief, mainly provided by the informal sector. Concerns about the health and well-being of mothers and children, as well as pro-natalist concerns, were strong motives for this greater intervention of the state as welfare provider. But, behind this general trend, strong inter-country differences had already emerged. While Germany, Austria, and Switzerland were taking the lead with regard to the provision of maternity leave, Belgium and France were taking the lead with regard to the provision of cash benefits. Britain and the United States tended to target their intervention to the most necessitous and deserving families (i.e. poor children, widows and orphans) while still leaving a room for philanthropic initiatives. On the other hand, Sweden emerged as a distinct case in acknowledging the principle of voluntary parenthood and the right of women to employment.

These early inter-country differences are important as they will tend to be maintained over the following decades. So, if state intervention of the pre-World War II appeared as limited and scattered, it nevertheless instituted some of the foundations of the post-war state support for families.

4

THE EXPANSION OF STATE SUPPORT FOR FAMILIES

With the return to peace, new economic and political conditions emerged, and favoured a major expansion of state support for families. In contrast to the scattered measures of the pre-World War II period, the post-war policy of governments towards families was to be characterized by the universality of its support and the comprehensiveness of its coverage. It was the golden era of the welfare state. It is this change in the governments' policy which is now examined for the three decades following the end of the war, up to the mid-1970s. The analysis begins with an examination of the changes in the demographic, social, and economic environment of families, which were to provide the new bases for an expanded state support for families. The cases of family allowances and maternity benefits are then examined in more detail. Despite the persistence of significant inter-country differences, this period witnessed a certain convergence across countries in the provision of state support for families.

4.1 The new social, political, and economic order

For citizens, the new political order meant the end of wartime sufferings, and hopes of a better future. Improved standards of living were expected, and with it a more active role for governments as welfare providers. They were now expected to provide citizens with an insurance; an insurance that there would be no return to the pre-war economic depression, or to wartime deprivation. For governments, the new political order also meant new ideologies. In particular, there was a commitment — at least in Europe — to repair the damages of the war, and to give citizens a new sense of security and prosperity.

Some initiatives taken at the international as well as national levels during the immediate post-war period would also convey these new expectations for a better future, and for a new relationship between governments and citizens. Among these was the adoption by the United Nations of the Universal Declaration of Human Rights in 1948 which laid down some of the foundations of the post-war welfare state by acknowledging the role and duties of the state towards its citizens, and enshrined the right of citizens to social security and state support. In particular, the Declaration acknowledged two main principles:

- The right to a just and favourable remuneration (article 23.3), as well as the right to an adequate standard of living (article 25.1).

- The right to social security in the event of unemployment, sickness, disability, widowhood, old age or other lack of livelihood in circumstances beyond the individual's control (article 25.1). (United Nations, 1948)

Welfare and social security were consequently no longer reserved for the neediest, but were considered as a citizen's right. A clear shift in the orientation of social and welfare policies was therefore advocated, from one of limited assistance and relief to a more comprehensive and supportive one.

For families, the acknowledgement of these new welfare-state principles was significant especially since mothers and children were identified as a sub-group deserving special protection (article 25.2). A greater support from governments could therefore be expected. In 1959, the special status of children and their rights to state protection were further emphasized with the adoption by the United Nations of the Declaration of the Rights of the Child, superseding the first Declaration adopted in 1924. This revised version again acknowledged the principle that the child shall 'enjoy special protection' (article 2) and 'enjoy the benefits of social security' (article 4) (United Nations, 1959).

Another major event which gave further weight to the principles of universality and citizen's right to social security was the publication of the Beveridge report in Britain in 1942. This report was the work of the Inter-departmental Committee on Social Insurance and Allied Services set up in 1941 in response to 'growing public pressure for a guarantee that there would never be a return to the poverty and inequalities of pre-war Britain' (Fleming, 1986: 85). To chair this Committee, the government asked for the services of William Beveridge, who was already known for his involvement in the cause of family allowances, in leading, with Eleanore Rathbone, the Child Endowment Society. His report, published in November 1942, had immediate success, selling over 100,000 copies within the first month of its publication (Leaper, 1991: 6). In itself, the report did not introduce many novel ideas, as the notion of social insurance already had a long history. Where it innovated, however, was in its principle of universality. In particular, Beveridge argued that 'no scheme of social security would work unless a system of children's allowances was introduced, a comprehensive health service established, and the fullest possible level of employment maintained' (Silburn, 1991: 84). This report had a decisive influence on the adoption of universal family allowance schemes.

Another event which contributed to the emergence of more comprehensive government support for families was the adoption by the ILO of specific norms concerning social security benefits through the 1952 Revised Maternity Protection Convention, the 1952 Convention on Social Security (Minimum Standards), and the 1962 Convention on Social Policy (Basic Aims and Standards). In the history of state support for families, these texts were important for at least four reasons. First, although they mainly applied to workers, the ILO texts approached the idea of universality of social security by including both workers and their dependents as beneficiaries of social security programmes. In particular, they stated the principle that, in the case of any contingency, the family composition of the afflicted person has to be taken into consideration. Second, these texts acknowledged the occurrence of maternity and the death of the breadwinner as subject to social security protection and income compensation. These contingencies had therefore to be covered by specific rules and benefits. Third, the ILO texts acknowledged society's responsibility in ensuring the well-being of children and families. And finally, for some of these measures, especially family allowances, the texts stated that they should be provided to all families, independent of parental resources and income. Again, this was a major departure from previous practices which had targeted these benefits at the most needy families.

Together the United Nations Declaration on Human Rights, the Beveridge report, and the International Labour Office conventions laid the basis for a major expansion of state support for families and contributed to the acknowledgement of the new role of governments as welfare providers.

4.2   The changing demographic situation and renewed familism

In this period of major social changes, there were also major changes in the family. Fertility, which had reached unprecedented low levels before the war, was now increasing, and the family, as a traditional institution, was experiencing a renewed popularity. While the pre-war policy of governments was partly driven by fears of population and family decline, the emerging welfare state instead reflected the return to a strong and traditional family.

The post-war baby-boom

Among the immediate post-war changes, one of the most spectacular was the complete reversal in fertility (see Table 4.1). In England and Wales, the increase in

Table 4.1 *Total fertility rate in selected countries, 1945-1960*

Country	Average number of children per woman			
	1945	1950	1955	1960
England and Wales	2.04	2.18	2.22	2.68
France	2.28	2.93	2.68	2.73
Germany	1.53	2.09	2.13	2.37
Japan	4.63[a]	3.65	2.37	2.01
Sweden	2.59	2.32	2.25	2.17
United States	2.48	3.03	3.50	3.61

[a]: 1947 data

the total period fertility rate exceeded one child per woman, from a low point of 1.75 children per woman in 1941 to a first peak of 2.69 in 1947, and eventually a maximum of 2.94 in 1964. In France, the increase was of a similar magnitude, the

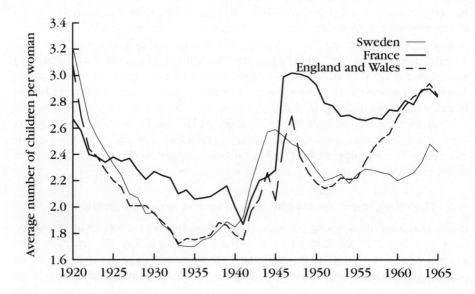

Fig. 4.1 *Total fertility rate, France, England and Wales, and Sweden, 1920–1965*

total fertility rate gaining more than one point from its lowest level of 1.87 in 1941 to its highest of 3.02 in 1947, and 2.90 in 1964. In the United States, the increase was even more spectacular, from a low point of 2.19 children per woman in 1936 to a maximum of 3.77 in 1957 (Sardon, 1990; Teitelbaum and Winter, 1985). The contrast with the 1920s and 1930s was therefore sharp. As can be seen in Figure 4.1 the post-war baby-boom marked a complete break with the previous trends.

Although the magnitude of the baby-boom varied across countries, in nearly all of them the pre-war and post-war trends were very different. There were however some exceptions. For example, the increase in fertility was delayed by several years in Germany, and reached a lower level than in most other countries. On the other hand, and contrary to most other countries, fertility in Japan declined from 1945.

In most countries, however, the baby-boom was both unexpected and spectacular. In retrospect, it is now obvious that the magnitude of the fertility reversal was artificially inflated. Post-war changes in the age at marriage and in the entry into motherhood distorted the total period fertility rate and suggested a higher fertility than that observed in cohorts. In fact, when one looks at fertility rates within cohorts, which is independent of changes in the timing of births, the post-war increase was much less spectacular, of the order of 0.3 to 0.5 child per woman. For example, in England and Wales, after reaching a minimum of 1.81 children per woman for the generation 1901–10, cohort fertility reached a maximum of 2.39 for the generation 1931–40 (Festy, 1979).

In general however, this new demographic situation was sufficient to eliminate earlier fears about population decline. A remedy to fertility decline apparently had been found, and there was no reason to be preoccupied still by this spectre.

The renewed family

The other major demographic change was the renewed popularity of marriage. While the celibacy rate among women aged 45–49 in 1921 was 27 per cent in Britain, it was reduced to 8 per cent for women of the same age group in 1971 (Coleman and Salt, 1992: 179). Similarly, in the United States, the proportion of ever-married women aged 25–29 increased from 75 per cent in 1910 to 92 per cent in 1965 (Spiegelman, 1968: 232).

The revival of the traditional family was also reflected in the very low levels of participation of women in the labour force, especially as compared to wartime. For example, while in the 1980s the labour force participation rate of women age 15–64 in Britain would reach more than 60 per cent, in 1950 it was still below 45 per cent. Similarly, in Sweden while the labour force participation of women would reach nearly 80 per cent in the 1980s, in 1960 it still averaged 50 per cent. Of course, the low level of participation of women in the labour force during this period was not only the result of a dominant traditional ideology. It also resulted from limited work opportunities. Viewed in combination with the increase in fertility and marriage, the low level of women's participation in the labour force reflected a genuine revival of the traditional housewife–male breadwinner family. This renewed familism was echoed in two other spheres: in the work of psychologists and sociologists, and in the family movement.

The mother–child relationship

In the immediate post-war period, a return to a stronger and traditional family was highly praised by new psychological and sociological studies. Among them, the work of the American sociologist Talcott Parsons was to be particularly influential in emphasizing the importance of the mother–child relationship. Although Parsons acknowledged that the family had lost some of its social functions, he argued that it remained the best institution to perform the functions of 'affection and companionship in the marital relationship and the socialization of children' (Popenoe, 1988: 26). Moreover, he argued that this socialization process was best achieved through a traditional sex-role segregation which strengthened the relationship between mother and child.

In Britain, the mother–child relationship, and the importance of 'good mothering', were stressed also. Full-time mothering was seen as having the utmost importance, and in a series of radio broadcasts in 1957 the psychologist Donald Woods Winnicott told his listeners about the nonsense of women refusing to take up their traditional role: 'talk about women not wanting to be housewives seems to me just nonsense because nowhere else but in her own home is a woman in such command' (Lewis, 1992: 18). In a similar vein, John Bowlby saw the mother–child unit also as of prime importance, while the father's role, although vital, was seen more for the emotional and economic security it provided. These theses became highly influential, especially through Bowlby's monograph published by the World

Health Organization in 1951 (reprinted in 1953 and 1965), and its paperback version *Child Care and the Growth of Love* (1953). These messages received a very favourable reception among the public. The war was over, 'normal life' was back, and furthermore, the economic recovery was allowing women to be freed from the labour market and able to devote themselves to their role of housewives and child-carers. Only in the mid-1960s was this new ideology to be challenged.

A new wave of the family movement

The renewed familism was also reflected in the revival of the family movement. As seen in Chapter 2, in the pre-war period the family movement had played a major role in protecting the interest of families and in calling for the introduction of more comprehensive support from governments. Similarly, in the immediate post-war period other family associations were set up to protect the interests of children, mothers, and families, and to put pressures on government for the adoption of additional measures. At the European level, the foundation of the Confederation of Family Organizations in the European Community (COFACE) in 1958 followed the adoption of the Treaty of Rome which laid down the foundation of a common European market. For the COFACE, a broad Europe was more than a common economic market, and consequently took up the task of campaigning for the adoption of a common family policy and the adoption of common standards for the protection and safeguarding of families.

At the national level, the family movement in France was given a major impetus following the creation by the government of the Union Nationale des Associations Familiales (UNAF) in 1945. The Gounot Law of 1942 had already given considerable power to family associations. In the same spirit, the decree of 1945 further empowered these associations by giving UNAF the status of 'a legally bound partner of the government for all questions related to families' (a.t., United Nations, 1989: 31). At its creation, UNAF included 661 national and regional associations, and subsequently played a significant role in the development of a family policy in France. Another national organization, the Fédération des familles de France, was also created during this period following the merging of several regional and national associations. Less closely linked with the political scene than UNAF, it was nevertheless strongly concerned about the standard of living of families; its objective being of 'allowing families to satisfy their vital needs in all fields: housing, health, education of children, culture, leisure . . . ' (a.t., Fédération des familles de France, 1989). These two organizations, along with their numerous local and regional branches, significantly contributed to keeping the family issue on the political agenda in France.

In a similar vein, families' interests were promoted in Luxembourg with the foundation of the Action Familiale et Populaire in 1947, and in the Netherlands with the Dutch Family Council in 1955. In the United Kingdom, on the other hand, major developments in the family movement took place only from the mid-1960s and tended to fall more under the banner of welfare organizations. This singularity, with its greater emphasis on families and children in need, was in line with earlier intervention. Actions were mainly focused on single-parent families, (e.g. Gingerbread Association founded in 1970), and poor children, (e.g. Child Poverty Action Group founded in 1965).

The immediate post-war period was undeniably a period of major changes: in the political and economic environment of families, and in their demographic situation. Together these changes were to alter radically the importance devoted to the family, and the basis of the governments support for families, and this, in at least three ways. First, there was the acknowledgement of the principle of citizens' right to welfare and state protection. Second, there was the increased visibility of the family as an institution deserving special protection. And third, there was the new praise for a traditional housewife–male-breadwinner family.

4.3   The new policy towards the population question

As a result of the return to high levels of fertility, fears of population decline, and more generally the whole population question, were eliminated from the political agenda of most countries. This was particularly the case in Germany, Italy, and Spain, where the experience of the Nazi's eugenic population policy led to censorship being applied to the whole population question. In fact, it is only from the 1970s onwards that the issue was raised again (see Chapter 8). The only exception is Germany in 1953 when the Chancellor referred explicitly to the demographic situation. Concerned about the persistence of relatively low fertility levels, and by their social and economic effects, the Chancellor stressed the need for the adoption of a population policy. This, he argued, was necessary 'because of the constantly growing proportion of older persons, the declining proportion of economically active, and the danger that declining production would make it impossible to care for the aged' (Schubnell, 1974: 695). The government was quick to bury the issue. If supporting and protecting the family was within the sphere of government responsibility, the fertility issue clearly fell outside it. Similarly, in Italy the government avoided for many years after the war specific references to population policy. The issue was only indirectly addressed by the Commission on Poverty and Employment in 1952. However, as reported by Berelson (1974: 659) the only results were a few timid suggestions for slowing the rate of population increase and many statements to the effect that the current population trends, with respect to unemployment and poverty, were of no consequence. Clearly, the population issue had been removed from the political agenda.

At the international level also, the population question did not receive much attention in the immediate post-war period. There were nevertheless some major initiatives, including the setting up of the United Nations Population Commission in 1946 (Symonds and Carder, 1973: 44). The Commission was the result of a joint British and American proposal and was mandated to conduct and commission studies on demographic trends, and to advise the Council on four distinct aspects: (i) the size and structure of the population; (ii) the interplay of demographic factors with economic and social factors; (iii) policies designed to influence the size and structure of the population; and (iv) any other demographic questions on which either the principal or the subsidiary organs of the United Nations or the Specialized Agencies might seek advice (Symonds and Carder, 1973: 44). Although the Commission did not play an immediate major role, it gradually paved the way for more significant action, especially in the 1960s (see Chapter 8). In particular, the publication of a series of documents (among which, the *Demographic Yearbook*, first published in 1948) contributed to a better knowledge of demographic trends.

The other main activity of the United Nations in the immediate post-war period, was the holding of the first post-war World Population Conference in Rome in 1954. A conference had already been held in 1927, but under the auspices of the League of Nations. Although it marked a continued interest in the population question, this first World Population Conference did not have the impact that subsequent ones were to have (see Chapters 7 and 8). In fact, there were no burning issues. The pre-war fears of population decline had vanished, and there was still no concern about the consequences of the new high fertility trend. Nor was the question of birth control an issue at that time. The reports by India, Egypt, and Japan concerning their family planning efforts were received apparently with respectful attention, but did not lead to any significant debate (Symonds and Carder, 1973: 86). This nevertheless paved the way for more significant actions and discussions from the 1960s onwards.

Against this general background, which gave a very low profile to the population question, there were two countries where the issue continued to occupy an important place in the immediate post-war period: France and Japan. In France, pro-natalism had been strongly promoted during the war. More babies were a guarantee of military power, and failure to bear babies was consequently putting in jeopardy the defence of the country. In the aftermath of the war, this position was reiterated when De Gaulle asked for 'twelve million beautiful babies' in order to restore the power of the country (Tomlinson, Huss, and Ogden, 1985: 31). Thus, in contrast to the other countries, the French government took significant actions in the immediate post-war period to strengthen its pro-natalist orientation and to maintain the profile of the population question. In particular, it set up in 1945 the High Consultative Committee for the Population and the Family. Initially composed of a dozen members, the Committee was seen as a major body which ought to be consulted by the government on all measures concerning the protection of the family and trends in fertility. In addition, its mandate included issues related to rural emigration, urban decentralization, the settling of immigrants and their integration into the French population (United Nations, 1989a: 34). In 1950, the Committee was then asked to produce a report on the French demographic situation and its future trends. In addition, the government set up in 1945 a demographic institute, the Institut National d'Etudes Démographiques (INED), in order to better monitor trends in the demographic situation.

In Japan also the population question continued to occupy attention in the immediate post-war period. But, in contrast to France, it was an anti-natalist attitude which was to prevail. The devastated economy, and the repatriation of a large number of Japanese nationals, led the government to believe that the rate of population growth had to be slowed down if economic recovery and improved standards of living were to be achieved (Muramatsu and Kuroda, 1974: 709). For Japan, this anti-natalist position marked a radical departure from the pro-natalist stance endorsed during the war. As a result, the Japanese government took action to better monitor the demographic trends and to be better advised concerning policy alternatives. Among these initiatives was the setting up of the Foundation Institute for Research on the Population Problem, in 1946. In its report, this quasi-governmental organization stressed the problems created by the unprecedented increase in population, and recommended the improvement of the country's capacity to sustain a fastly growing population, as well as the regulation of the rate of population growth (United Nations, 1984: 272). In 1949, the Population Problems Research Council was set up at the request of the Prime Minister. As part of its interim recommendations, the Council stressed the need for a reduction in the population growth rate. In particular, it made specific suggestions concerning the provision of family planning facilities (United Nations, 1984: 271).

Responding to these recommendations, the Japanese government launched in 1951 a national family planning programme and so was among the first countries to acknowledge explicitly the problem of rapid population growth rate, and to take concrete action to counteract this trend. This action moreover was in sharp contrast to the pro-natalist policy adopted in the early 1940s. The next major government initiative came in 1953 with the setting up of a new Population Problems Advisory Council. In its series of reports between 1954 and 1963, the Council pointed to the difficulties created by a fast-growing population, and suggested relevant policies to cope with these problems (United Nations, 1984).

4.4 The new policy towards the family

The renewed familism was to change the nature of the governments' policy towards the family. In particular, the new policy placed a greater emphasis on the protection of families, and especially on the mother and child relationship. The policy thus emphasized the central role of the family as a societal institution, and praised the traditional male breadwinner and housewife structure. This renewed interest in the family, and the governments' commitment to better support it, were reflected in a series of actions taken at both the international and national levels. Some of these initiatives for the period 1945–59 are reported in Table 4.2.

At the international level, the setting up of the United Nations Children's Fund (UNICEF) in 1946 marked a major development. Started as a temporary fund to provide relief for the children suffering in war-devastated Europe, it was eventually given a more permanent basis when the United Nations decided to undertake long-range and far-reaching programmes targeted at children and women. At the national level, the new importance given to the family was reflected in the creation of Ministries for the Family in Germany (in 1953) and Luxembourg (in 1952) so as to better protect the interests of families. In Switzerland also, particular attention to the family question was given through the setting up of a Group for Family Protection in 1946. Its mandate included the development of a federal family allowance scheme, as well as the monitoring and development of questions related to family policy (Switzerland, Office Fédérale des assurances sociales, 1982: 23-4). In Sweden, the renewed commitment to the family was to lead to concrete initiatives, among which was the setting up of a Family Commission in 1954 concerned

Table 4.2 *Family-related governmental initiatives, 1945–1959*

Country	Start-up year	Title of initiative
France	1945	High Consultative Committee for the Population and the Family
	1945	Law for the Protection of Mothers and Children
Germany	1953	Ministry for the Family
Luxembourg	1952	Ministry for the Family
Sweden	1954	Family Commission
Switzerland	1946	Group for Family Protection
United Kingdom	1948	Children's Act and Children's Departments
United States	1950	White House Conference on Children
International	1946	United Nations Children's Fund

with the standard of living of families and mandated to examine the adequacy of the government's financial support for families (Liljestrom, 1978: 27–8).

In France, the 1945 *Loi Protection Maternelle et Infantile* was to generalize state protection to pregnant women, mothers after delivery, and children until their sixth birthday. The Law was an expanded version of a decree on the protection of very young children adopted in 1935. The new law marked a real shift from an assistance policy to a more comprehensive, protective, and supportive one. According to Norvez: 'The objective was no longer to support only deprived categories, but to protect the whole population' (a.t., 1990: 85).

In the United States, pursuing the tradition of White House Conferences on children, a further conference was held in 1950 under the title of Mid-Century Conference. According to Steiner (1976), this conference as well as its successors (in 1960 and 1970) lacked focus and led to the adoption of numerous recommendations which had no impact on the government's policy towards families. The hostility of the American government to taking a more active role in the provision of support for families seemed to pre-empt the potential impact of these conferences. As will be seen in chapter 5, more action was taken in relation with the war against poverty. Similarly, in Britain the action of the government towards families took a very specific orientation. The Children's Act adopted in 1948, while reflecting the interest in government for family issues, paved the way for the policy which was to characterize the intervention of the government, that is, a policy concerned with children in need rather than all children. More precisely, the Act created the Children's Department, which was seen as a step towards the creation of a comprehensive and integrated social services agency for families (Handler, 1973: 34). Above all, it was the more limited issue of standards of care and supervision for children in local authority care that this Act was addressing (Eekelaar and Dingwall, 1990: 5).

Undeniably, the immediate post-war period witnessed significant changes in the public and official attitude towards the population and family questions. The experience of the war had strengthened family bonds and resulted in a stronger commitment of governments to support and protect families. The setting up of ministries devoted to the family and the launch of various initiatives reflected this endorsement of a more public responsibility towards the well-being of families. Behind this general trend there were however strong inter-country differences. While countries such as the United States refused to expand significantly their boundaries of public responsibility for families through universal family allowances and comprehensive maternity benefits, others adopted a more interventionist approach to families by emphasizing public rather than private responsibility.

4.5   The expansion of family allowances

Early family allowance schemes had already been introduced in some countries before the onset of the Second World War. In most cases, however, their coverage was limited. For instance, in New Zealand, Italy, and Germany, family allowances were means-tested, and were designed only for children of large families (except in Italy where all children were covered). Moreover, with the exception of New Zealand, the schemes were linked with the employment status of the breadwinner, and did not cover groups such as the self-employed, agricultural workers, and the unemployed. Starting with the Second World War, more general schemes were introduced, gradually covering all residents and categories of workers.

The determinants

Two main factors seem to have influenced this development. There was first the ILO texts referred to earlier, which included specific references to universal family allowances. Second, there was the Beveridge report in Britain which undeniably strongly influenced the adoption of universal family allowances. The widespread support that this report received from the public had an obvious influence on the government, and already in 1944, the wartime coalition government was tabling a Family Allowance Bill. As initially conceived, however, the bill did not please activists such as Eleanore Rathbone, since allowances were not to be paid for the first child, and more importantly, they were to be paid directly to the father. For supporters of a mothers' wage, this was a severe blow. Rathbone, then a member of Parliament, made it clear that she would vote against the bill if the allowances were to be paid to fathers. The battle on that front was eventually won, and the modified Child Allowance Bill was adopted with allowances paid to mothers.

Other countries followed rapidly, and universal family allowances became the cornerstone of the new state support for families. Even in the Nordic countries, where the Myrdals' preference for in-kind over in-cash benefits had prevented the earlier adoption of such allowances, family allowances were eventually introduced. In fact, when one looks at the sequence of the introduction of family allowances across countries, it is clear that the new development took place over a relatively short period of time (see Table 4.3).

Table 4.3 *First family allowances schemes*

Period	Year of introduction	Country	Type of benefit	Coverage
Pre-1900	1926	New Zealand	U	3+
	1930	Belgium	E	A
	1932	France	E	A
	1937	Italy	E	A
	1938	Spain	E	A
1939–45	1939	Netherlands	E	3+
	1941	Australia	U	A
	1942	Portugal	E	A
	1944	Canada	U	A
	1944	Ireland	U	A
	1945	United Kingdom	U	2+
Post-1945	1946	Norway	U	2+
	1947	Luxembourg	E/U	A
	1947	Sweden	U	A
	1948	Austria	E	A
	1948	Finland	U	A
	1952	Denmark	U	A
	1952	Switzerland	E	A
	1954	Germany	E	3+
	1958	Greece	E	A
	1971	Japan	E/U	3+

Key: U = Universal; E = Employment-related; A = Allowances paid for all children; 2+: Allowances paid only from second child; 3+: Allowances paid only from third child. Notes: Austria: Restricted to employees. Extended to self-employed (1955), and all workers (1967). Belgium: Restricted to wage-earners. Extended to self-employed (1937). France: Restricted to workers. Extended to all employed and unemployed persons (1939). Germany: Restricted to private sector employees. Extended to all workers (1955). Initial scheme restricted to third and subsequent children. Extended to second child (with means test) in 1961, to all children (without means test) in 1974. Greece: Restricted to workers. Italy: Restricted to workers in industry, commerce, and agriculture. Extended to state employees (1952), self-employed persons and agricultural workers (1967), unemployed (1968), and all workers (1980). Japan: Distinct schemes for public employees, private sector employees, and unemployed persons. Restricted to third and subsequent children (with means test). Extended to second child (with means test) in 1986. Luxembourg: Restricted to employees. Extended to self-employed (1959), and all workers (1964). Netherlands: Restricted to employees (3+ children). Extended to wage-earners (first and second children) (1946); self-employed (first and second children) (means-tested) (1951); all workers (3+ children) (1962); public service employees (first and second children) (1963); all workers (all children) (1979); unemployed persons (all children) (1982). New Zealand: Restricted to third and subsequent children. Extended to second child (1940), and first (1941). Means-test abolished in 1946. Norway: Restricted to second and subsequent children. Extended to first child (1969). Portugal: Restricted to employees. Spain: Restricted to employees. Switzerland: Restricted to agricultural workers. United Kingdom: Restricted to second and subsequent children. Extended to first child (1975).

Nearly half the countries introduced a family allowance scheme between 1944 and 1948. Three points need to be made here, however. First, although welfare considerations and the well-being of children were among the main motives behind the adoption of these schemes, their introduction was not entirely exempt from other considerations. In a period subject to high inflationary pressures, these allowances were also seen as means of avoiding a new inflationary wage–price spiral (Lindgren, 1978: 284). In Britain, in particular, 'the wartime coalition government accepted them primarily as a means of combating wage inflation by reducing the need and demand for larger wages for workers with families' (Land and Parker, 1978: 345). Such an argument had been used in the 1930s during earlier discussion about cost-of-living bonuses and family allowances. But, in contrast to the earlier period when the inflationary argument had led to the setting up of temporary schemes, the new allowances were given a more permanent character.

The second point to note is that the adoption of family allowances was not unrelated to other pro-natalist, pro-family, and welfare considerations. For example, in Britain, the adoption of family allowances was aimed at:

encouraging parents to have more children . . . At the same time they were seen as preserving work incentives for men by recognizing family responsibilities both in and out of work . . . Family allowances were also aimed at reducing poverty among children. Only a minority of the political interests supported them as a means of recognizing and improving the status of mothers as a worthy end in itself. (Land and Parker, 1978: 346)

Finally, it should be noted that the coverage of the initial schemes remained limited with regard to the first child, and with regard to some categories of families. For example, in 1950 the first child was still uncovered in five countries (France, Ireland, Netherlands (for some categories of workers), Norway, and the United Kingdom). With the exception of France, these schemes were expanded to cover all children during the following years. In Germany, the initial scheme introduced in 1954 (the scheme introduced under the Fascist regime having been abolished after the war) only covered the third and subsequent children. It was expanded to cover all children in 1961 and 1974. In Ireland, family allowances were extended to the second child in 1952, and to the first one in 1963. With regard to the coverage of families, the schemes in several countries still excluded certain categories of workers, or gave differential treatment (payment) to different categories of workers. At that level too, there was over time a gradual expansion and harmonization of the schemes. For example, in the Netherlands, the initial scheme only applied to employees. After a succession of reform, the allowances were equalized across all categories of workers by 1979. A similar pattern was to be found in Italy, with the gradual extension of the allowances to all categories of workers, and equalization in 1980.

The exceptions

Against this general trend towards a more universal coverage, three countries stood out as exceptions: Japan, Switzerland, and the United States. In Japan, the adoption of family allowances had already been recommended by an official committee in 1947. It was only in 1971 however that allowances for the third and subsequent children were introduced (Muramatsu and Kuroda, 1974: 722). Financial constraints, among other factors, seem to have prevented the earlier adoption of a general scheme. In Switzerland, on the other hand, a family allowance scheme was adopted at a relatively early stage, in 1952. In contrast to the other countries, it covered only agricultural workers and small farmers, while the coverage of the other categories of workers was left to cantonal authorities. This decentralized system was justified on two grounds. First, since the federal government was responsible for the agricultural policy, it was only natural that state support for that category of workers also fell under its responsibility. And secondly, since farmers had played a vital role in feeding the entire population during the war, it was considered as a duty for the federal government to support them (Tschudi, 1985: 60). In 1957, a commission of experts was mandated by the government to examine the possibility of extending the scheme to all families. In its report, in 1959, a majority of the commission members spoke in favour of the introduction of a general scheme for all categories of workers. The related legislation prepared by the Federal Council, which would have introduced a general family allowance scheme, was however rejected by Parliament (Switzerland, Office Fédérale des assurances sociales, 1982: 42). An aversion to political centralization, a belief that public sector intervention should be kept as limited as possible, coupled with the belief in the self-sufficiency of the family, seem to have prevented the adoption of a general federal family allowance scheme.

The third exception was the United States. The ADC (Aid to Dependent Children) programme, which was introduced in 1935 as part of Roosevelt's New Deal, provided federal grants to the states for lone-parents. But unlike other countries, the scheme was never extended to other types of family. The only major change came in 1950 when the programme was renamed AFDC (Aid to Families with Dependent Children) and amended to provide benefits to the custodial parent of the dependent child as well as to the child (Garfinkel and McLanahan, 1986: 106). In 1961, the programme was amended again to provide states with the option of extending eligibility to children of unemployed parents (ibid.). Political ideology, in terms of belief in the autonomy of the family and in limited state intervention, is believed to have prevented further expansions. Furthermore, as suggested by Berkowitz (1991), the experience of the war had been felt completely differently in Europe and the United States. In Europe, the destruction and suffering paved the way for universal state support for families, but in the United States, the war put further faith in the private sector:

Since we did not regard the war as the same sort of landmark as did the British, it was not as important for us to build an alternative to the warfare state as it was for the British. No bombs dropped on New York as they did on London, and, although the war demanded considerable sacrifice by America, it brought considerable profit as well. For us, the war did not produce a revolution in social relations so much as it restored the prosperity to which we had been accustomed. The American government, unlike the British, owed its citizens nothing more than continuing prosperity; the private market, charity, state and local government, and voluntary associations would take care of the rest. (ibid. 51-2)

Family allowance rates

Despite the general trend towards universal family allowance schemes, strong inter-country differences remained in terms of levels of benefit paid to families. These disparities are revealed in Table 4.4 which compares monthly values of family allowances for a two-child family in successive decades.

The variability in the levels of benefits is remarkable. For a two-child family in 1950, the levels varied between less than 3 per cent in Norway and 28 per cent in Portugal (as a percentage of the average male wage in manufacturing). Over time, this disparity was greatly reduced. For example, by 1975 the gap between the lowest and highest levels had been reduced to 9 percentage points (1 per cent in Australia and 10 per cent in Belgium). In fact, it is the very high levels which have tended to disappear during this period, thus resulting in a greater convergence across countries. For example, while in 1950, France, Italy, and Portugal appeared as unchallenged, with benefits exceeding 15 per cent of the average wage for a two-child family, in all three cases the relative value of the allowance was strongly reduced during the following years. By not keeping up with increases in wages, it fell to levels close to or below the country average in 1975. During this period, the relative value of family allowances also strongly declined in Belgium (between 1960 and 1975), Luxembourg (between 1960 and 1975), and New Zealand. On the other hand, the value of benefits strongly increased in Austria during the early part of the period. From a value of 5 per cent of the average wage in 1950 for a two-child family, benefits reached 10 per cent of wages in 1960.

Similar inter-country variations appear when the monthly value of allowances for a two-child family is expressed in US dollars. As of 1975, the levels varied from more than 40 dollars in Belgium, the Netherlands, Austria, and Luxembourg, to less than 12 dollars in Greece, Australia, and Japan (see Figure 4.2).

The cases of France and Britain deserve some specific comments. As we have seen before, Britain took a major lead in the immediate post-war period in introducing universal benefits. However, the level of benefits in Britain remained relatively low compared with that of other countries. In fact, the recommendation of the White Paper on children's allowances in 1944 to the effect that family allowances should be related to the subsistence costs of children was largely ignored, and the allowances were set at five shillings per week instead of the suggested eight shillings (Jordan, 1991: 19). In terms of the average male wage, this meant that benefits for a two- child family remained below 4 per cent for the entire period. The benefits were upgraded following the adoption of the Child Benefit Act in 1975 which extended allowances to the first child, and which replaced the tax allowance for children by more generous levels of family allowances. In France, following the adoption of the Family Code in 1939, the allowances for the first child were eliminated, while being increased for the third and subsequent children. The relative ranking of France would therefore be considerably higher if the comparison was made on the basis of a three- child family rather than a two-child one.

Table 4.4 *Family allowances for a two-child family, 1949-1975*

	Allowances as percentage of average male manufacturing wage			
Country	1949	1961	1970	1975
Australia	6.1	4.2	2.1	1.0
Austria	5.3	10.3	10.8	8.5
Belgium	11.2	16.5	13.5	10.4
Canada	5.9	3.8	2.1	4.5
Denmark	—	0.0	6.4	4.4
Finland	7.1	6.2	4.3	4.8
France	18.7	13.2	7.5	5.5
Germany	—	—	2.2	6.7
Greece	—	7.1	8.4	3.8
Ireland	0.0	2.0	2.2	2.7
Italy	16.8	21.5	10.1	5.9
Japan	—	—	—	—
Luxembourg	10.0	11.9	7.8	6.0
Netherlands	10.4	0.1	9.4	7.6
New Zealand	3.0	11.0	5.4	5.4
Norway	2.8	2.5	5.2	3.4
Portugal	—	20.2	10.7	7.5
Spain	2.7	2.2	5.6	2.6
Sweden	9.6	6.4	6.1	5.1
Switzerland	—	4.5	2.4	4.6
United Kingdom	3.9	2.9	3.5	2.7
United States	—	—	—	—

—: No national family allowance scheme in force. Notes: For the calculation, an average of 40 hours of work per week was assumed in all countries. Data were converted in US dollar using the standard exchange rate in 1949 and 1961. For 1970 and 1975, the parity purchasing power index was instead used. Belgium: In 1961, increasing rates by birth-order. Rates for the second child assumed to be equal to that of the first child. Denmark: In 1961, variable rates according to area of residence (Copenhagen, other towns, rural areas). An average value was used. France: Family allowance set as a percentage of base wage. In 1949, these percentages were 0% and 10%, respectively for the first and second child, and 0% and 22% for 1961, 1970, 1975. The corresponding monthly base wage for each of these years was 120 FF, 234 FF, 378 FF, 632 FF. Ireland: In 1949, variable rates according to sector, and employment status (i.e. wage-earners and salaried employees). Japan: The scheme introduced in 1971 covered only the third and subsequent children Luxembourg: In 1949, variable rates according to resources. In 1961, variable rates according to employment status (i.e. employees and non-employees). Rates for employees are used. Netherlands: In 1961, increasing rates by birth-order. Rates for the second child assumed to be equal to that of the first child. Portugal: In 1949, variable rates according to funds. In 1961, rates varied between 40-100 Esc. An average of 70 Esc. was used. Spain: In 1949, allowances available only for employees (means-tested). Switzerland: Rates used correspond to those provided under the Federal scheme. Rates under cantonal schemes may in some cases be higher.

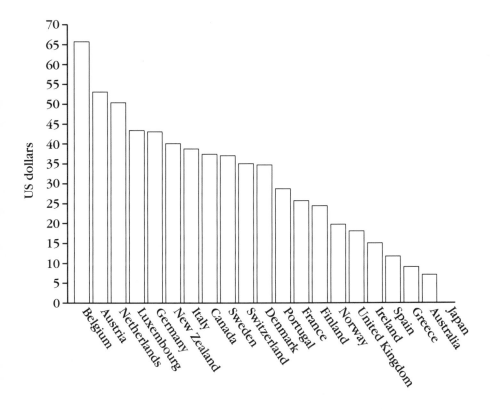

Fig. 4.2 *Family allowances to a two-child family, 1975*

Note: Monthly value of family allowances calculated on the basis of parity purchasing power indices (value in 1975 US dollars).

In the field of family allowances, major reforms were introduced in the post-war period, especially with the adoption of universal coverage schemes. While not specifically responding to demographic trends, these reforms were driven by considerations about the well-being of families, especially in the context of emerging welfare states.

4.6 Maternity benefits

As mothers had been identified in the immediate post-war period as a sub-group deserving special protection and care, it was to be expected that provision for maternity leave and benefits would be considerably upgraded. These benefits were indeed upgraded, but against a background relatively unfavourable to women's employment. In view of the renewed familism and the new emphasis on the mother–child relationship, women's employment was not encouraged and it was instead a more traditional family that the post-war policy promoted.

Attitude to working women

If the war had drawn numerous women into the labour force, the closure of wartime industries was eventually to lead to considerable redundancies, mostly at the expense of women. Anticipating this problem, the ILO had adopted in 1944 a recommendation to the effect that the transition from a wartime to a peacetime economy should be made according to a principle of complete equality between men and women: 'The redistribution of women workers in each national economy should be carried out on the principle of complete equality of opportunity for men and women in respect of admission to employment on the basis of their individual merit, skill and experience' (ILO, 1949).

Despite this recommendation, the reality was very different. Following the end of the war, a large number of women actually lost their jobs. Reports from the United States in 1945 and 1946 confirmed that not only a larger proportion of women than men were victims of lay-offs, but that it was also more difficult for women than men to find new jobs (ILO, 1946: 259). As a result, 'by January 1946 ... men were replacing women in industries where the latter had been extensively employed during the war' (ibid.). In the United Kingdom, a similar situation was observed with women being encouraged to quit jobs, with the exception of some key reconstruction sectors where, because of an acute shortage of skilled labour, women were asked to stay in employment (ibid. 33–7).

The solution to this problem was not easy, and beyond the ILO recommendation for complete equality, all other policy alternatives suggested ways of eliminating the need for a second salary, i.e. for female employment. These alternatives included:

• Social security measures being developed so that a family could survive on a single salary.
• Male workers being offered salaries high enough to provide for their own needs and those of their family.
• Full employment being aimed at, to minimize unemployment among male bread-winners and to eliminate the need of their wives to seek employment.

Obviously, the prevailing attitude was against female employment. The closure of wartime nurseries, such as in Britain, further contributed to this situation by denying women access to ways of combining work and family. While during wartime the number of nurseries in England and Wales had been increased from 14 (in October 1940) to 1,300 at the end of the war –providing places for over 62,000 children– their number had been reduced to 914 already within one year of the end of the war (Cohen, 1988: 2). By the mid-1950s day nurseries had been reduced by half, and by the mid-1960s by two-thirds (Penn and Riley, 1992: 5). A combination of financial constraints and a belief in the beneficial effect of parental care, as opposed to out-of-home care, seem to have motivated this political withdrawal (Lewis, 1992: 21).

For a large number of women, however, the return to home was not unwelcome. Not only did it signify the end of routine jobs in unpleasant conditions, but above all, it allowed them to devote their time entirely to their children, for whom the full-time presence of their mother was now highly praised.

Maternity benefit schemes

Despite this situation, which was not supportive of women's employment, maternity leave benefits were significantly upgraded in the immediate post-war period. This reform was partly influenced by the adoption of new standards by the ILO. Compared with its 1919 version, the 1952 Revised Maternity Protection Convention represented considerable improvements. For instance, instead of the 12-week leave suggested in the 1919 Convention, the new one stipulated a leave of 14 weeks. Moreover, while the previous Convention fixed no precise level with regard to cash benefits, the new one explicitly linked them to the woman's earnings, fixing them at not less than two-thirds of the woman's previous earnings. In fact, the introduction of benefits equal to 100 per cent of the woman's previous earnings was suggested in the supplementary Recommendation (Maternity Protection Recommendation no. 95, 1952).

In the immediate post-war period, reforms of the maternity leave schemes followed three main lines: (i) introduction of compulsory schemes (several of the pre-war schemes were voluntary); (ii) extension of the duration of the maternity leave period; and (iii) adoption of wage-related cash benefits instead of the previous flat-rate or lump-sum payments. From a limited and often voluntary version, maternity leave schemes therefore emerged as a major component of state support for families.

It was in the Nordic countries that the most extensive reforms were brought about. As will be recalled, on the eve of the Second World War, very restricted schemes were in force in these countries. In Denmark, reforms adopted in 1956 introduced for the first time a compulsory scheme, and provided women with flat rate benefits for a period of 11 weeks. The scheme was subsequently increased to 14 weeks in 1972, in addition to replacing the flat rate benefits by wage-related ones equal to 90 per cent of the woman's previous earnings. In Sweden, major reforms came in 1955 through the introduction of the first compulsory scheme which provided women with flat rate benefits for a period of 3 months (an additional 3 months could be taken as unpaid leave). From 1963 this scheme was further upgraded, especially through the introduction of wage-related cash benefits equal to 60 per cent of the woman's previous gross earnings for the whole of the 6-month period. It was subsequently increased to 80 per cent of gross earnings in 1967, and to 90 per cent of net earnings in 1974. In addition, the Swedish government took a major step in 1974 by transforming the maternity leave scheme into a parental one. From there on, parents would be allowed to share the 6-month leave. The leave could be taken on a full-time or part-time basis any time before the child's eighth birthday (Sundstrom, 1991). This reform was particularly innovative. As will be seen in Chapter 10, similar parental schemes were introduced by some other countries in the post-1975 period.

In Finland and Norway too significant reforms were introduced. In Finland, where the pre-1945 scheme was restricted to a lump sum maternity benefit paid only on a means-test basis, a new scheme introduced in 1963 included a paid leave of 54 days with daily benefits representing 0.15 per cent of annual income (the equivalent of weekly benefits of around 40 per cent of the woman's previous earnings). In 1971, the period of leave was then extended to 72 working days and to 174 in 1975. With these reforms, Finland and Sweden were taking the lead by providing women with the most extensive maternity benefit scheme. In Norway the duration of the maternity leave was increased from the pre-war 8 weeks to 12 weeks in 1956. While on the eve of the Second World War the Nordic countries were clearly lagging with regard to their maternity leave scheme, they emerged as leaders in the following period. This situation was strongly influenced by a movement in support of working women.

The other countries which were lagging behind in 1945, and which greatly upgraded their schemes thereafter, were Canada, Ireland, and the United Kingdom. In Canada, the reform came very late with the adoption of a first scheme of paid leave in 1971. The scheme provided women with 15 weeks leave during which benefits representing two-thirds of regular earnings were paid.[1] In Ireland, where the pre-war scheme was still restricted to a lump-sum payment, a new scheme adopted in 1952 introduced a leave of 12 weeks along with flat rate benefits. A similar reform was brought about in the United Kingdom in 1946 with a new 18-week leave with flat rate benefits.

In Austria, France, Italy, and Portugal major extensions of the maternity benefit schemes also took place after 1945. In Austria, benefits equal to 100 per cent of the regular earnings were introduced in 1955, while in 1974 the duration of the leave was extended from 12 to 16 weeks. In addition, the Austrian government introduced an innovative scheme in 1956 allowing women to extend their maternity leave by an extra six months during which benefits, equal to 50 per cent of unemployment benefits were paid. This leave was extended until the child's first birthday in 1957. In France, the first reform introducing benefits proportional to wages (50 per cent) was adopted in 1945. It was then upgraded to confer benefits equal to 90 per cent of wages in 1971. In Italy, the government took a major lead in 1950 by adopting a scheme which provided women with a leave of 14 to 20 weeks (depending on their occupation) and with benefits equal to 80 per cent of previous earnings. In 1971, a uniform 20-week leave was introduced.[2] In addition, new legislation adopted in 1971 provided women with the opportunity of taking an extended leave of 6 months during which they would receive cash benefits representing 30 per cent of previous earnings. Finally, in Portugal, a new scheme was introduced in 1962 providing 60 days of leave with full wage compensation.

[1] Under the new scheme, 17 weeks of leave could be taken but only 15 would be paid as a result of a 2-week waiting period.

[2] The 1950 legislation included 8 weeks of leave after childbirth for all women. Before childbirth, the leave was of 3 months for women in industry, 8 weeks for those in the agricultural sector, and 6 weeks for others. In 1971, all women became entitled to 2 months of leave before childbirth, and 3 months after.

The only countries which did not devote similar effort to the upgrading of their maternity benefit schemes in the immediate post-war period were Australia, New Zealand, Switzerland, and the United States. In Australia, and New Zealand, leave remained unpaid during the whole 1950–75 period. Similarly, in the United States, no national legislation granting women a maternity leave was adopted during this period (although schemes were introduced in some states). In Switzerland, the scheme introduced in 1911 which provided minimal flat rate benefits remained virtually unchanged. From 1975, the law provided women with a period of only 8 weeks of leave after confinement. Of these, there was an obligation for the employer to provide pay during the period covered by the sick leave scheme (minimum of 3 weeks). Provision for longer payment was left to collective agreements, or private health insurance schemes. Although the Swiss Federal Constitution provides for the introduction of a maternity insurance, no action in this direction has yet been taken (Switzerland, Office Fédérale des assurances sociales, 1982: 134).

The trends with regard to the duration of maternity leave and related cash benefits between 1945 and 1975 are summarized in Table 4.5.

With regard to the duration of the leave, and leaving aside the cases of Australia, New Zealand, Switzerland, and the United States, there was already a clear concentration around a 12-week leave by 1950. By 1975, divergence can be observed especially in view of the leading position taken by the Nordic countries. With regard to cash benefits, by 1950 most schemes were still limited to lump sum payments or flat rate benefits. In only a few cases were benefits proportional to wages. By 1975, on the other hand, all countries with the exception of Ireland, Norway, and the United Kingdom, had introduced wage-related benefits.

From a very disparate situation on the eve of the Second World War, a clear convergence in maternity benefit schemes was therefore to be observed in the 1950s. The situation was subsequently altered with the emergence of the Nordic countries as leaders. On the other hand, little progress in the field of maternity benefits was observed during the 1945–75 period in Australia, New Zealand, Switzerland, and the United States. In these countries, the provision of maternity benefits was instead left to private initiatives through collective agreements. This position is in sharp contrast with the Nordic countries where full responsibility was taken by governments in the provision of these benefits. The situation in 1975 thus differed largely from that charted in Chapter 3. Not only had most countries introduced wage-related benefits, but the duration of the leave had also been upgraded. The results are illustrated in Figure 4.3 using an index of maternity leave which corresponds to the number of weeks fully compensated for.

Sweden appeared unchallenged, followed a long way behind by Italy and Germany. The precursors of maternity leave in the 1880s — Austria, Germany, Switzerland — had lost their leading position.

4.7 Conclusion

In the pre-World War II period, several countries experimented with some forms of state support for families but they were of limited scope, and left a large room to philanthropic organizations. The events of World War II, and its aftermath, changed

Table 4.5 *Maternity leave benefits, 1950–1975*

Country	Maternity Benefits							
	1950		1960		1970		1975	
	Duration in weeks	Pay	Duration in weeks	Pay	Duration in weeks	Pay	Duration in weeks	Pay
Austria	12	FR	12	100	12	100	12	100
Belgium	12	60	12	60	14	60	14	80
Canada	—	—	—	—	—	—	15	66
Denmark	4	FR	4	FR	11	FR	14	90
Finland	6	LS	6	LS	11	39	35	39
France	14	FR	14	50	14	50	14	90
Germany	12	50	12	75	12	75	14	100
Greece	12	33	12	50	12	50	12	50
Ireland	4	LS	12	FR	12	FR	12	FR
Italy	10	LS	14	80	14	80	20	80
Japan	10	60	12	60	12	60	12	60
Lux.	12	50	12	75	12	75	12	100
Neth.	12	100	12	100	12	100	12	100
Norway	8	FR	12	FR	12	FR	12	FR
Portugal	a	—	a	—	9	100	9	100
Spain	10	FR	10	FR	12	60	12	75
Sweden	8	LS	12	FR	26	60	30	90
Switz.	6	FR	6	FR	8	100	8	100
UK	4	FR	18	FR	18	FR	18	FR

Key: – = No scheme in force; FR = Flat rate benefits; LS = Lump-sum; x (e.g. 60) = Percentage of regular earnings. a: Variable provisions according to the insurance funds, as stipulated by the Corporative Social Insurance Decree 1933. Note that there was no national maternity leave scheme in force in Australia, New Zealand, and the United States. Finland: Leave extended over time from 6 weeks in 1950 to 174 working days in 1975. Italy: From 1950 to 1971, the duration of the leave was variable according to the employment sector (see text). Portugal: 60-day leave introduced in 1962. Sweden: From 1955 to 1967, 3 months of paid leave and optional 3 months unpaid, gradually extended to 7 months. Switzerland: Until 1965, under Federal Code, 6 weeks with flat rate benefits. Increased to 8 weeks thereafter. Benefits are payable for between 3 to 8 weeks at full wage depending on the collective agreement. Women covered by a health insurance scheme are entitled to sick pay for a total of 10 weeks.

this situation considerably. There was, first, the new commitment of governments to repair the damage of the war and to improve the standard of living of their citizens. There was also the acknowledgement, at the international level, of the right of citizens and families to state support, as well as the adoption of new standards with regard to the levels of social security benefits. There was, finally, the acknowledgement of mothers and children as deserving special state protection.

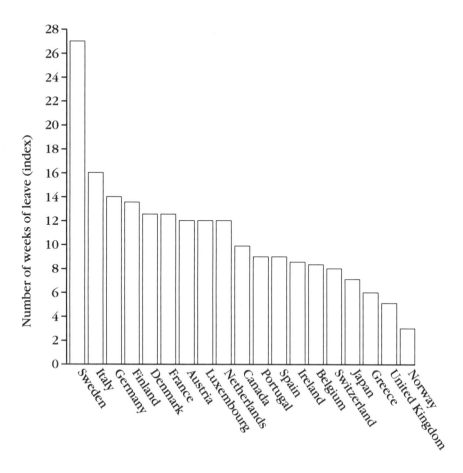

Fig. 4.3 *Maternity leave scheme, 1975*

Note: The index used represents the number of weeks fully compensated for. It is obtained by multi-plying the number of weeks of leave by the percentage of salary received during this period (e.g. 14 weeks x 100% = 14).

The experience of the war, along with the revival of the traditional family, had led to a situation in which the mother–child relationship was highly praised — a situation which was to influence significantly the subsequent development of policies.

The role of the state as welfare provider, which had so far been marginal, was greatly expanded during the immediate post-war period. It was the golden era of welfare states. New cash benefits for families were provided, as well as new services. Behind this general trend, there were however significant inter-country differences. While most countries took full responsibility in the provision of sup-port for families, other countries opted for a much more restricted approach. This was particularly noticeable in the provision of maternity leave benefits. While the Nordic countries emerged as leaders in providing women with extensive schemes, no national paid scheme was adopted in the United States, Australia, and New Zealand where the responsibility of providing benefits for working mothers continued to be left to private employers. Such a policy of limited state intervention was also reflected in the refusal of the American government to adopt a universal family allowance scheme.

Yet, despite these exceptions, for the majority of countries, the expansion in state support for families in the immediate post-war period represented a considerable departure from earlier trends.

5

THE REDISCOVERY OF POVERTY

If the end of the war had raised hopes of a better future and improved standards of living, these hopes had apparently been fulfilled. The post-war economic recovery, and the expansion of the welfare state had brought general prosperity, and above all, had eliminated poverty. This at least was widely believed. The reality however proved to be very different. The rediscovery of poverty in the mid-1960s showed that not only had the post-war developments failed to eliminate poverty, but more startling, that poverty had even increased.

Governments did not remain indifferent and from the 1960s onwards a series of reforms were introduced to the system of state support for families. Breaking with the post-war policy of universalism, these reforms aimed instead at better supporting families in greatest need. This shift of emphasis, from a universal approach to a more targeted one, gave a completely new direction to state support for families.

5.1 Forgotten realities

Belief in the beneficial effects of the post-war economic and welfare state developments was widespread, and moreover, was supported by clear empirical evidence. For instance, while in Britain at the turn of the century it had been estimated that around 10 per cent of the population was living in poverty, studies had shown that this level had been reduced to 4 per cent in 1936, and to below 2 per cent in 1950 (Ringen, 1987: 44). This belief was seriously challenged in the 1960s when new estimates put the incidence of poverty at 10 per cent among British households in 1953–54, and at 18 per cent in 1960 (ibid. 148). These results, disclosed in the study of Abel-Smith and Townsend entitled *The Poor and the Poorest* (1965), had a major impact on public opinion. For believers in the market and welfare state success, it was a severe blow. In Britain, as in several other countries, this rediscovery put poverty back on the political agenda. In the United States, the magnitude of the problem was revealed by the rising trend in the number of recipients of the means-tested AFDC (Aid to families with Dependent Children) benefit. From a case-load of 700,000 in 1945, the number of beneficiaries increased to 3 million in 1960, 4.5 million in 1965, 8.5 million in 1970, and 11.5 million in 1975 (Berkowitz, 1991: 86, 93). Post-war prosperity had obviously not eliminated poverty. For a society which strongly believed in self-reliance, this increasing dependence on welfare benefits was clearly unacceptable. But this was not the only worry. While at the beginning of the AFDC programme, the overwhelming proportion of beneficiaries were widows and orphans, a large majority of cases now involved never-married, separated, and divorced mothers. If widows and orphans deserved state support, public opinion was split with regard to the deserving or undeserving nature of the other recipients. And while at the beginning, the AFDC case-load was overwhelmingly composed of White children, the situation was completely reversed by the 1960s. The fact that the majority of cases now involved Black children led the public and the government to question the legitimacy of this programme and its use of public funds.

The situation was complex, and the solutions not self-evident. There was on the one hand the problem of the high incidence of poverty, but there were also the uncomfortable facts that (i) the increase in AFDC beneficiaries was suggesting a breakdown of the traditional family; (ii) some families were now using AFDC as a main source of income rather than as an emergency means; and (iii) these problems were most acute among the Black population. The publication of *The Negro Family: The Case for National Action* by the politician Daniel Patrick Moynihan in 1965 was to give further weight to these concerns. Black families, Moynihan argued, were unstable, had high ratios of illegitimate births, high levels of divorce and lone-parenthood, and had moreover developed a high incidence of crime and welfare dependency (Berkowitz, 1991: 125). More attention had therefore to be given to the Black family, in particular to reduce its welfare dependency, and to reinforce a family structure which gave husbands a more important role in the family. Although Moynihan's report was heavily criticized in some circles, it added to other evidence which pinpointed the undesirable and unintended effects of the AFDC programme. On the one hand, it destabilized families by encouraging them to split up (since the benefits were limited to lone-mothers), and on the other, it carried strong work disincentives (working earnings being heavily taxed) (ibid. 122–3). Two main reforms were seen therefore as urgently needed. First, the state had to strengthen the family by 'keeping families together and preventing mothers from having illegitimate children' (ibid. 101). Second, work disincentives had to be removed, and replaced by work-conditional, or 'workfare' benefits .

This was the forgotten reality, the fact that contrary to the popular belief the post-war period had not brought general prosperity. Conversely, substantial proportions of the population remained in poverty. This discovery had a major impact, leading to significant reforms of the system of state support for families.

5.2 Public and state responses

How did the public and governments react to this new reality? The reaction was in fact mixed. There was, first of all, a sense of emergency, a feeling that something had to be done in order to alleviate poverty. But there was also concern about the unintended effects of policies, and a feeling that some poor people deserved more support than others. In particular, there was generally a sympathetic attitude towards children, whose high levels of poverty moved public opinion. In Britain, it was under this banner, of family and child poverty, that activists rallied from the mid-1960s. Among the related organized groups, the Child Poverty Action Group (CPAG), set up in 1965, had an undeniable effect on both public and government in raising the profile of the poverty issue. For example, its first campaign, launched in

December 1965, was highly successful and rallied public opinion around the need for immediate government action. In fact, its timing, just before Christmas, was excellent as it hit public opinion at its most receptive to humanitarian causes, and at a time when competition with other news was at its lowest. The reaction of the government was quick, and the matter was said to be 'receiving urgent attention' (Banting, 1979: 74). In fact, the matter even eclipsed other social issues previously considered as paramount.

The government indeed rapidly launched a specific initiative. Following the campaign of CPAG, the British government commissioned a study on the circumstances of families in 1966, and eventually set up a committee on one-parent families (the Finer Committee) in 1969. Both aimed at evaluating the number of families in greatest financial need, as well as the inadequacies of the existing system of state support for families. The report of the Finer Committee was to be particularly critical of the existing system of cash support for families, recommending the introduction of a means-tested tax credit for dependent children, and of a guaranteed maintenance allowance for lone-parents (Britain, 1974). Through these poverty initiatives, the family was therefore put back on the political agenda; not all families, however, but only those in greater need. This aspect is important as it was to give a new orientation to the policies of government towards families. In contrast with the immediate post-war period, when the policy embraced all families, it was now to be targeted at families in greater need. In Britain, the poverty issue was again addressed some years later through the Royal Commission on the Distribution of Income and Wealth (in 1974). Although no precise recommendation was formulated by this Commission, it stressed the higher incidence of poverty among the elderly and children.

This rediscovery of poverty, and the greater attention paid to families in need, was not limited to Britain. As can be seen in Table 5.1, initiatives concerned with poverty and the economic situation of families were also launched in several countries from 1960.

In the United States, the poverty issue received sufficient attention to lead President Johnson to launch in 1964 a 'War against Poverty': 'This administration today, here and now, declares unconditional war on poverty in America' (Berkowitz, 1991: 11). The objective was twofold: to reduce both poverty and welfare dependency. This objective was not new, as the idea of greater self-support and lower state dependency had already been brought forward by President Kennedy in 1962 (Garfinkel and McLanahan, 1986: 107). What was new was the strong will of the government to tackle the problem, along with the numerous reforms and measures that it introduced (see Section 5.3).

Following this first initiative, the problem of poverty was then further examined through a series of specific commissions and committees. Among them the 1968 Income Maintenance Commission was appointed by President Johnson in order to make recommendations on the nation's maintenance system. This appointment was significant as it was the first presidential commission since the Economic Security Committee appointed by Roosevelt (ibid. 113–14). In its report, published in 1969, the Commission was critical of the prevailing system: 'existing welfare

Table 5.1 *Governmental initiatives related to poverty and the economic situation of families, 1960–1974*

Country	Start-up year	Title of initiative
Australia	1972	Commission of Inquiry into Poverty
Canada	1971	Senate Committee on Poverty
Ireland	1973	Pilot Schemes to Combat Poverty
Sweden	1965	Family Policy Committee
	1965	Low Income Commission
United Kingdom	1967	Study on the Circumstances of Families
	1969	Finer Committee on One-Parent Families
	1974	Royal Commission on the Distribution of Income and Wealth
United States	1968	Income Maintenance Commission
	1973	Sub-committee on Fiscal Policy

programmes are inadequate, inequitable, and inefficient'. Furthermore, the Commission believed that 'failure to aid the working poor not only precluded the elimination of poverty but also led to family breakup' (ibid. 114). Once again poverty and family dislocation were linked, in addition to the denunciation of the inadequacies of the government policies. In 1973 the whole system of cash transfers and its interplay with family policy and poverty came once again under close scrutiny, this time by the Sub-Committee on Fiscal Policy. In its report, the Sub-Committee made a series of recommendations for public assistance reform, as well as devoting attention to the alleged impact of welfare programmes on individual and family behaviour (Kamerman and Kahn, 1978: 443).

In other countries poverty also emerged as a major issue. In Australia, Canada, Ireland, and Sweden, initiatives were launched by governments to examine the nature and magnitude of the problem. In Canada, the setting up of a Senate Committee on Poverty in 1971 was a response to increasing concern about the higher incidence of poverty among families with children, especially among one-parent families. The situation, according to the government, deserved great attention especially in view of its impact on the standard of living of families. Furthermore, it was feared that poverty might introduce major dysfunctions into families, and result in long-lasting effects on children. To tackle these problems, the Committee listed among its recommendations the development of a negative income tax support for all families; a concept which had also received support in the United States (Armitage, 1978: 386).

In Australia, the Commission of Inquiry into Poverty was set up in 1972 with the mandate of investigating 'the extent, incidence and cause of poverty and the effectiveness of existing measures in the alleviation of poverty' (Kaim-Caudle, 1976: 401). Among its recommendations, the Commission suggested the abolition of tax relief for dependent children, and its replacement by tax credits. According to

Kaim-Caudle (1976), although the existing political climate made it unlikely that many of the recommendations would be adopted, the report of the Commission nevertheless constituted a landmark in the development of social policy in Australia. In Ireland, poverty also received considerable attention through the launch in 1973 of a programme of action aimed at combating poverty (Dennett *et al.*, 1982: 4). As will be seen in Chapter 9, this programme was to be the source of inspiration of a larger programme by the European Community in 1975 (i.e. the first European Community Poverty Programme).

In Sweden, the poverty issue was specifically examined by the Low Income Commission set up in 1965. The conclusions of the Commission were revealing. Not only was low income widespread, but the system of cash transfers had a negligible redistributive effect (Liljestrom, 1978: 28). These conclusions further reinforced the government's concern about poverty and, together with the report of the Family Policy Committee in 1972, led to a significant shift in Swedish policy. At this point, the government took, as a matter of principle, the position that it would strengthen the financial support to single parents and large families, while slightly reducing it for higher- income earners with few children (ibid. 27). Again, this position marked a major departure from the government immediate post-war policy.

In France, the poverty issue also attracted considerable attention during the 1960–74 period. As in other countries, it was to lead to a major re-orientation of the government's policy towards families. The turning point came in 1969 when the government announced its decision to transfer financial support to the worse-off (Laroque, 1985: 23). Support for the traditional family policy had apparently been lost. As reported by Laroque, from the 1960s: 'family policy no longer mobilizes the forces which gathered in support of other neighbouring, but partially contradictory, policies . . . It now seems natural to integrate family benefits in a global policy of reduction of inequalities through social transfers' (a.t. ibid. 18, 22).

For a government committed to universalism and pro-natalism, this marked a major departure. The changes in the economic situation of families, or more precisely the rediscovery of poverty, was therefore to lead governments in several countries to revise substantially their policy towards the family. If the post-war return to peace and the revival of the family had called for general and universal schemes, the rediscovery of poverty was instead calling for a more targeted approach. Two main types of actions were needed: one to increase the financial support for families, and the other to combat the so-called 'culture of poverty'.

5.3 Financial support for families

In response to the poverty problem, three main objectives were endorsed by governments: (i) reduction of inequalities inherent to the existing welfare system; (ii) increase in support to families in greater need; and (iii) elimination of work disincentives. With these reforms, universal support would still be provided for all families, but families in greatest need would receive extra support.

Reduction of welfare inequalities

The post-war development of the welfare state was based on the principle of equality of support and opportunity. There was, however, no awareness of the fact that the welfare state might itself generate inequalities. Such inequalities became clear from the 1960s, especially with regard to the system of tax relief for dependent children. Introduced in several countries before or shortly after the war, in most cases this relief took the form of a tax allowance, that is, an amount deductible from taxable income. Combined with progressive marginal tax rates, this system was intrinsically unfair since it meant higher relief for higher-income families than for low- or middle-income ones (since higher-income families were subject to higher marginal tax rates). Even worse, it discriminated against the very low income families who could not benefit from this form of state support since they did not pay any taxes (if their income fell below the taxable income threshold). In the 1960s, this inequality of the tax allowance system was denounced by several of the government commissions referred to earlier. Reform was obviously needed. Several policy alternatives were possible ranging from a complete abolition of tax allowances, to their replacement by a more equitable form of tax credit. In several countries, reforms along these lines were implemented from the 1960s, marking a first step towards a more egalitarian system and, furthermore, reflecting the growing concern of governments about poverty. Some of the main changes in the system of tax relief for dependent children are reported in Table 5.2 for the period 1947–75.

Such changes were introduced in eleven countries (Austria, Belgium, Denmark, Finland, Germany, Ireland, Italy, Netherlands, New Zealand, Norway, and Sweden), although not all in the expected direction. Sweden was the first to abolish tax allowances before 1950. Denmark followed in 1961, along with Austria, Finland, New Zealand, and Norway, before 1975. In contrast, tax allowances were introduced in Germany shortly after the war and were maintained throughout the period studied here. A similar reform can be observed in Ireland and the Netherlands. In Belgium and Finland, a tax credit was added to the existing tax allowance scheme before 1975, while in Italy a new tax credit was introduced before 1975. While in 1960 a tax allowance was still in force in thirteen countries, this was reduced to ten countries by 1975. As will be seen in Chapter 10, additional countries would eliminate the tax allowances during subsequent years.

Although no reform was implemented in the United States in the 1947–75 period, there was much discussion about the concept of a negative income tax, which was in essence another form of cash benefit, to be paid on a means-tested basis to low-income families. Such a measure was strongly supported by economists in the early 1960s, especially by the conservative economist Milton Friedman who suggested the replacement of all transfer programmes by a negative income tax (Garfinkel and McLanahan, 1986: 111). Although the government initially rejected such a proposition, it eventually reappeared on the agenda through President Nixon's proposed Family Assistance Plan. The plan, which included the introduction of a variant of the negative income tax for all families with children, proposed

Table 5.2 *Tax relief for dependent children, 1947-1975*

Country	Type of relief				
	1947	1950	1960	1970	1975
Australia	A	A	A	A	C
Austria	A	A	A	A	C
Belgium	A	A	A	A	AC
Canada	A	A	A	A	A
Denmark	A	A	—	—	—
Finland	AC	A	A	A	AC
France	Q	Q	Q	Q	Q
Germany	—	A	A	A	A
Greece	na	na	na	na	na
Ireland	—	—	—	A	A
Italy	—	—	—	—	C
Japan	A	A	A	A	A
Luxembourg	na	na	na	na	na
Netherlands	—	—	A	A	A
New Zealand	A	A	A	A	—
Norway	A	A	AC	—	—
Portugal	na	na	na	na	na
Spain	na	na	na	na	na
Sweden	A	—	—	—	—
Switzerland	A	A	A	A	A
United Kingdom	A	A	A	A	A
United States	A	A	A	A	A

Key: — No scheme in force. na: Data not available. A: Tax allowances. C: Tax credit. Q: Family quotient.

Source: Wennemo (1992).

to extend state support to two-parent families, and to provide them with a federal minimum benefit (ibid. 114). The related bill passed the House twice, but failed to pass the Senate each time. Concerns about the potentially negative effect of this plan on work incentives seem to have prevented its adoption. But the notion of a negative income tax still had its supporters, and in the early 1970s the American government agreed to conduct four experiments: the Seattle–Denver, New Jersey, Rural Income Maintenance, and Gary experiments (Bishop, 1980). The results of these experiments turned out to be controversial. Not only did they suggest that a guaranteed income carried strong work disincentives, but also that it encouraged marital breakup. In particular, it was found that families eligible for the experimental Negative Income Tax had a marital instability 50 percent higher than that of the control group, which was eligible only for the existing AFDC and Food Stamp programmes (ibid.). In view of these results, it is not surprising that no further attempt took place to implement a negative income tax on a national level.

Further helping families in greatest need

If the above reforms were favourable to middle- and low-income families, they were obviously insufficient to eliminate poverty. Breaking with the principle of universalism, several countries consequently introduced a series of means- tested benefits from the late 1960s which aimed explicitly at better supporting families in need. These benefits took several forms, including means-tested cash benefits (targeted at families with children), benefits for lone-parent families, and housing benefits. Some of the measures falling under the first and second categories and adopted during the 1960–74 period are reported in Table 5.3.

Table 5.3 *Targeted cash benefit schemes for families, 1960–1974*

Country	Start-up year	Title of scheme
A: Scheme targeted at low income-families		
Belgium	1963	Minimum Resources Allowance scheme
	1971	Means-tested allowance
Denmark	1974	General Sufficient Resource scheme
Germany	1961	Social Assistance scheme
Netherlands	1963	General Relief scheme
New Zealand	1968	Means-tested Family Maintenance Allowance
United Kingdom	1966	National Insurance scheme
	1970	Family Income Supplement
United States	1960	Food Stamp Programme
B: Scheme targeted at lone-parent families		
Denmark	1973	Supplementary family allowance
France	1970	Orphan allowance
Ireland	1970	Means-tested allowance for deserted wives
New Zealand	1973	Supplementary family allowance
Norway	1969	Supplementary family allowance
Sweden	1964	Advance Maintenance Payment scheme
United States	1962	Maintenance obligation scheme

In Denmark, Germany, and the Netherlands the new schemes were part of new measures targeted at all low-income households. Other measures were directly targeted at low-income families with dependent children. In Britain, the new Family Income Supplement introduced in 1971 was a response to earlier concerns about the high incidence of poverty among families with children. Paid on a means-tested basis to parents with low income and full-time work, this scheme was seen as a preferred alternative to a negative income tax or a general increase in family allowance rates. In the United States, further support for families was provided through a new Food Stamp programme. The programme, which had been introduced on an experimental basis at an earlier stage under President Roosevelt, was revived under Kennedy (in 1960) and significantly expanded under Johnson (Garfinkel and McLanahan, 1986: 110). The Food Stamp Programme was in fact an alternative to the failed Family Assistance Plan and the Negative Income Tax proposal. The programme was amended in 1971 and 1973 in order to extend it to all States (until then it had been available only in some of them) and to provide benefits to all those meeting the eligibility criteria (ibid. 115). The Food Stamp Programme thus constituted a concrete measure of the American government to combat poverty.

In addition to the above measures, a series of others were targeted at lone-parent families. The introduction of these measures was motivated by two factors: by the increase in the divorce rate and the prevalence of lone-parent families; and by studies revealing the higher level of poverty among these families. Once again government action was influenced by demographic changes (especially the prevalence of lone-parent families) and changes in the economic circumstances of families. In Denmark, France, Ireland, New Zealand, and Norway specific cash benefit schemes were introduced in order to better support lone-parent families. In addition, other measures were adopted in relation to maintenance payments. Since the poverty problem experienced by lone-parents was often associated with the failure of the non-custodial parent to pay regularly the maintenance allowance, actions were taken in order to correct the situation. In Sweden and Denmark, governments introduced an advance maintenance payment scheme by which government would pay the maintenance allowance and claim the amount back from the liable parent. Sweden had introduced such a scheme already in 1937, and further reinforced it in 1964. Through this advance maintenance scheme, the government took full responsibility in supporting lone-parent families, by acting as an intermediary between the custodial and the non-custodial parent.

In the United States, on the other hand, the government decided to tackle the problem of non-payment of maintenance allowance completely differently. Rather than advancing payment, Congress enacted legislation which reinforced the obligation of the liable parent. The amendment of 1962, and the legislation of 1965 and 1967, aimed at enforcing child support (maintenance obligation) and establishing paternity (ibid. 119). Thus, while in Sweden and Denmark the new legislation emphasized public responsibility with regard to support of lone-parents, the American legislation instead emphasized private responsibility.

A last set of measures aimed at better supporting families through housing benefits. Subject to means-tests, such benefits had been introduced after the war in response to housing shortages. From the 1960s, these schemes were reformed in several countries in order to make them more advantageous to low-income families. Examples of such reforms were found in Denmark, Germany, Finland, Norway, Sweden (Flora, 1986–87), as well as in France (Prost, 1984), thus adding to the new targeted orientation of the policies of governments towards families.

Reducing work disincentives

The high incidence of poverty had been viewed in the United States partly as the result of failure to work and to seek employment. Removing work disincentives and making the receipt of benefits conditional on being in work, or being available to work, were consequently central in the reforms introduced by the American government from the 1960s. The first action was taken in 1962 when, following a series of amendments to the Social Security Act, the deduction of work-related expenses from earnings was authorized in the calculation of eligibility for benefits. This contrasted with the previous situation in which benefits were reduced by one dollar for each dollar earned (Garfinkel and McLanahan, 1986: 107). In 1967, this system was further reformed by allowing AFDC beneficiaries to keep a small part of their earnings before facing benefit reduction (the first thirty dollars earned each month plus one of every three dollars earned in excess of thirty dollars) (ibid. 113). Incentives to take up employment were further reinforced in 1964 with the introduction of the Work Experience Programme for AFDC mothers, and in 1972 with the requirement to register for work for AFDC mothers with no children under the age of 6. This last measure is important since it was the first time that the receipt of benefits was linked to an obligation to work. According to Garfinkel and McLanahan, however, this policy was never effectively enforced, the reason being that 'there were always more AFDC recipients who wanted to avail themselves of the services offered by the work registration programme than there were funds available to finance these services' (ibid. 116). The implementation of work-related, or workfare, benefits turned out therefore to be difficult. These first experiments were nevertheless to influence subsequent reforms, especially under the Reagan administration.

Together, these various actions reflected the willingness of governments to better support families in greatest need. Although universal benefits had not been abolished, a new priority had emerged: that of reducing inequalities between income groups. From a policy aimed at helping all families irrespective of their income and structure, the addition of means-tested benefits from the 1960s had added another dimension to the governments' state support for families.

5.4 Educational services

The introduction of means-tested and targeted cash benefits was one response of governments to the emerging problem of poverty. Another one was through the channel of education. The increase in poverty, it was argued in some circles, had been accompanied by the development of a poverty 'culture'. Educational measures, by attacking the problem at its roots, were believed to be essential to break this culture of poverty by exposing children to different values. Actions in this field were strongly influenced by the American and British debates about poverty and the role of education. In its simplest form, the culture of poverty thesis insisted that 'the poor are different not primarily because of low income, but because they have been habituated to poverty and have developed a sub-culture of values adapted to these conditions which they then pass on to their children' (Halsey, 1972: 16). Parts of the American War against Poverty was driven by this theory, while reports on education such as the Coleman report in the United States in 1966, and the Plowden report in Britain in 1967, explicitly referred to it. The Plowden report, in particular, stressed the desirability of nursery school attendance for children from deprived neighbourhoods: 'they need above all the verbal stimulus, the opportunities for constructive play, a more richly differentiated environment and the access to medical care that good nursery schools can provide' (Britain, 1967: 63).

In terms of concrete action, the Head Start Programme launched by the American government in 1965 was to provide education, health, nutrition and other social services to 3–5 year-old children and their families (Halsey, 1972: 21). Its impact proved disappointing as revealed by the Westinghouse report of 1969. The Head Start programme, the report concluded, had not make any substantial long-term impact on children's intellectual and social development. Believers in the value of education as a means to combat poverty, had fallen from a high optimism to profound pessimism (ibid. 20).

In England, the publication of the Plowden report and its recommendation on educational priority areas (EPAs) was also to initiate a series of discussions. Schools in deprived areas, it was argued, should be given priority in order to compensate for the little support and stimulus that children from these areas receive from their homes and neighbourhoods (ibid. 31). This recommendation was broadly endorsed by both the government and the House of Lords and led to significant action, including the building of new schools in targeted EPAs as well as a budget for local authority initiatives. From 1972, however, lack of money, lack of political support, and doubt about the effectiveness of education as a means to combat poverty, brought to a halt the initial enthusiasm for this form of state support (Smith, 1987).

If the immediate post-war period had seen the emergence of a 'support-for-all' policy, the rediscovery of poverty in the 1960s, along with the increasing prevalence of lone-parent families, resulted in a new targeted orientation to the policies of governments towards families. The adoption of a series of means-tested and targeted cash benefits, the reform of the tax system along more equitable lines, and the introduction of specific educational programmes, all reflected this new orientation.

5.5 Conclusion

The rediscovery of poverty in the 1960s, and the realization that the post-war recovery had failed to deliver the expected general prosperity, cast a shadow on the golden era of the welfare state. New selective and targeted measures had to be adopted, thus sharply contrasting with the post-war tradition of universalism. With regard to financial support for families, three main types of actions were under-taken: measures to eliminate the inequalities inherent in the existing programmes (in particular with regard to the tax system), measures to better support families in greatest need (i.e. low-income and lone-parent families), and measures to rein-force the principle of work for welfare. Although these actions were to lead to a greater proportion of the state budget being devoted to means-tested benefits, this was done through an incremental policy rather than a radical abandonment of the principle of universality. Universal measures, such as family allowances, were main-tained but were complemented by a series of means-tested benefits. In addition, measures in the field of education were introduced to break the so-called culture of poverty. Children, it was argued, had to be exposed to new values to give them the necessary tools to bring them out of this culture of poverty.

Although these new policy orientations were common to most countries, ma-jor inter-country differences nevertheless emerged. While governments in some countries emphasized their full responsibility in the provision of welfare and in the combat against poverty, others emphasized instead the private responsibility of individuals. For instance, the introduction of advance maintenance payment schemes in Sweden and Denmark reflected the major role assumed by govern-ments in the protection of lone-parent families. In contrast, the American policy of reinforcement of maintenance obligation illustrated a limited public responsibility and a belief in the principle of self- support. Similarly, the adoption of a guaranteed sufficient resource scheme in some European countries contrasted with the much more selective nature of the American cash benefit programmes, and their empha-sis on workfare, or work related eligibility conditions. Thus, while the combating of poverty in the United States was dominated by issues such as welfare dependency, family breakdown, and poverty, in several European countries it was dominated by issues such as the insufficiency of existing welfare programmes.

6

WOMEN'S ISSUES: THE SECOND WAVE

Through their involvement in charities, lobbying groups, and eventually through their representation in Parliament, women played a major role in the pre-World War II period in the development of measures to better support families. Their involvement and effort were not in vain, and led to the adoption of several welfare measures. In the field of family planning and equality in the labour market however, their success was minimal. It was this situation, and its underlying inequalities, which were questioned by women from the 1960s onwards. Freedom, equality, and independence would be the major themes of this second wave of the women's movement. In particular, the battle was to be organized on two fronts: to gain liberal access to contraception and abortion, and to gain equality on the labour market. Once again, this movement was not confined to a single country, but rapidly acquired an international dimension, and was marked by considerable success.

6.1 The renewed birth-control question

The fight for birth-control in the pre-World War II period had led to stricter legislation on contraception and abortion in most countries. This situation was challenged by several parties from the 1960s. Six main groups contributed to the discussion concerning the abortion and contraception question: the international organizations, women's groups, various interest groups, the Churches, the medical profession and experts, and the public. The position and role of each of them are briefly reviewed below.

1. *International organisations*: From the 1950s, there was a rising concern about the risk of over-population among international organizations, and a growing acknowledgement of the need for general access to, and support for, family planning. Population in both developed and less developed countries was growing at an alarming rate, and was to lead to an undeniable change in the attitude of international organizations, such as the United Nations, towards family planning. In particular, the decision by the United Nations to acknowledge the right to family planning as a human right in the 1960s gradually rallied other international actors behind the need for liberalization of access to means of family limitation.

2. *Women's groups* : If the first women's movement had lost its momentum with the outbreak of the war, it re-emerged forcefully in the late 1960s, bringing the right to family planning to the forefront of the agenda (Chafetz and Dworkin, 1986). The issue was raised by several women's groups, and major campaigns were organized in order to liberalize access to abortion and contraception. For instance, in France

following the initiative of the Women's Liberation Front, more than 300 women
known to the public spoke in favour of abortion in 1971, and declared having
had, at least once, recourse to abortion (Bourgeois-Pichat, 1974: 566). Similarly,
in Italy in 1974, following the government's charge against 262 women in Trente
(accused of having had illegal abortions), over 2,500 women signed a petition
declaring that they had also had an abortion. The following year, over 500,000
women and men signed petitions calling for a referendum on abortion (Andersson
and Zinsser, 1988: 419). In Italy, as in France and in other countries, these initiatives
considerably influenced subsequent legislative developments.

3. *Interest groups* : In the fight for more liberal access to family planning, several
interest groups conducted active campaigns from the 1960s. Groups such as the
International Planned Parenthood Federation (founded in 1952), the American
National Abortion Rights Action League (founded in 1969), and the American
National Family Planning and Reproductive Health Association (founded in 1971),
played an active role in this field. On the other hand, they were opposed by
several pro-life groups such as the British Society for the Protection of the Unborn
(founded in 1967) and the Christian Americans Pro-Life Association (founded in
1972). The individual's right to family planning and abortion, against the right to
life of the unborn, was at the core of the debate. In France, the publication of *Des
enfants malgré nous* in 1956 (Derogny, 1956), which exposed the whole problem
of clandestine abortions, added much to the debate, in addition to leading to the
setting up of several private family planning clinics (United Nations, 1989a: 37).

4. *Churches*: Adding to these voices were those of the Churches and religious
leaders. The Church of England had accepted contraception in certain marital
situations in 1931. In 1958, the Anglican Church further softened its position in
acknowledging that contraception was permitted in special cases. Abstinence and
self-control were however still promoted as the primary and most obvious methods
of family planning (Kaiser, 1987: 33–4). In 1971, the Protestant Federation in France
then took a major step in giving its official support to abortion in cases of danger
to the health and life of the mother, and in judicial cases (e.g. rape and violence)
(Bourgeois-Pichat, 1974: 565). On the other hand, the Greek Orthodox and Catholic
Churches remained strictly opposed to family planning (Louros, Danezis, and Trichopoulos, 1974: 184–5). Dissatisfaction was however growing among Catholic
ranks, and in 1963 Dutch bishops proposed that the contraception question be
debated by the Vatican Council (Kaiser, 1987: 41). At that time, there was a growing awareness that in view of the demographic problem, 'the church ought to try
to help the human race by approving in certain parts of the world, at least, the
production of fewer babies' (ibid. 42). The response from Rome took the form
of a Commission on Population, Family, and Birth in 1964–66 which raised hopes
that the Church was ready to change its position. The final position, which was
expressed in the 1968 *Humanae Vitae*, and which re-affirmed the Church's strong
opposition to artificial contraception, was thus received with mixed feelings. While
it was endorsed by bishops in countries such as Australia, New Zealand, Poland,
Spain, and Yugoslavia, the reaction was more mixed in Austria, Canada, France,

the Netherlands, Scandinavia, Switzerland, and West Germany, where several implicit references were made to the 'encyclical's non-infallible character' (ibid. 249). Elsewhere, in Japan, Italy, and England and Wales, a certain ambivalence towards the Vatican's position was expressed.

5. *Medical professionals and other experts*: Among the medical profession, there was a growing dissension from the 1960s with regard to abortion and contraception. While in Belgium, France, and Spain, medical associations spoke against any legislation which would liberalize abortion, in Canada, Italy, Japan, the Netherlands, and the United Kingdom, the medical profession called for some relaxation of the legislation on abortion and expressed strong support for greater and easier access to contraception (Berelson, 1974: 518). The reduction in the number of unwanted births, and the potentially harmful effects of illegal and repeated abortions, were their main arguments. This position was endorsed by experts in several countries. For instance, a specifically appointed commission in Sweden in 1965 recommended authorization of abortion for health, genetic, or 'unreasonable hardship' reasons (Jonsson, 1974: 130). It should be recalled that the Swedish abortion law had already been liberalized to a certain degree in 1938 but was still not available on request. In France, a liberal position was adopted in the 1967 report of the High Consultative Committee on Population and the Family in concluding that abortion was justifiable on self-protection grounds, including cases in which childbirth would have an adverse effect on the health of the mother (Bourgeois-Pichat, 1974: 561). Finally, in the Netherlands, the 1970 Commission on Abortion gave its entire support for more liberal legislation on abortion (Van Praag, 1974: 308).

6. *The public*: Among the public there was a clear shift in attitude in favour of abortion and contraception, although a strong split still existed. For example, a survey conducted in 1967 in Sweden revealed that 50 per cent of the population supported a more liberal policy on abortion (Jonsson, 1974: 131). In contrast, the majority of women interviewed in Spain in 1971 said that they would persist in their negative attitude to the pill even if the Church were to authorize Catholics to use it (del Campo, 1974: 511). In Ireland too 63 per cent of the respondents to a survey carried out in 1971 said to be opposed to the authorization of the sale of contraceptives (Walsh, 1974: 34). In reality, however, the use of contraception was rapidly increasing in most countries. In the United States, for example, while only 10 per cent of women used 'modern' contraceptives in 1960, this proportion was up to 33 per cent by 1965, and 52 per cent by 1970 (Westoff and Ryder, 1977: 333). In the United Kingdom, a similar trend was observed with 15 per cent of women using modern contraceptives in 1967 (pill, IUD), 23 per cent in 1970, and 40 per cent in 1976 (Murphy, 1993: 223). As will be seen in Section 6.2, changes in the legislation contributed strongly to this trend.

From this brief review, it is clear that from the 1960s a real change was taking place in the attitude of the public, experts, and several key groups towards the family planning question. Although some groups remained strongly opposed to any relaxation of the legislation in this area, at least four factors further shifted the balance in the direction of legislative reform. There was, first, the acknowledgement of family planning as a human right at the International Conference on Human Rights in 1968. Parents, it was acknowledged, 'have a basic human right to determine freely and responsibly the number and spacing of their children' (Johnson, 1987: 30). This was a major development, especially since the resolution was apparently adopted without opposition, even from the Holy See. Its interpretation was variable. While for some it implied a more active state involvement in family planning, for others, including the representatives from the Holy See, the resolution recognized family planning as an individual human right, but not as a state responsibility (ibid. 30–1).

The second event was the decision in 1973 to include support for family planning activities among the mandate of the United Nations Fund for Population Activities (ibid. 72). A recommendation to this effect had already been made by the American National Policy Panel on World Population (in its report in 1969) when acknowledging that the existing 'high rates of population growth [could] jeopardize national goals' and consequently that the United Nations should 'take the lead in dealing with one of the world's most serious problems . . . without arousing the fear that family planning is a device of the rich nations to avoid their obligations to the poor' (ibid. 50). The recommendation of this report was fully endorsed by the American government which further stated that it would co-operate fully with the United Nations, its specialized agencies, and other international bodies in the initiation and implementation of related programmes (ibid.). Thirdly, the technical development of the pill completely changed the situation. The breakthrough in this field came in 1956 when the first clinical trials of the pill were carried out in Puerto Rico, and in 1960 when the first contraceptive pill manufactured by Searle Cie was approved by the United States Food and Drug Administration (McLaren, 1990: 240). Other companies quickly followed with Ortho in 1962 and Parke-Davies in 1964 (Djerassi, 1979: 250). If public opinion was already favourable to family planning, this scientific and commercial development obviously made greater control over family size within the reach of more people.

The last development was the holding of some judicial test cases. Among the cases which received much publicity, the Bobigny case in France in 1972 was to have a major influence on public opinion. The acquittal of a 16-year old girl accused of having illegally obtained an abortion marked a turning point in the history of the access to abortion (Andersson and Zinsser, 1988: 418). In Italy, a major judicial case was held in 1974 with the trial of more than forty women accused of having illegally opened an abortion clinic in Florence. The demonstrations and debates surrounding this trial were such that the government was eventually forced to hold a referendum on abortion. The results, which marked an important victory for the pro-abortionists, eventually led to the liberalization of abortion in 1977 (ibid. 419). Other well known cases include the Melbourne trial in 1970 (Borrie, 1974: 287), and the Rose v Wade case in the United States in 1973 (Tietze and Henshaw, 1986). In several other countries, test cases also led to the adoption of a more liberal legislation.

6.2   Government responses and legislation

In view of the circumstances described above, governments eventually took steps to liberalize the legislation concerning access to contraception and abortion. Although the trend was common to all countries, the changes took place with different time lags, and reached different degrees of liberalization, ranging from complete access to contraception only on medical prescription, and from abortion on request to abortion only for medical reasons.

Legislation on contraception

With regard to contraception, three points should be noted. First, while in most countries explicit legislation forbade access to contraception in 1945, including the sale, import, manufacturing, and display of contraceptives, in others, such as Finland and Greece, these activities were not covered by any law. Consequently, when the demand for contraception increased from the 1960s, and the technology made modern contraceptives available, there was no legal opposition to the use of these new modern devices in these countries. Secondly, in countries where prohibitive laws existed, they were enforced to varying degrees, and the number of convictions tended to be minimal. Thirdly, in the liberalizing process which took place from the 1960s, contraception became widely available without prescription in several countries, while in others legislation remained conservative by authorizing access to contraception only under medical prescription or in forbidding the display of contraceptives.

Between 1945 and 1974, liberal access to contraception was authorized in eleven countries: Japan (1949, 1952), Austria (1952), France (1967, 1974), Britain (1967), Germany (1968), Canada (1969), Netherlands (1969), Italy (1971), United States (1971), Finland (1972), and Belgium. (1973) The initial reform in the post-war period was brought about by the Japanese government in 1949 with a law which authorized the manufacture and sale of condoms, diaphragms, and sponges. It was followed in 1952 by the adoption of the government Official Family Planning Programme. As seen in Chapter 4, concerns about the high rate of population growth in the immediate post-war period had led the government to endorse such a family planning programme. The Austrian government also liberalized access to means of contraception in 1952 through the authorization of the advertisement of contraceptives. The French government followed in 1967 with the Loi Neuwrith which, while authorizing the use of contraception, obliged users of pills and IUDs to declare their names and addresses, and required parental authorization for minors (United Nations, 1989a: 37). Opposed by pro-natalists, the Church, and even initially by the Medical Association, the law was passed mainly on medical grounds, as part of measures to combat illegal abortions (ibid.). Greater freedom of access to contraceptives, including supply to minors, was introduced through new legislation in 1974.

In Britain, legislation allowing local authorities to provide free advice on contraception and free supplies of contraceptives was adopted in 1967 as part of the National Health Service (Family Planning) Act (Simons, 1974: 635). It followed pressure from birth-control campaigners, and the recommendations of various studies to reduce the number of unwanted pregnancies. In 1968 and 1969, sale of contraceptives was authorized in Germany and Canada. In the Netherlands, the Penal Code was amended in 1969 to allow the display and sale of contraceptives to minors under 18 years of age. In Italy, it was in 1971 that the use and sale of contraceptives became legal following the verdict of the Constitutional Court which declared as unconstitutional previous laws and decrees prohibiting them (Ferrari, 1975: 439). Similarly, in the United States, the repeal of the Comstock Law in 1971 abolished most restrictions on the display and advertising of contraceptive products (Westoff, 1974: 737).

In Finland in 1972, family planning was given a major impetus with the Family Planning Act which recognized family planning as an integrated part of other public health services provided for citizens (Piepponen, 1974: 102). The Act furthermore required each local community to provide free advice on family planning. Finally, in Belgium an amendment to the Penal Code in 1973 abolished the article prohibiting the dissemination of contraceptive information and the distribution of contraceptives.

The end of the 1960s thus marked a turning point in access to contraception. Influenced by a public opinion increasingly in favour of its use, and by the manufacture of modern contraceptives, governments eventually lifted the prohibition that they had imposed in the pre-World War II period. Only in countries such as Ireland and Spain was the liberalization to take place later.

Legislation on abortion

The lead on abortion legislation was taken by Japan in 1948 with the Eugenic Protection Law which significantly liberalized abortion. Abortion was allowed for health and economic reasons, and left the performance of an abortion to the discretion of one medical practitioner (Muramatsu and Kuroda, 1974: 711). The main justification of this policy was to improve public health, but was also part of the government's new anti-natalist policy (see chapter 4).

This Japanese initiative was only followed by other countries from the late 1960s onward. In Britain, it was in 1967 that legislation was liberalized, authorizing abortion on medical, judicial, and social grounds. One of the innovative aspects of this legislation was that, for the first time, was abortion allowed not only to save the life of the woman or to prevent grave permanent injury to her physical or mental health, but also if the continuance of the pregnancy would involve greater risks to the mental and physical health of the woman and of the existing children of the family than if it were terminated (Simons, 1974: 640). In Australia the move towards the liberalization of the abortion law came in 1970 through a legal case in Melbourne. Shortly before, the state of South Australia had amended its law relating to abortion to allow it on similar terms to the British law, that is, in cases in which 'the continuance of the pregnancy would involve greater risk to the life, physical, or mental health of the pregnant woman than if pregnancy were terminated' (Borrie, 1974: 287). Finland then followed in 1970 with the authorization of abortion for social reasons, while abortion on request was introduced in Denmark and the United States in 1973, and in Sweden and Austria in 1974 (in Austria effective 1

January 1975) (Kirk, 1981).

In contrast to the above, legislation in other countries remained strict despite some attempts to liberalize it. It was for example the case in Belgium, where attempts were made in 1971 to introduce more liberal legislation following the Scandinavian example. The proposed legislation was never adopted, following strong opposition by the government, the Church, and the medical associations which, according to Lohlé-Tart (1974: 216) were extremely conservative both politically and morally. Similarly, in Germany a law adopted by Parliament in 1974 authorizing abortion to be performed with the consent of the woman and approved by a doctor until the twelveth week of pregnancy, was suspended by the Federal Constitutional Court (Schubnell and Rupp, 1975: 310). As a result of the above changes, in 1974 the following situation applied (see Table 6.1). While abortion was available on request, or for broad medical and social reasons in Australia (New South Wales), Denmark, Finland, Japan, Sweden, United Kingdom, and the United States, the legislation remained much stricter elsewhere.

The post-war liberalization in legislation on contraception and abortion in several countries represented a considerable success for women and other pro-family planning activists. Women had been granted control over their fertility and the principle of voluntary parenthood had been recognized. Yet, behind this general trend, the refusal of some governments to endorse this principle was to leave women in different countries in very different positions.

6.3 Women's employment: trends and views

The move towards greater liberalism in access to contraception and abortion was just one facet of a much deeper societal change. As women gained further control over their fertility, they also challenged the traditional sex role pattern by entering the labour market *en masse* from the 1960s. The increase in the participation of women in the labour force was not without precedent as women had participated actively in the labour force during both world wars. But each time, their participation was only temporary, and women returned home shortly after the return to peace. In a similar way, the entry of women into the labour force in the early 1960s was not permanent, or at least was not initially viewed as such. Women were still seen as a 'reserve army' of labour to be drawn upon in periods of rapid economic growth. Soon, however, it appeared that the participation of women in the labour force was not temporary. Major changes had occurred and women were to stay in the labour force. These changes were to lead to significant reform in government policy towards families.

The increase in women's participation in the labour force was impressive. After having stagnated between 1945 and 1960, the participation rate of women aged 15–64 increased between 1960 and 1975 by more than 15 percentage points in countries such as Austria, Canada, Denmark, Norway and Sweden, and by 10 to 15 points in countries such as New Zealand, Spain, and the United States. Instead of being confined to a limited number of countries, the trend was shared by all countries — although to varying degrees of magnitude. The increase in labour force participation varied also according to the age and family responsibilities of women.

Table 6.1 *Abortion legislation, 1974*

Reason for termination	Country	Year of introduction	Limit of pregnancy for authorization of termination
On Request	Sweden	1974	18 weeks
	Denmark	1973	12 weeks
	United States	1973	12 weeks
Medical and socio-economic reasons	Finland	1970	12 weeks
	Australia[a]	1969	ns
	United Kingdom[b]	1967	24 weeks
	Norway	1960	ns
	Japan	1948	24 weeks
Medical reasons	Canada	1969	ns
	Greece	1950	ns
	Switzerland	1937	ns
	Italy	1926	ns
	Germany	1926	ns
	Austria[c]	na	ns
To save a woman's life	New Zealand	1961	ns
	Spain	1941	ns
	France	1920	ns
	Netherlands	1881	ns
	Luxembourg	1879	ns
Prohibited	Portugal	1886	ns
	Belgium	1867	ns
	Ireland	1861	ns

[a]: State of South Australia only. [b]: With the exception of Northern Ireland where abortion is authorized only for other maternal health reasons. [c]: Illegal under old Criminal Code. Reformed in 1973 with new abortion law effective 1 January 1975. Key: ns = Duration not specified. na = Information not available.

For example, in Britain in 1974 70 per cent of women aged 16–59 and without dependent children were part of the labour force, while the corresponding figure was less than 50 per cent for women with dependent children. Furthermore, while the majority of women without dependent children were working full-time, rather than part-time, it was the other way round for women with dependent children (Foster, Wilmot, and Dobbs, 1990).

The main determinants

Several factors contributed to this increase in the number of women in the labour force. One was the development of the service and public sectors, which created numerous work opportunities for women. In fact, from the 1960s the shortage of labour in these sectors was such that employers in some countries strongly encouraged women to join the labour force. This situation is well illustrated in the case of Sweden where the expansion of the public sector led employers to adopt a series of incentives to encourage women to join the labour force. But, as Baude described it, this was still viewed by many as only a temporary situation:

> When the labour market Board in the early 1960s flooded much of the country with advertisements, conferences, and other efforts aimed at stimulating women at home to seek employment, many regarded the entrance of women in the labour market as a temporary expedient. Women were considered a marginal labour supply to be drawn on during periods of prosperity. (1979: 166)

A second factor which contributed to the increase in women's labour- force participation, and in its more permanent character, was the increase in the salary being offered, and the consequent reduction of the gap between women's and men's wages. For women staying at home, this new situation signified an increase in foregone earnings, and made their traditional role more costly.[1] A third factor was the increasing need of families to live on two salaries instead of only one, especially in view of their rising material aspirations.[2]

In addition to these economic factors, social ones, such as the women's claims for greater independence and equality, also contributed to the increase in women's employment. If the housewife role had been welcomed by many in the immediate post-war period, it was no longer deemed satisfactory. Having benefited from the post-war expansion in post-secondary education, women had obviously developed new career and life aspirations which could no longer be fulfilled with the traditional sex role pattern. Furthermore, the development of the pill and the greater acceptance of family limitation meant that women could better control their fertility and more freely join the labour market.

This was the economic and social background. But superimposed on it, traditional views opposed to the entry of women into the labour force still persisted.

Government attitude towards working women

If not entirely opposed to the entry of women into the labour force in the early 1960s, governments in several countries expressed the view that this new trend should not prevent women from fulfilling their traditional role. This attitude was

[1] This is based on Becker's theory of fertility which assumes that the increase in the opportunity cost of childbearing (i.e. foregone earnings incurred by women who withdraw from the labour market for childbearing) was the main determinant of the increase in female employment and the decline in fertility (Becker, 1981).

[2] This is based on Easterlin's theory of fertility which assumes that the desire to maintain relative income (material aspirations versus earnings opportunities) was the main driving factor of the decline in fertility and the entry of women into the labour force (Easterlin, 1987).

revealed in a survey conducted by the International Labour Office in 1963. The reply of the Irish government summarizes well this position:

The Government agrees that in many countries today shortage of manpower has created a situation where material prosperity and industrial growth are dependent to a growing extent on the employment of women with family responsibilities ... It is the view of the Government, however, that ... social and economic policy should primarily be designed to ensure that women with family responsibilities will not be obliged to engage in employment to the detriment of their duties and responsibilities in the home. (ILO, 1964: 6)

The view that women, especially women with young children, should stay at home was also expressed by the British government: 'It would not be right to provide facilities for a woman with family responsibilities to take up employment if the health and welfare of the mother and young children thereby suffered' (ibid. 19). In contrast, no explicit objection to women's employment was expressed in several other countries. Instead, women's right to employment was acknowledged, and it was consequently the duty of the state to provide them and their children with adequate benefits and facilities. While the British and Irish governments expressed the view that policies should avoid women with young children having to seek employment, in countries such as Sweden and Finland the view was that policies should provide women with a genuine choice between home-care or gainful occupation. It should however be stressed that in several countries, including Sweden and Finland, the presence at home of the mother during the first years of her child's life was still highly valued. According to the Finnish government:

The creation of conditions which enable women with family responsibilities to choose whether they wish to work outside their homes or to remain at home is in harmony with the recognition of the principle of individual freedom. Besides, as in most cases it is still nowadays important that mothers with young children remain at home, particularly during the first years of life of their children, there should be possibilities for such choice in general. (ibid. 14)

Some major differences between countries were therefore noticeable in the attitudes of governments towards the participation of women in the labour force. What most governments still seemed to agree upon was that the participation of women in the labour force was less desirable when young children were present. Obviously, governments at that time were not anticipating the subsequent developments which would lead to a major increase in the participation in the labour force of mothers with young children.

Attitude towards state responsibility

If in the 1960s governments were still partly opposed to women in the labour force, what were their views concerning the role of the state? Again, such views are important for they partly conditioned the legislation which was to be subsequently adopted. Four aspects of the question are considered here which reveal major inter-country differences.

There was first the principle of non-discrimination in employment on the basis of sex. Already in 1944 the ILO had adopted a recommendation stressing the principle of non-discrimination against women in the process of the return to peace. This principle was reiterated in the 1951 Equal Remuneration Convention and the 1958 Discrimination (Employment and Occupation) Convention. According to the ILO survey referred to earlier, while most governments agreed with the principle that it was unlawful to discriminate against young women or pregnant women, several underlined the danger of potential discrimination if special protective measures were adopted. For example, the Danish, Finnish, and Swedish governments all stressed the point that special care had to be taken in order to prevent adverse effects of special regulations related to the employment opportunities of female workers. The Swedish government argued that, in order to avoid such discrimination, measures should not be restricted to women, but should instead apply to both men and women with family responsibilities: 'to avoid discrimination, special measures for facilitating re-entry into employment should not be limited to women workers but should apply to the entire labour force, i.e. both men and women. The same argument applies also to part-time employment, which should not be deemed an issue concerning women workers only' (ILO, 1964: 9).

The second aspect related to the principle of equal pay for equal work. While most countries agreed with the principle that women should be paid the same wages as their male counterparts (for the same work and qualification), the ILO survey revealed considerable disagreement with regard to the treatment of part-time workers. Several countries argued that while such a principle may be desirable, in practice it might be difficult for employers to ensure that part-timers (often women) received the same treatment as full-timers with regard to pay and social security benefits. In particular, the United Kingdom pointed out that: 'as regards equality of opportunity and treatment in employment there are some factors in part-time employment which militate against such equality' (ibid. 62). Furthermore, governments in countries such as the United States insisted that while part-timers should receive the same rates of pay as full-timers, their social security protection should be proportional to their contribution and attachment to the labour force.

The third issue referred to the principle of protection of female workers before and after childbirth. The ILO had already acknowledged the principle that pregnant women should be protected against hazardous and heavy work, and that they should be granted leave of absence from work immediately before and after confinement (1919 and 1952 Conventions). All countries had introduced legislation to conform to these principles. However, considerable disagreement remained as to (i) whether these benefits should be extended to a much longer period; (ii) whether the state should ensure the job protection of women during this period; and (iii) whether special measures should be introduced in order to facilitate the re-entry of women into the labour force after a prolonged withdrawal from the labour market.

With regard to the first point, major differences were expressed in the ILO survey concerning the possible extension of maternity leave. The question asked referred to the desirability and feasibility of introducing a one-year leave during which the employment rights of women would be maintained. Only governments in Austria and Italy responded favourably, stressing that such a measure was already in force in their countries, and did not seem to be creating practical difficulties. Governments in other countries, however, such as Australia, Canada, Denmark, and Sweden, underlined the additional burden that such a measure would impose on employers who would need to find temporary substitutes for the absent workers. At the other end of the spectrum, governments in Japan, the Netherlands, Portugal, the United Kingdom, and the United States remained formally opposed to the suggestion; the arguments being that such a long period of leave would inevitably increase the number of workers engaged as replacements without any guarantee of stable employment, that this would create unjustifiable job turnover, would consequently put in jeopardy the productivity of firms, and ultimately have adverse effects on the employment opportunities of women. Finally, governments in countries such as New Zealand and Switzerland, without being opposed to an extended maternity leave, supported the view that such a benefit should not be regulated by the state but should be left to private initiatives, and should therefore be negotiated between employers and employees.

Finally, the fourth aspect referred to the principle of state responsibility as provider of other benefits for working mothers. Again, major differences between countries were apparent. For instance, with regard to the provision of child-care facilities, the Swiss government made explicit the point that a large role should be left to private initiatives, and that the state should play only a minor role: 'The provision of child-care facilities and services should be planned in relation to local circumstances and should be entrusted to private initiative, including that of the parties directly interested, with the help, where necessary, of the State' (ILO, 1964: 32). In contrast, the state's responsibility in the provision of adequate child-care facilities was acknowledged by other countries. However, the Finnish government expressed the view that a traditional element should remain because it was undesirable if the provision of child-care facilities was to lead to a major increase in female employment: 'Developments in this matter [child-care facilities] should not lead, however, to a situation where the mothers of infants are tempted to enter gainful employment outside the home to a greater degree than is desirable from the standpoint of society' (ibid. 30). Moreover, in several of these countries, the view was that the state should not only organize these services and ensure their standards, but should also heavily subsidize them in order to minimize the cost to parents.

Despite the fact that the participation of women in the labour force strongly increased in all countries between 1960 and 1974, sharp differences persisted between governments with regard to the desirability of this trend, and towards the role of governments as facilitators of this process. While most governments acknowledged that the current economic growth demanded an increased participation of women in the labour force, some clearly saw this situation as undesirable for women with children. Furthermore, while some governments considered as their responsibility the provision of facilities and measures to ensure equality between workers with and without family responsibilities, others instead left the provision of such facilities to the private sector.

6.4   State support for working women

Despite the persistence of opposition to the participation of women in the labour force, and the reluctance of some governments to endorse full responsibility for the provision of benefits and services for working mothers, some measures were introduced from the 1960s. The International Labour Office was once again to play a leading role in acknowledging the state responsibility in the provision of measures for working mothers. This position was outlined in the Recommendation on Women Workers with Family Responsibilities adopted in 1965. Although this recommendation did not have the same weight as a convention, it nevertheless clearly acknowledged the presence of mothers in the labour force, and the state's responsibility in the provision of related measures. In particular, the recommendation stressed the importance of providing public information and education on the problems of working mothers, developing public child- care services and facilities, and introducing measures to facilitate the entry or re-entry of women into the labour force. The recommendation was however confined to working mothers and, in a sense, maintained the view that the care of children was still a woman's responsibility. As will be seen in Chapter 10, the ILO revised this view in 1981 through the adoption of the Convention on Workers (Men and Women) with Family Responsibilities.

Provision for public child-care

At the beginning of the 1960s, provision for public child-care, as a form of state support, was little developed. In fact there was little demand for it since the level of participation of mothers with young children in the labour force was still very low. But, with the increase in women's economic activity, there was increasing pressure for a greater state intervention. In addition, studies stressing the merit of pre-primary school education contributed to the emergence of more favourable attitudes to the development and provision of this type of state support. For example, the first report of the Swedish Child Centre Commission, in 1972, underlined the pedagogical and educational merits of early programmes for children aged 5 to 6 years old. Every child, it was argued, should be given access to such programmes as part of his or her right to 'good development potentials' (Liljestrom, 1978: 42).

A selected list of government initiatives related to child-care and early education launched between 1960 and 1975 are reported in Table 6.2. Again, the Nordic countries were to take the lead. While acknowledging the educational value of early learning and socializing experience, governments in the Nordic countries also viewed the provision of public child-care facilities as an essential component of state support for working mothers. Major action was therefore taken. For example, a law on pre-schooling adopted in Sweden in 1975 obliged local authorities (municipalities) to allot places to all 6-year olds (ibid.). Moreover, acknowledging the serious shortage of day care provision for very young children, the Swedish government launched a programme aimed at creating 100,000 more places during the period 1976–80 (ibid. 43). Through this programme, the government was explicitly placing the provision of child-care facilities, as well as the formulation of adequate standards, under its responsibility.

Table 6.2 *Governmental initiatives related to child-care and early education, 1960–1975*

Country	Start-up year	Title of initiative
Australia	1972	Child Care Act
Denmark	1964	Child Care Law
Finland	1971	Child Day Care Committee
	1973	Children's Day Care Act
Italy	1968	National Regulation on Kindergartens
	1971	National Child-Care Plan
Norway	1975	Law on Day Care Institution
Sweden	1968	Child Centre Commission
	1975	Law on Pre-Schooling
United Kingdom	1967	Plowden Report on Education
United States	1964	Head Start Programme
International	1962	Joint United Nations-World Health Organization Expert Committee on the Care of Children

In Finland, a similar view was expressed that also led to increases in the provision of child-care facilities. In particular, following the report of the Child Day Care Committee in 1971, the government adopted the Children's Day Care Act (in 1973) which aimed at making the provision for day care a public social service available to anyone in need of it (Lindgren, 1978: 287). In contrast, the Norwegian government did not respond rapidly to the question of child-care. Conflicting views about the participation of married women in the labour force delayed the involvement of the government in this matter. In 1975, however, the government decided to go ahead with major legislation, stating that 'municipalities are responsible for securing children a good life situation by constructing and operating day care institutions or by financially supporting the maintenance and operation of such facilities' (Ve Henriksen and Holter, 1978: 63). The government's plan was to increase the coverage of the provision from about 11 per cent of children in 1975 (40,000 spaces) to 25 per cent by 1981 (100,000 places) (ibid.). Finally, in Denmark the government placed a particular emphasis on the developmental and pedagogical functions of public child-care institutions through the adoption of the Child Care Law 1964 (Langsted and Sommer, 1993: 149–50).

Elsewhere in Europe, the question of child care was also raised during the 1960s. In Italy, a first step was taken in 1968 with the recognition of the government's right to be directly involved in pre-primary education (Pistillo, 1989: 162; Donati, 1989: 152). The child-care question was also given some attention through the launch, in 1971, of a national plan for the creation of around 3,800 day nurseries throughout the country (Pistillo, 1989: 200). This early involvement of the Italian government may seem surprising considering the very low level of participation of women in the labour force at that time. In fact, and contrary to the Nordic countries, the involvement of the Italian government in the provision of child-care facilities was not so much driven by consideration for working mothers, as for the value of early education. As will be seen in Chapter 10, pre-primary school education for children age 3 and above is still more highly developed in Italy than in most other countries.

Outside Europe, and especially in the United States, the provision of early education facilities was part of the governments' fight against poverty. The launch of the Head Start Programme in 1964, already referred to in Chapter 5, was part of this strategy. The programme however was limited to children of AFDC mothers. Proposals for further development of publicly funded child care were then tabled in the early 1970s and eventually blocked when President Nixon vetoed the Comprehensive Child Development Bill in 1971. The bill, which would have established a national child care programme, was refused on the ground that 'it would commit the vast moral authority of the National Government to the side of communal approaches to childrearing over and against the family-centred approach' (Olmstead, 1989: 372–3). In Australia, on the other hand, a public commitment to the development of child-care was made by the government in 1972 through its Child Care Act. The government, it was argued, should be a major catalyst in the development of children's services, as well as a major provider of funds (Brennan, 1993: 13). Subsequent governments in Australia were to depart from this policy in emphasizing the private nature of child-care responsibilities.

A clear three-way split therefore emerged between governments: (i) the Nordic ones, which showed great willingness to support working mothers and to pursue an objective of sex equality through extensive maternity leave schemes and child-care facilities; (ii) the Italian and French governments, for which support in the field of maternity leave and child care was driven by other sets of considerations, either pronatalist, welfare or educational; and (iii) the American government, which viewed support for working mothers as falling beyond governmental responsibility, with the exception of families and children in greatest need.

6.5 Conclusion

Following the rediscovery of poverty and the first round of re-assessment and reorientation of state support for families, women's demands for greater equality and independence led to significant reforms in government programmes from the 1960s. These changes were twofold: (i) liberalization of abortion and contraception legislation, and (ii) greater support for working mothers in the form of improved maternity leave benefits and child-care facilities. In addition to marking a departure from the immediate post-war policy, which supported traditional families, these reforms illustrated again the interplay between demographic changes and policies. The increasing willingness of women to limit their family size, as well as their increasing participation in the labour force, created new needs which called for government intervention. Although these trends were observed in most countries, the specific responses of governments to them reflected different attitudes to the issues of sex equality and the role of governments as welfare providers. While governments in Sweden and Finland took a decisive lead in the support for working mothers, through the provision of extensive maternity leave benefits and child-care facilities, resistance to such state involvement was expressed in countries such as the United States where the provision of such facilities was seen as a private rather than as a public responsibility. Moreover, while governments in Denmark and Sweden were adopting a liberal attitude to family planning by authorizing abortion on request, in countries such as Belgium, Ireland, Portugal, and Spain, conservative views prevented any early liberalization of this legislation.

7

RENEWED DEMOGRAPHIC CONCERNS

The period from the 1960s witnessed major reforms and re-orientations in the policies of governments towards families. New economic and social circumstances prevailed, and were making obsolete some of the measures adopted in, and adapted to, the immediate post-war period. Similarly, the demographic changes which were to take place from the mid-1960s were also to call for policy reforms. If the post-war fertility reversal had eliminated earlier fears of depopulation, the sudden onset of fertility decline was to put the population issue back on the political agenda. In addition, the increase in divorce rate, lone-parenthood, and the prevalence of dual-earner families, were also revealing the inadequacies of a system of state support aimed at very traditional and stable families. Together these demographic changes were therefore to stimulate the launch of significant action by governments.

Responses to this new demographic situation were not uniform across countries. While some governments raised the flag of pro-natalism and opted for interventionist actions, others welcomed the onset of fertility decline as a solution to earlier fears of over-population.

7.1 A changing demography

In contrast to the immediate post-war baby-boom and family revival, the period from 1960 witnessed a strong fertility decline along with a gradual weakening of the traditional family. Both these changes attracted the attention of governments and led to major initiatives. It is in the mid-1960s that the era of high levels of fertility suddenly came to an end. As can be seen in Table 7.1, although fertility was still increasing between 1960 and 1965 in most countries, it declined rapidly thereafter. While in 1960 all countries, with the exception of Japan, had fertility above or equal to the replacement level, it was the case in only seven of them by 1975 (Austria, Greece, Ireland, Italy, New Zealand, Portugal, Spain). From a cross-national average (based on 22 countries) of 2.85 children per woman in 1960, fertility had declined to 2.01 in 1975. This sharp decline undeniably reflected strong changes in fertility behaviour. It also reflected postponement in the entry into motherhood, which further deflated the value of the fertility index.[1]

Another major change to take place from the 1960s was the decline in the popularity of marriage. From near universality immediately after the war, marriage

---

[1] See Section 4.2 for further details about fertility indices.

Table 7.1 *Total fertility rate in selected countries, 1960-1975*

Country	Average number of children per woman			
	1960	1965	1970	1975
England and Wales	2.68	2.85	2.40	1.78
France	2.73	2.83	2.48	1.93
Germany	2.37	2.51	2.02	1.45
Japan	2.01	2.14	2.13	1.91
Sweden	2.17	2.41	1.94	1.78
United States	3.61	2.88	2.48	1.77

rates were now declining rapidly. Already in 1975, the total first marriage rate[2] among women was down to 0.70 in Denmark, Sweden, and Switzerland(suggesting a celibacy rate of 30 per cent) and between 0.70 and 0.80 in Austria, Finland, and Germany. As compared to the post-war period, this decline revealed a lower inclination of young people to get married at an early age, along with an increase in the prevalence of cohabitation. During this period, the stability of the family was also increasingly threatened by the rising divorce rates. In Britain, the divorce rate increased from 7 divorces per 100 marriages in 1960 to 32 in 1975.[3] In France, the increase was more modest from 10 per cent in 1960 to 17 per cent in 1975, while in Sweden it reached unprecedently high levels, from 17 per cent to 51 per cent. In 1975, the highest divorce rates were observed in Denmark, Sweden, and the United States, while very low levels were still observed in Greece, Italy, and Portugal. In parallel to the above changes, the increase in the prevalence of births outside wedlock from the 1960s also reflected deep family transformations. From a cross-national average of 5 per cent in 1960 (i.e. 5 children born out of wedlock out of 100 new-born children), it had already reached 9 per cent in 1975. It was in Sweden that the highest level was observed with 32 per cent of children born out of wedlock in 1975. On the other hand, the percentage of births outside wedlock remained, in 1975, very low (below 5 per cent) in countries such as Belgium, Greece, Ireland, Italy, Japan, Luxembourg, Netherlands, Spain and Switzerland.

Finally, the other major transformation to take place from the 1960s was the increase in the participation of women in the labour force. Together, these changes were to fundamentally alter the traditional family, and the demographic situation which had prevailed in the immediate post-war period. During this period of major transformations, some substantial inter-country differences were observed. While the Nordic countries experienced the most extreme transformations, the

---

[2] Calculated on the basis of age-specific marriage rates. It is a period measure highly sensitive to changes in the timing of the age at marriage.

[3] Data based on the total period divorce rate, i.e. number of marriages to be dissolved by divorce if the current conditions were to be maintained.

family in southern European countries still appeared to be partly immune to such transformations. These divergent demographic trends resulted in divergent attitudes towards the population question among governments.

7.2   Fears of over-population

In contrast to projections carried out in the 1930s suggesting an eventual decline of population, projections carried out in the 1960s revealed a completely different scenario. The unexpected long-lasting baby-boom in industrialized countries, along with the rapidly increasing population in less developed countries, had resulted in a 1.6 times increase of the world's population between 1920 and 1960. Moreover, projections were now suggesting a further increase of the same magnitude in half the time, that is between 1960 and 1980. This situation was unexpected, and in several countries was to raise fears of over-population.

Catalytic elements

Several factors contributed to the emergence of this new concern. First, there was already at the international level in the 1950s growing concern about the rapid rate of population increase, especially in the developing world. Censuses carried out in the early 1960s further confirmed these fears. The world's population was grow-ing at a much faster rate than anticipated and was in fact heading towards a real explosion. So far, however, these concerns had been limited to some specialized circles. They spread to a much wider public following the publication of two major books: *The Population Bomb* by Ehrlich, in 1968, and *Limits to Growth*, by Mead-ows *et al.* for the Club of Rome, in 1972. Both were alarmist: population growth had to be halted in order to avoid disastrous ecological, social, and economic con-sequences. As argued by Meadows *et al.*: 'If the present growth trends in world population, industrialization, pollution, food production, and resource depletion continue unchanged, the limits to growth on this planet will be reached sometime within the next one hundred years. The most probable result will be a rather sudden and uncontrollable decline in both population and industrial capacity' (ibid. 23).

Although both Ehrlich's alarmist interpretation and the model used in the Club of Rome report proved to be highly controversial, [4] their impact was considerable. Discussions about the threat of rapid population growth became widespread, and there were calls for the adoption of immediate measures to slow down population growth. The foundation of the pressure group Zero Population Growth Inc. in the United States, founded in 1968, with Paul Ehrlich as its first honorary president, reflected this increasing concern for population and ecological issues. Together with other ecological organizations, the Zero Population Growth Inc. was to be very active through its campaigns aimed at sensitizing the public and governments to the detrimental effects of population growth.

---

[4] Among the main criticisms, it was pointed out that the model used in the Club of Rome report had failed to take into account the possibility of corrective feedback mechanisms, as well as having seriously underestimated scientific and technological progress. For a recent re-analysis of the Club of Rome report, see Pestel (1989).

Government responses

Governments once again did not stay indifferent to this new problem, and launched a series of initiatives to examine the question. Some of these initiatives are reported in Table 7.2. The American government was among the first ones to respond to

Table 7.2 *Governmental initiatives related to over-population, 1960–1974*

Country	Start-up year	Title of initiative
Australia	1970	Commission on Population
Canada	1972	Study on Population Growth and Environment
Japan	1959	White Paper on Population
	1974	White Paper on Population
Netherlands	1972	Royal Commission on Population
United Kingdom	1965	Study on Population and Land Availability
	1970	Committee on Population Growth
	1971	Expert Panel on Population
United States	1967	Commission on Urban Problems
	1968	Commission on Family Planning
	1969	Commission on Population Growth and the American Future
United Nations	1964	World Population Conference
	1974	World Population Conference

the new demographic concern with the launch of the Commission on Population Growth and the American Future in 1969. The setting up of such a commission had in fact been recommended some years earlier by the Committee on Population and Family Planning (Westoff, 1973). The scale of the new commission was impressive: more than 100 research reports, a national survey on public attitudes towards demographic issues, public audiences held in five major cities, the production of a film on the topic, and the publication of a six-volume report. But, perhaps most significantly, the Commission marked the first official recognition that the problem of rapid population growth was not only a Third World problem, but was also affecting the developed world.

The report, published in 1972, was indeed to prove the ZPG (Zero Population Growth) activists right, in concluding that: 'in the long run, no substantial benefits will result from further growth of the Nation's population, [conversely] ... the gradual stabilization of our population through voluntary means would contribute significantly to the Nation's ability to solve its problems' (United States, 1972: 4).

In particular, the Commission recommended that in view of the high number of unwanted births, extensive family planning service, and free abortion should be introduced. This last point turned out to be highly controversial and was strongly opposed by the President. In fact, the President's response to the work of the Commission was disappointing. Made public two months after the publication of the report, his response contained no reference to the commission's main conclusion concerning the stabilization of the population (Westoff, 1973). Between the launch of the Commission and its report, fertility had declined to just below replacement level, and fears of over-population were apparently no longer justified.

Outside the United States, a similar story was to take place. Fears of over-population were strong enough to initiate some government action, but led to few concrete policy measures. By the time the commissions reported, fertility had already started to decline and there was no longer any immediate need to intervene. This sequence of events is well illustrated by the case of the Netherlands. Faced with a rapidly growing population and one of the highest population densities in Europe, the Dutch government launched in 1972 a Royal Commission on Population. The conclusion of the commission was unequivocal: 'We recommend that the government aims at ending natural population growth as soon as possible' (Leeuw, 1986: 310). The government was to respond favourably to this report, removing the ban on the advertisement and sale of contraceptives, improving the access to family planning, and stating its objective of reaching a stationary population. Noting that fertility had by then already declined below replacement, it stated that no further policy intervention was required during the next few years (ibid. 311).

In the United Kingdom, the question of rapid population growth also led to major concern in the late 1960s and early 1970s, but, it was followed by little concrete action. The first initiative in this field was a specially commissioned study on population and land availability in 1965–71. It was followed in 1970 by the setting up of a sub-committee of the Parliamentary Select Committee on Science and Technology, mandated to examine further the consequences of population growth. From the sub-committee's enquiry, it became clear that government officials were by no means alarmed by the current demographic trends and believed that there would be plenty of time to adapt to the new situation (Simons, 1974: 630-1). The committee did not share this view and considered that it was in society's best interest that the government should act now in order to prevent 'the consequences of population [growth] becoming intolerable for the everyday conditions of life' (ibid. 631). The government took the conclusions of the committee seriously and in 1971 decided to appoint a small panel of experts to further examine the question. The report of the panel did not however carry much weight. Although the panel concluded that Britain would do better in the future with a stationary rather than an increasing population, it also concluded that the situation did not require immediate action to reduce the rate of population growth. Only a reduction in the number of unwanted pregnancies was recommended for social and not necessarily demographic reasons. In a way, the conclusion of the panel, and its aftermath, recalled the events which surrounded the 1944 Royal Commission on Population. Not only did the commission take a non-alarmist stance with regard to the population question, but by the time its report was completed, the demographic situation had changed and made previous fears appear ill-founded.

These early initiatives nevertheless attracted considerable attention, and in Australia, Canada, and Japan, governments also launched initiatives to examine the population question. In Australia, the annual population growth rate of 1 per cent (2 per cent in Melbourne and Sidney), together with relatively high levels of immigration, were creating concern in terms of their impact on the country's environmental resources. A review of the situation was needed; a task which was undertaken by a specially appointed commission in 1970. The final report, published in 1975, was reassuring: the future growth of the population was so modest in relation to the country's capacity and resources, that a growing population could be accommodated without risk to the environment or the economy. In any case, since fertility had already started to decline, there was no need for a population policy (Fortier, 1988). In Japan on the other hand, the Council on Population Problems took a firmer stance. Already the problem of over- population and rapid population growth had been stressed by the Population Advisory Council in its 1954 and 1955 resolutions, and in its 1959 White Paper. In its 1971 and 1974 reports, the council stressed further the potentially detrimental effect of rapid population growth, and the need to reduce the rate of population growth (United Nations, 1984: 275).

At the international level, the question of high population growth rates was also given a high degree of visibility, especially through the events surrounding the United Nations World Population Conferences in 1964 and 1974. Without imposing the adoption of measures to slow down population growth in the less developed countries, the World Population Plan for Action adopted in 1974 nevertheless stressed that: 'Countries which consider that their present or expected rates of population growth hamper their goals of promoting human welfare are invited, if they have not yet done so, to consider adopting population policies, within the framework of socio-economic development, which are consistent with basic human rights and national goals and values' (United Nations, 1975: 9).

With these initiatives, the population question was therefore back on the agenda of governments. However, the fact that fertility had already started to decline in developed countries meant that the over-population problem was increasingly seen as a Third World problem rather than as a world-wide one.

7.3 Fears of depopulation

While the question of rapid population growth was receiving a high level of attention in some countries, concerns of a completely opposite nature were being raised in others. Fertility, which had reached record high levels in the mid-1960s, had started to decline and was causing alarm. In a way which recalled the 1930s, fears of depopulation were back on the agenda. The degree of concern varied considerably across countries, and only in some cases was an explicit alarmist and pro-natalist position adopted. Some of the main initiatives launched during the 1960–74 period are reported in Table 7.3.

Not surprisingly, it was in France that the first alarm about declining fertility was raised. A tradition of pro-natalism had made the government very sensitive

Table 7.3 *Population-related governmental initiatives, 1960–1974*

Country	Start-up year	Title of initiative
Australia	1965	Committee on Economic Development
Belgium	1962	Sauvy Report on the Walloon Population
	1962	Delpérée Report on the Belgian Population
Finland	1966	Commission on the Equalization of Family Burdens
	1972	Committee on Emigration
France	1960	Commission on Ageing Problems
	1967	Study on Ways to Increase Fertility
Germany	1971	Ad hoc Commission on Fertility Decline
	1974	Governmental Working Group on Population
Greece	1968	Ad hoc Committee on Population Policy
	1971	Study on Emigration
	1971	Adoption of Population Policy
Japan	1969	Population Problems Advisory Council's Interim Report
	1971	Council Report on Population Trends and Problems
New Zealand	1968	Conference on National Development
Spain	1968	Bureau of Population
United States	1973	Federal Council on Ageing

to the population question, and the onset of fertility decline consequently did not pass unnoticed in official circles. The military argument, which linked high fertility and strong military power, no longer prevailed but a continuous renewal of the population was still seen as essential to a dynamic society. In fact, as early as 1967, when fertility was still well above replacement level, the government commissioned a study on ways to increase fertility, and especially the birth of a third child (United Nations, 1989a). The government then went ahead with a further initiative in 1969 by setting up a study group on demographic problems. The adoption of an active and selective family policy was strongly recommended by this group; a recommendation which was endorsed by the government in its VIth Plan in 1971. Society, it was argued, ought to be more child-friendly, to better support families in need and families with three and more children (ibid.).

The other country where fertility decline led to early concern was Belgium. It was in the French- speaking community that the alarm was initially raised in view of the strong fertility deficit as compared to the Dutch- speaking community (Catholic University of Louvain, 1975: 68). In a context of strong linguistic-based rivalries, this fertility differential led the Walloon Economic Council to commission a report on the Walloon population in 1962. The task of writing up the report was given to the French economist-demographer Alfred Sauvy, and reflected the pro-natalist orientation of its author. Outlining the potentially negative consequences of low fertility, Sauvy recommended the adoption of a series of financial and fiscal measures in order to stimulate fertility (Fortier, 1988). This report received wide coverage, and led the Belgian government to commission an independent study on the population question shortly after its publication, in 1962. The report of this second study (the Delpérée report) was less alarmist and pro-natalist than the former one. Supporting Sauvy's recommendation concerning the adoption of a population and family policy, this second report also recommended the adoption of a series of measures to improve the quality of life of citizens (ibid.). Pronatalism however proved to be a politically highly sensitive concept, and as a result the measures eventually implemented by the government made no reference to the demographic situation.

In addition to France and Belgium, the other country in which population issues were given considerable attention was Germany. In the immediate post-war period, the population question completely disappeared from the political agenda in Germany, and any reference to it was clearly avoided. In view of the decline in fertility, and the reaching of unprecedented low levels of fertility (1.45 children per woman in 1975), the government decided that it could no longer ignore the situation and put the population question back on the agenda. In particular, there was concern about the consequences of the continuous fertility decline on the future labour force supply and future financing of pensions. As a response to this concern, and breaking with its post-war stance, the government set up a first Ad Hoc Commission on Fertility Decline in 1971. The conclusion of the report was reassuring: fertility decline was no threat to the economic development of the country nor to the elderly's social security (ibid.). More research on the demographic situation was nevertheless advocated. Despite this non-alarmist conclusion, the publication (in the early 1970s) of projections showing the likely decline of the population led the government to once again raise the population question. The task was this time given to a working group on population, set up in 1974, whose report was never published. Subsequent official statements suggested that, although the fertility decision was seen as out of the scope of any government intervention, the government now intended to adopt measures to create a more child-friendly society (ibid.).

Concern about population growth was raised at an early stage in Greece, Finland, and Spain. Low population growth, especially due to high levels of emigration, was the main concern. The setting up in Greece of an Ad Hoc Committee on Population Policy in 1968, and the conduct of two official studies on population in 1968 and 1970, reflected this early anxiety. The adoption of a pro-populationist policy in 1971 gave further visibility to these issues. The objectives of this policy were clear: to increase fertility and immigration, and to decrease emigration (Louros, Danezis, and Trichopoulos, 1974: 189). This position was partly echoed in Finland, where a combination of low fertility and high emigration led the 1966 Commission on the Equalization of Family Burdens to call for measures to ensure an annual population

growth of more than 1.5 per cent (Lindgren, 1978: 278). The problem of emigration was also given attention in 1972 through the setting up of a Committee on
Emigration. Finally, in Spain, similar demographic problems captured the attention
of the government where, under a dictatorial regime, high population growth and a
strong family were considered essential for the future of the country. In 1968, these
issues were given further visibility through the setting up of a Population Bureau.
Since it was becoming clear that the government's objective of reaching 40 million inhabitants was unattainable, it was becoming urgent to find ways to increase
population growth (del Campo, 1974: 499). In Spain, these pro-populationist ideas
came to an abrupt end in 1975 with the return to a democratic regime.

Outside Europe, population issues also received attention. In Japan, the Population Problems Advisory Council examined the problem of low fertility in its
1969 interim report and recommended the restoration of Japan's net reproduction
rate to unity in order to avert possible labour shortages (United Nations, 1984:
273). This viewpoint was subsequently abandoned in view of rising concern about
the ecological consequences of population growth. In Australia, the question of
fertility decline was also causing anxiety, especially among the Catholic Members
of Parliament. Suggestions were even made that Australia should adopt a policy
similar to the French Family Code in order to encourage the birth of a third or
subsequent child (Borrie, 1974: 280). The government was cautious, and decided
to first set up a committee to examine the question. This was done through the
Committee for Economic Development (1965) which devoted part of its study to
the structure and growth of the population. Demographic trends, it was argued,
were likely to have an impact on all aspects of the economy, and consequently
required specific examination. The report of the study did not reflect the fears
of depopulation expressed by some Members of Parliament. Acknowledging that
changes in the age structure of the population will necessitate some adjustment,
no reference was made to the need for increasing fertility (Borrie and Spencer,
1965).

In New Zealand, the population question was also raised at the governmental
level, but only indirectly as part of the Conference on National Development (1968-
9). More rapid economic growth was seen as desirable, and the demographic
situation was one of several elements which could influence this development
(Fortier, 1988). Finally, in the United States, the only initiative taken with regard
to low population growth in the pre-1975 period was the setting up of a Federal
Council on Ageing in 1973 which addressed issues related to welfare programmes
for the elderly and to their need for long-term care. In the United States fears of
over-population, rather than declining fertility, dominated the political agenda at
this time.

These early responses to fertility decline not only represented a major departure
from the attitudes which had prevailed since the Second World War, but they were
also precursors of a more generalized concern about the demographic situation
which emerged from the mid-1970s. These responses revealed clear inter-country
divergences in the attitudes of governments. While the French government once
again adopted an explicit pro-natalist stance, governments in other countries such

as Germany and Belgium were much more hesitant to endorse such a stance. As in several other countries, the responsibility of supporting families, from a welfare point of view, was seen as falling under government responsibility, but not from a pro-natalist point of view.

7.4   Concerns about the family

Fertility decline was only one of several changes which transformed the traditional family from the 1960s. Changes in marriage, divorce, and female labour force participation were also deep, and prompted the emergence of the family question on the political agenda. Again, concern about the future of the family in the 1960s and 1970s bore some similarities with that raised in the 1930s. In general, however, a less alarmist attitude tended to prevail this time. The family, history had shown, could survive periods of major economic and social transformations. It could therefore be assumed that the family would survive the new changes. However, it was becoming evident that if it were to survive, it would be under a plurality of forms. The traditional family was no longer the only type, but had been supplemented by others, including unmarried cohabitants, lone-parent families, and reconstituted families. Undeniably, these transformations were making obsolete some aspects of the post-war state support for traditional families.

To examine these transformations, initiatives were launched by governments in several countries, some of which are reported in Table 7.4. In France, where

Table 7.4 *Family-related governmental initiatives, 1960–1974*

Country	Start-up year	Title of initiative
Austria	1967	Family Policy Advisory Council
	1969	First Report on the Family
Denmark	1971	Children's Commission
Finland	1974	Committee on Maternity Allowance
France	1960	Commission on Family Problems
	1971	Consultative Committee for the Family
Germany	1968	First report on the Family
Netherlands	1967	Department on Family Policy
Norway	1974	Report on Families
Sweden	1965	Family Policy Committee
United Kingdom	1963	Children and Young Persons Act
	1969	Children and Young Persons Act
	1969	Commission on One-Parent Families
United States	1960	White House Conference on Children
	1970	White House Conference on Children
	1973	Sub-Committee on Fiscal Policy

pro-natalism dominated the political agenda, the family issue was closely linked with the fertility one. Both issues were perceived as requiring improved state support for families. Such a view was for example expressed in the report of the Commission on Family Problems (set up in 1960) and chaired by Robert Pringent. The recent transformations undergone by the family, the report argued, called for a renewed family policy. In particular, major reforms were needed with regard to cash benefits, including family allowances, pre-natal and maternity allowances, housing benefit, and housewife's allowance (Laroque, 1985: 221-2). Recommendations concerning some of these measures were also formulated in the 1967 study on ways to increase fertility (referred to in the previous section). If the Family Code had been well suited to the demographic situation which prevailed at the time of the Second World War, reforms were now needed in order to better reflect the new demographic situation. The setting up of the Consultative Committee for the Family by the French government in 1971 further reflected this perceived need for major reform of the existing system of state support for families.

In Germany too, family issues were raised at an early stage. This was done through a report on the family in 1968 — the first of a series of reports which were published at irregular intervals during the following years. The report, which discussed at length the transformations of the family, reflected the importance that the German government attached to the family question. In Austria, a series of family reports was also initiated, with the first report in 1969. Two years earlier, the Austrian government had launched a major initiative through the setting-up of the Family Policy Advisory Council whose task was to provide expertise on economic, social, legal, and cultural matters affecting the family (Krebs and Schwarz, 1978: 199). This initiative was especially significant in view of its precursory use of the term 'family policy' which was at that time still little used in political circles. The Swedish Family Policy Committee set up in 1965 and the Dutch Department on Family Policy in 1967 were among the rare exceptions.

The family question attracted considerable attention from the 1960s in the Nordic countries. Here the issue was closely linked with that of female employment, with deliberate efforts made to encourage women to join the labour force. The 1974 Committee on Maternity Allowance in Finland and the 1965 Family Policy Committee in Sweden addressed this issue. Both acknowledged the right of women to employment and examined ways of better combining employment and family responsibilities (Liljestrom, 1978: 40; Lindgren, 1978: 291). In Norway, the view was that women had the right to employment, but above all, the participation of women in the labour force was seen as beneficial to the standard of living of families. As suggested in a report on the situation of families with children published in 1974, giving women the means of joining the labour force was seen as the most effective way of supporting families, much more effective than increasing cash payments and subsidies to families. The provision of child-care facilities was essential to achieve this goal (Ve Henriksen and Holter, 1978: 60-1).

While acknowledging the importance of providing public child-care, the Finnish government took a slightly different stance. Women had the right to work but such a right could be exercised only if they were given the means to join the labour force or to stay at home to look after their young children. Consequently, child-care facilities had to be provided for women wishing to join the labour force, but a child-care allowance was also essential in order to allow women, if they wished, to stay at home. Such a call was made by the Committee on Maternity Allowance in 1974: a child-care allowance should be paid for the care of all children under the age of 3, that is, the age when home is their most natural growth environment (Lindgren, 1978: 291). The measure was never fully implemented. Instead the government limited the introduction of a child-care allowance to a 3-year experiment in some municipalities. The new measure gave women the right to cash benefits if their children did not attend an all-day care centre supported by the state (ibid.). Only years later was the government to generalize this form of state support to all families (see Chapter 9).

In the Anglo-Saxon world, the family issue received considerable attention. In Britain, it was raised through two initiatives: a report in 1967 on the circumstances of families, and the setting up of a Commission on One-Parent Families in 1969. As seen in Chapter 5, these initiatives were launched in relation to the issue of poverty. Attention was also paid during the 1960s to children and families in need, especially through the adoption of a series of Children's Acts. For example, the 1963 and 1969 Children and Young Persons Acts further reinforced this selectivity by devoting particular attention to children in need, especially maltreated, delinquent, and other children in need of care and protection (Eekelaar and Dingwall, 1990).

In the United States, attention to the children's cause was maintained through the holding of two further White House Conferences on children, in 1960 and 1970. As in the 1950 conference, their impact was limited. As argued by Steiner (1976), participants at these conferences had grown both critical and sceptical of their value. Their scale (7,600 participants at the 1970 conference, distributed among 210 work-groups over five days), and the number of recommendations produced (670 recommendations at the 1960 conference) undermined their value. According to Steiner: 'The White House Conference is a better technique for bolstering the ego of many of its participants than for formulating a workable policy programme' (ibid. 130). In fact, of the 1970 conference recommendations, no legislation was enacted and no concrete programmes followed. If through these conferences the American government was aiming to acknowledge the importance that it attached to children and the family, its subsequent inaction revealed instead a lack of commitment to state support for families. For, if the well-being of families and children were important, it was an issue which called for private and philanthropic initiatives rather than state ones. Through these conferences, the state was therefore adopting the role of an intermediary, facilitating contact between professionals, social workers, and other concerned groups. The state was not to play a more interventionist role in providing or regulating benefits for children and families.

If the immediate post-war period had seen the disappearance of family issues from the political agenda, the transformations of the family from the 1960s put them back on the agenda of governments. The new situation, as well as its related calls for policy reforms had to be assessed. The post-war state support for families had been developed to suit the traditional and stable family, but was now in need of major reform to better suit the new and unstable families. In particular, the transformations of the family were to lead governments to pay particular attention to lone-parents and working mothers. Despite the fact that these demographic trends were observed in most countries, the specific responses of governments were once again highly divergent. While in France, the family issue was closely linked with that of population growth and pro-natalism, in Germany it was approached from the angle of family welfare. In the Nordic countries, on the other hand, the family issue was linked to that of female employment and paved the way for significant measures to support working mothers.

7.5   Conclusion

This Chapter concludes the period which may be entitled 'From golden age to first re-assessments'. The rediscovery of poverty, women's claims for greater equality and independence, fertility decline, and the transformations undergone by the family, were all elements which, without bringing to an end the post-war development in state support for families, forced governments to reassess their attitude and policies towards families. The 1960s and early 1970s represented a transitory phase in the history of the politics of population and family. Both population and family issues were back on the political agenda, but with considerable inter-country variants in terms of the perceived degree of seriousness of the situation and the role of the state as welfare provider. If the immediate post-war era had seen a certain convergence across countries, the period from 1960 was marked by considerable divergences.

8

THE NEW POPULATION QUESTION

In contrast to the mid-1960s, when the onset of fertility decline had raised alarm in only a few countries, the subsequent reaching of below-replacement fertility levels resulted in widespread concerns. The new questions of population ageing and population decline paralleled to a certain extent those raised in the 1930s, when fears of depopulation were heard. But while in the 1930s, the situation of below-replacement fertility persisted for only a few years, during the 1970s and 1980s there was little sign of fertility reversals. Below-replacement fertility was seemingly here to stay, thus giving rise to some anxieties concerning the economic and social consequences of such a situation.[1]

8.1 Persistent below-replacement fertility

In contrast to the early 1960s when record high levels of fertility were observed, well above replacement, fertility subsequently declined rapidly in several countries to levels as low as 1.3–1.4 children per woman. From a cross-national average (based on 22 countries) of 2.0 in 1975, fertility declined to 1.7 in 1990. While in 1970 levels above replacement were observed in 17 of the countries, it was the case in only 3 of them by 1990 (Ireland, New Zealand, Sweden). These trends for selected countries are presented in Table 8.1 and Figure 8.1.

The break with the previous baby-boom was unmistakable but with significant inter-country differences. While fertility in countries such as Australia, France, United Kingdom, and United States remained relatively stable, around or above 1.8 children per woman (during the 1975–90 period), in other countries such as Austria, Germany, Luxembourg, the Netherlands, and Switzerland, it declined to very low levels. Furthermore, while fertility in southern Europe was still well above replacement level in 1975, it subsequently fell drastically and reached unprecedented low levels. In 1990, fertility in Greece, Italy, Portugal, and Spain had reached levels below 1.6 children per woman — that is, some of the lowest levels ever observed in the industrialized world. As will be seen later in this chapter, this drastic fertility decline raised particular concern in southern Europe. On the other hand, fertility increases had been observed in some countries since the mid-1980s, bringing countries such as New Zealand and Sweden above replacement level. This new

---

[1] As discussed in Section 8.1, fertility in some countries has increased since the mid-1980s. In most cases, this increase is modest, of some fraction of children, and may well reflect a catching up of postponed births. In some other cases, notably in Sweden, the increase has been such that one may suspect a genuine cohort fertility increase.

Table 8.1 *Total fertility rate in selected countries, 1975–1990*

Country	Average number of children per woman			
	1975	1980	1985	1990
England and Wales	1.78	1.88	1.78	1.84
France	1.93	1.95	1.82	1.78
Germany	1.45	1.44	1.28	1.48
Japan	1.91	1.75	1.76	1.54
Sweden	1.78	1.68	1.73	2.14
United States	1.77	1.84	1.84	2.08

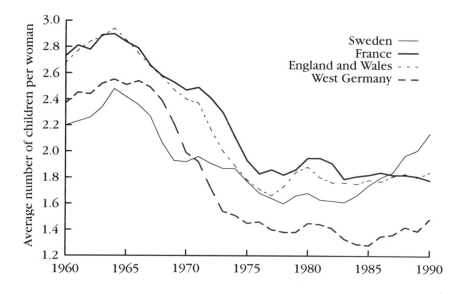

Fig. 8.1 *Total fertility rate, selected countries, 1960–1990*

trend, and especially the case of Sweden, led to different interpretations. While some specialists viewed this increase as a result of a 'catching up' of postponed births, others viewed it as a result —here referring to Sweden- – of social policies particularly favourable to parenthood (Hoem, 1993).

As a result of these diverging trends, the inter-country ranking was strongly altered. As can be seen in Figure 8.2 the predominantly Catholic countries of Italy, Portugal, and Spain had fallen to the bottom end, while the English-speaking countries (Australia, Canada, Ireland, New Zealand, United Kingdom, United States) appeared to be forming a distinct cluster of high fertility countries (although still

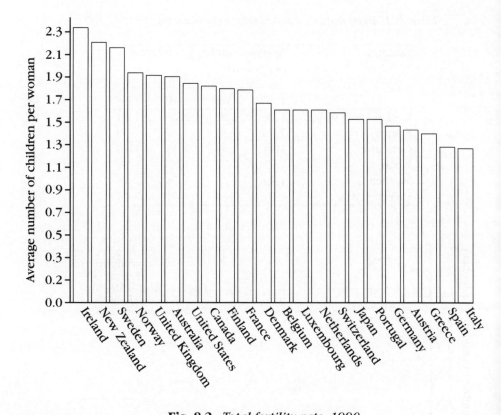

Fig. 8.2 *Total fertility rate, 1990*

below or close to replacement level).

Two major points therefore characterized the fertility situation in the early 1990s, the fact that (i) with few exceptions, fertility had reached levels well below-replacement (including in southern European countries); and (ii) in several countries, this situation of below-replacement fertility had been in place for more than fifteen years. It should however be added that the nature of the total period fertility rate (i.e. sensitivity to changes in the timing of births) may be underestimating the true cohort fertility.

In view of this new era of below-replacement fertility, it is not surprising to find that the fertility and population questions were addressed by governments in all countries during the 1975–90 period. However, the fact that there is no unanimity among specialists concerning the effects of persistent below-replacement fertility has complicated the discussions surrounding these questions. Before going on to analyse the attitudes and responses of governments to the new demographic situation, it may be useful to review some of the main arguments put forward. There is first the economic argument. As seen in chapter 2, in the pre-World War II period population growth was seen as a guarantee of military power and political dominance. Following the experience of World War II, and especially the Nazi's population policy, no further explicit reference was made to the link between population growth and political dominance. The link between population growth and economic growth was however to remain strong in the opinion of several specialists and non-specialists. Low population growth or declining population, it was and still is believed, may jeopardize economic growth. Three main arguments are usually put forward to justify this position:

1. Low fertility will reduce the number of entrants into the labour force, and will consequently lead to labour shortages. Such shortages will slow down the economy, or force governments to be heavily reliant on foreign workers — a position which is usually not favoured by governments.
2. Low fertility will reduce the size of the active population, and will consequently make difficult the financing of social security. In particular, the future imbalances between the elderly population and active workers will jeopardize the current financing schemes of pensions and health care.
3. Low fertility will also make it difficult to cover the cost of other services in view of a declining number of tax payers.

There is however much disagreement among scholars about the degree of severity of these problems. For instance, adopting an explicit pro-natalist position, Sauvy repeatedly stressed the danger associated with population ageing. An increase in the number of young people was the only remedy (Sauvy and Hirsch, 1990). In contrast, scholars like Thane (1989) have been much less alarmist, instead pointing to the potential contribution of the elderly to the economy.

Another argument put forward in the discussion surrounding the population question is the ecological one. As seen in Chapter 7, this argument had already been used in the early 1970s by the zero population growth lobby. From an ecological point of view, the recent decline in fertility is therefore desirable as it reduces the problem of environmental degradation associated with high population growth and high population density. Any government action to counter this trend is therefore undesirable. But, here also there is no unanimity concerning the degree of severity of the world's population problem. For example, Ehrlich and Ehrlich in *The Population Explosion* (1990) points to a disastrously rapid increase in the population between 1960 and 1990, and renewed their call for urgent and immediate actions.[2] On the other hand, Meadows *et al.* (1992), in a follow-up study of the 1970s Club of Rome report, are less alarmist, pointing to a possible sustainable future if a series of measures are taken rapidly.

Finally, the discussion surrounding the population issue has also included some social arguments, which have tended to be used mainly by fervent pro-natalists. Fertility decline has been viewed as synonymous with the loss of desire for children, and as a precursor of the disappearance of the family as an institution and a fundamental pillar of society. For example, Sauvy has been very alarmist in his

---

[2]See Chapter 7 for a discussion of Ehrlich's 1968 book.

interpretation of the situation, arguing that the ageing of the population was undermining the capacity and willingness of societies to innovate, and would result in their degeneration: 'the loosening of the social fabric, the sclerosis of our organs, the blocking of society, the degeneration of several institutions, the cancer of violence, all this is the result of the anaesthetic ageing of the population' (a.t., 1979: 106).

The population question is therefore a complex one, and no unanimity has been reached among scholars. As will be seen in the following sections, this disagreement has led most governments to be very careful in their interpretation of the new demographic situation.

8.2   The perception of the demographic situation

At the international level, the population question since the mid-1970s has tended to be mainly focused on less developed countries. Although in recent years fertility decline has been observed in several Latin American, Asian, and African countries, there have been repeated calls for improved efforts in family planning services. For example, at both the 1984 and 1994 World Population Conferences, calls were made for a reduction in population growth rate and for the attainment of a level of sustainability between population growth, economic development, and the environment. Similar calls for the adoption of strong family planning programmes were made at a meeting of representatives from twenty industrialized countries in 1992. The adopted European Agenda for Action on World Population recommended that: 'population priorities be urgently turned into action . . . and that family planning be made universally available before the end of the decade, with the resulting decrease in population growth rates' (British All-Party Parliamentary Group on Population and Development, 1992).

On the other hand, increasing attention has been paid in recent years to the demographic situation faced by developed countries. For example, a series of resolutions adopted by representatives of governments at the 1993 European Population Conference reflected increasing concern about the consequences of persistently low levels of fertility. These resolutions underlined the need to pay greater attention to the changing age structure of the population, and called for the adoption of adjustment measures:

The continued low levels of fertility and declining mortality at higher ages have direct consequences for population growth and the age structure of the countries . . . These trends have important socio-economic and political implications . . . The development of specific 'ageing policies' is all the more important as the already high expenditure for health and retirement benefits is likely to increase with ageing . . . This . . . leads to new development in the nature of the social contract which binds generation together (article I.12).
Governments should give high priority to the development of human resources as a way of dealing with the adverse effects of population ageing . . . Governments should consider, as appropriate, social security system reforms to ensure greater inter-generational and intra-generational equity and solidarity (recommendations 24 & 26). (United Nations and Council of Europe, 1994)

A clear distinction is thus drawn between the First and Third World population problem. On the one hand, a too-rapid population growth is seen as threatening the development of Third World countries, and on the other, a too-slow population growth is seen as threatening the development of First World countries. As mentioned earlier, the assumed link between population growth and economic development is subject to much controversy, especially with regard to low population growth. Partly due to this uncertainty, radical and explicitly pro-natalist positions are rarely expressed in official circles. For example, at the 1993 European Population Conference no reference was made to the possible adoption of pro-natalist measures. The only exception was a resolution adopted by the European Parliament in 1983, which called for the adoption of measures to reverse the demographic trends. The resolution, which was initially proposed by France, was without precedent. Not only did it acknowledge the gravity of the demographic situation, but in addition explicitly linked it to the society's economic, political, and social situations:

The European Parliament, ... aware that Europe's standing and influence in the world depend largely on the vitality of the population and on the confidence placed by parents in the future well-being of their children ... Considers that population trends in Europe will have a decisive effect on the development of Europe and will determine the significance of the role which Europe will play in the world in future decades ... Considers that measures to combat this marked trend towards population decline, which is common to all Member States, could usefully be taken at the Community level and would be of both political and social significance. (European Community, 1983; Population and Development Review, 1984)

Its call for the adoption of measures to reverse this trend thus constituted a first in the history of the European Parliament. No concrete measures were subsequently taken.

In fact, although the new demographic situation raised concern in most countries, governments still tended to consider the situation as relatively satisfactory. This attitude was apparent in the responses collected as part of the Population Inquiry Survey conducted by the United Nations in 1989. Asked about their perception of the demographic situation in their country, all governments in western industrialized countries, except seven, said that they were satisfied with both their population growth rate and fertility level. Only governments in France, Germany, Greece, Italy, Luxembourg, and Switzerland expressed dissatisfaction in view of their perceived too-low fertility. On the other hand, the Dutch government was alone in perceiving its population growth rate (but not its fertility) as too high (United Nations, 1990).

The results of this survey are reported in Table 8.2 and are cross-tabulated against the fertility level in 1989. A number of points emerge. First, in view of the disparities in fertility levels in both the satisfied and dissatisfied groups, it is clear that fertility level in itself was not the sole determinant of the attitude of governments towards the demographic situation. For example, while both Austria and Germany had fertility levels below 1.5 children per woman in 1989, Austria was satisfied with its demographic situation and Germany dissatisfied. On the other hand, France with its fertility level above 1.8 children per woman was also

Table 8.2 *Perception of the demographic situation according to fertility level, 1989*

Average number of children per woman	Perception by country	
	Dissatisfied	Satisfied
>1.80	France	Australia
		Ireland
		Norway
		Sweden
		New Zealand
		United Kingdom
		United States
1.50–1.79	Luxembourg	Belgium
	Netherlands[a]	Canada
	Switzerland	Denmark
		Finland
		Japan
<1.50	Germany[b]	Austria
	Greece	Portugal
	Italy	Spain

[a]: Considers that population growth is too high. [b]: Is unwilling to intervene to raise fertility.
Source: United Nations (1990).

dissatisfied with its demographic situation. Obviously other demographic factors, such as the rapidity of fertility decline, the number of years of below-replacement fertility level, the level of fertility compared to that of neighbouring countries, population density, the composition of the population in terms of native- and foreign-born citizens, as well as other political, economic, and social factors, can influence perceptions. Secondly, although the attitudes of governments towards the demographic situation have remained unchanged in most countries since the first United Nations inquiry in 1976 (data not shown here), in two of them, Italy and Switzerland, dissatisfaction was expressed for the first time in 1989 (United Nations, 1989b). Finally, the singularity of the Dutch and German cases ought also to be underlined. The Netherlands was the only country to view its population growth rate (not its fertility level) as too high and to express a desire to reduce it, while Germany was the only country to view its fertility as too low but at the same time to be unwilling to intervene to raise it.

Despite the apparent satisfaction of a majority of countries towards their demographic situation, the population question has nevertheless been the recurrent subject of discussion in official and non-official circles since the mid-1970s. Even in southern Europe, where relatively high fertility levels were observed until recently, the new demographic situation has aroused great interest. For instance, in both Spain and Italy, public opinion has viewed very negatively the recent fertility decline. While in 1983, 51 per cent of Italians saw the decline in fertility as favourable, only 19 per cent did so in 1987. Similarly, while 57 per cent approved the decline in fertility in a survey conducted in Spain in 1985, only 23 per cent did so in 1988 (Moors and Palomba, 1991). Japan provides another example of growing concern about the new demographic situation. Commenting on the country's fertility level, the Japanese Minister of Health stated in 1990 that urgent action was needed and that such action was part of the government's responsibility (*L'Actualité*, 1990). Japan's empty cradles and vanishing workers have emerged as a top priority problem, and have been the subject of concern both in the public and private sectors (*Financial Times*, 1991). In fact, beyond these limited examples, governments in all countries have put the population question back on their agendas.

8.3   Population-related initiatives

Since 1975 initiatives have been launched by governments in all countries in relation to the population question. Once again, these initiatives vary considerably in nature. One common feature is the very wide context in which the population question has been addressed through these initiatives. The population question has not been confined to a strict description of population growth or changes in the age structure of the population, but has been seen more generally in relation to a whole series of sectors including regional planning, environment, economy, labour market, social security, education, culture, family, health, and national security. As compared to earlier periods, and especially the 1930s, the population question has therefore been approached in a more comprehensive way. Some of these initiatives are reported in Table 8.3.

General studies on population trends

Confronted with an unprecedent demographic situation, governments in several countries have launched initiatives to assess its causes and consequences. In several cases these initiatives took the form of small scale studies or meetings. In others, the initiatives were of a larger scale involving the commission of several years' studies or the setting up of permanent groups to monitor and report regularly on the population question. Such large scale initiatives were found, for example, in Australia with the setting up of the Australian Population Issues Committee (in 1990), and in New Zealand with the setting up of the Population Monitoring Group (in 1982). The first of these initiatives was launched in order to provide a comprehensive framework of analysis for population matters, especially in the context of ecologically sustainable development (Australia, Population Issues Committee, 1991). The second was also given a broad mandate, that of studying the past and future population trends, and assessing their consequences, as well as possible government intervention (Fortier, 1988). Similarly, in Canada the government launched a major initiative in 1987 in the form of the National Review of Demographic Trends, to clarify the diverse long-term links between a changing population and a changing economy (Canada, Health and Welfare, 1990). Through these initiatives, governments were therefore aiming at accumulating more knowledge about the demographic situation in order to better assess the need for policy interventions.

Table 8.3 *Population-related governmental initiatives, since 1975*

Country	Start-up year	Title of initiative
Australia	1984	National Council of Population
	1990	Population Issues Committee
Austria	1988	Meeting on the Long-Term Consequences of Population Trends
Belgium	1975	Report of the Walloon Population Commission
	1987	Report on Population and Social Security
Canada	1980	National Advisory Council on Ageing
	1987	National Review of Demographic Trends
Denmark	1978	Commission on Ageing
	1985	Study on Low Fertility
Finland	1983	Study of the Effects of Population Trends on Labour Force Supply
France	1975	Study on Ways to Halt Fertility Decline
	1985	High Council on Population and the Family
Germany	1978	Working Group on Population
	1984	Report on the Population
Greece	1988	Working Group for the Study of Demographic Problems
Ireland	1983/4	Reports on the Implications of Demographic Changes by the National Economic and Social Council
Japan	1980	Report of the Special Committee on Fertility Trends
	1992	Study on Fertility trends and Family Policy
Luxembourg	1977	Report on Population
	1991	Report on Population and Family Benefits
Netherlands	1982	Committee on Demographic Policy
	1983	Study on the Consequences of Demographic Trends
	1985	Commission on Social Security
	1988	Second Report of the Working party on Population Questions
New Zealand	1981	Study on Population

Table 8.3 *(Cont.)*

Country	Start-up year	Title of initiative
	1982	Population Monitoring Group
Norway	1981	Commission on Population Trends
Portugal	1988	National Commission on Ageing
Quebec	1985	Report on the Consequences of Demographic Trends
Sweden	1978	Committee on Fertility Trends
Switzerland	1984	Commission on Population Policy
United Kingdom	1979	All Party Parliamentary Group on Population and Development
United States	1978	Select House Committee on Population
	1981	White House Conference on Ageing
European Community	1993	European Year of the Elderly
United Nations	1982	International Assembly on Ageing
	1984	World Population Conference
	1994	World Population Conference

Major research-type initiatives have also been launched in recent years in the Netherlands and Norway. Already in the 1970s, the Dutch government had been particularly concerned by the prospects of over-population and had launched a series of initiatives to examine the question. In the period from 1975, the government was to stay active in this field with a series of other initiatives including the setting up of a Committee on Demographic Policy (in 1982) and a Study on the Consequences of Demographic Trends (in 1983). In Norway, a major initiative was launched in 1982 through the Commission on Population Trends, mandated to study demographic trends, assess their consequences, discuss possible measures which could influence these trends, and assess their potential effect and their justification (Fortier, 1988).

Finally, Germany provides another example of a country where the population issue received increasing attention. Following the initiatives of the early 1970s, the issue of fertility decline was raised again in 1978 as part of an inter-ministerial working group on demographic questions. Two reports were produced by this group: the first, published in 1980, described the demographic situation, and the second, published in 1984, assessed its socio-political consequences. The second report covered a variety of areas including regional planning, the environment, foreign residents, the economy, the labour market, social security, education, culture, the family, young people, health, national security, and international relations. Following these two reports, a further study was commissioned by the government in 1986 to examine the different options with regard to population policy. No official report was submitted (ibid.).

Despite the multi-faceted perspective under which the consequences of fertility decline were examined in these studies, in very few of them has an alarmist and pro-natalist attitude been adopted. Although the new demographic situation, if maintained, was believed to require some adjustments, there was no perceived need for pro-natalist intervention. For example, in its recommendations the New Zealand Population Monitoring Group made no reference to the adoption of measures to modify the current demographic trends. Adjustment measures rather than direct pro-natalist interventions were recommended (ibid.). Similarly, in its final report the Norwegian Commission on Population Trends acknowledged the fact that future transformations of the population would create serious planning problems, especially with regard to labour force supply, education, and health care. However, the authors were careful with regard to the possibility of influencing fertility, instead concluding that the effects of specific measures were uncertain. No pro-natalist recommendation was consequently formulated, the authors instead limiting their comments to pointing out that the changes in the age structure of the population will need to be taken into consideration by the government (ibid.). In contrast, in Australia the Population Issues Committee endorsed an explicit pro-intervention stance in its report in 1992, expressing the view that: 'the Government should develop a population policy which seeks to influence and respond to population change so as to advance economic progress, ecological integrity, social justice and responsible international involvement' (Australia, Population Issues Committee, 1991: p.ix). The adoption of both pro-active measures, that is measures deliberately aiming at influencing population size, characteristics, or distribution, and adaptation measures were consequently recommended. The authors of the report were careful however to underline the uncertainty surrounding the economic effects of population growth: 'because of our limited present direct knowledge of economies and dis-economies of scale, it is not possible to state on this basis that population growth per se enhances or reduces the productivity basis for economic progress' (ibid. p.xiv).

Population ageing

Other studies addressed the population question more specifically by focusing on the problems associated with population ageing. Examples of such initiatives include the Canadian National Advisory Council on Ageing (in 1980), the Danish Commission on Ageing (in 1978), the Portuguese Commission on Ageing (in 1988), the American White House Conference on Ageing (in 1981), the United Nations International Assembly on Ageing (in 1982), as well as the decision by the European Community to give to 1993 the theme the 'European Year of the Elderly'. More concerned with the outcome of demographic trends, rather than the trends themselves, these initiatives aimed at assessing the needs of elderly people, and more generally at elaborating a policy for the Third Age. Through them, governments were thus once again responding to need created by demographic changes rather than attempting to influence the demographic trends. The Belgian report on Population and Social Security (in 1987) and the Dutch Commission on Social Security (in 1985) are further examples of what can be labelled adjustment initiative.

Policy alternatives

Most of the initiatives reviewed above were not mandated by governments to formulate a population policy —although in some cases they were viewed as a first step to the formulation of such as policy. In contrast, a series of other initiatives addressed more specifically the issue of policy interventions. This was, for example, the case of the Walloon Population Commission (in 1975), the French study on ways to halt fertility decline (in 1975), the Luxembourg Report on Population (in 1977), and the Swiss Commission on Population Policy (in 1984). The Walloon report was commissioned by the Walloon government and carried out by demographers of the Université Catholique de Louvain-la-Neuve (known as the Poliwa report). Demographic disparities between the French- and Dutch- speaking communities had already raised concern in the 1960s and a similar situation prevailed. Year after year, the Walloon region was emerging as a loser in its migratory exchanges with Flanders, and furthermore faced a higher mortality level and lower fertility level than its Dutch- speaking counterpart. It was in this context that a new Population Commission was set up. While the previous report on the Walloon population (1962 Sauvy Report) had adopted an explicit pro-natalist stance, this one diverged substantially from it. Population decline in the near future was likely, but according to the authors of the report, this situation did not justify the adoption of a pro-natalist policy. No scientific criterion, they argued, would justify such a policy. A declining population was not necessarily associated with a declining economy or social structure. Instead, the authors recommended the adoption of measures to adapt existing institutions to the new demographic situation, together with measures to reduce existing social inequalities.

The qualitative aspect of the population, (i.e. its welfare), as opposed to its quantitative one, (i.e. its size), they argued, ought to be given preference. In particular, they emphasized that in view of the uncertainties surrounding the economic and social effects of low population growth, attention ought to be devoted to more pressing social issues such as the reduction of infant mortality, a better integration of immigrants, and the improvement of the care of the elderly. The adoption of various measures of social policy was therefore recommended, rather than the adoption of a strict pro-natalist policy. This report thus marked a complete departure from the Sauvy report published some ten years earlier. This report also contrasted sharply with the political atmosphere which prevailed in France during the same period, which emphasized the need for the adoption of a pro-natalist policy. Such a pro-natalist orientation was, for example, reflected in the decision of the French government, in 1975, to commission a study on ways to halt fertility decline. Since a moderate growth of the population was judged as desirable, the aim of the study was to 'assess the effectiveness of various measures which could be taken to slow down, and if possible halt, the decline in fertility' (a.t., INED, 1976: p.xvii). The study was carried out by the Institut National d'Etudes Démographiques. Although acknowledging the desirability of a fertility increase, the authors of the report were cautious concerning the possibility of influencing fertility. The decline of fertility, they argued, was the outcome of deep social changes and left little room for manœuvre for any pro-natalist action (ibid. 44). More extensive cash and in-kind benefits could possibly have a positive effect on fertility in reducing obstacles to fertility, but their success was not guaranteed.

In Luxembourg the possibility of introducing measures to better support families as a way of increasing fertility was considered in the 1977 report on population. The report was commissioned by the government in response to the unprecedented low level of fertility (1.6 children per woman in 1975). In the context of a small population like that of Luxembourg, this situation obviously raised concern about the demographic future of the population. But, in a country with one third foreign-born residents, low fertility meant also a greater reliance on foreigners for population growth, with a consequent decline of those in the population with a Luxembourg origin. For the government, the conclusion was clear: 'denatality' was excessive, the population of Luxembourg nationality was dying, and consequently, action had to be taken (Fortier, 1988). It was in this context that the government asked the French demographer Gérard Calot in 1977 to write a report describing the country's demographic situation, its likely future, and possible solutions. The report reflected the pro-natalist orientation of its author: pro-natalist measures had to be taken in order to bring a reversal of the fertility trend. In particular, Calot recommended the removal of obstacles which prevented couples from having the number of children that they would like to have, including better ways to combine parenthood and paid employment. In addition, equity had to be reached between childless couples and families with children in terms of standard of living and state support (ibid.).

The report was received favourably by the government; all parties acknowledging the need for urgent demographic intervention. In particular, the government agreed that it was essential to create a social climate favourable to families. In 1991 in view of a persistently very low fertility level, the government again requested Calot to examine the demographic situation and to review the system of state benefits and social security contributions. His report again emphasized the social inequalities that the state had introduced by penalizing families with children as compared to childless couples. Suggestions were consequently made in order to partly correct this situation and to make the state more supportive of families.

Finally, in Switzerland, faced with an unprecedented low level of fertility, and a high proportion of foreign-born residents, the government also expressed dissatisfaction about its demographic situation. The setting up in 1984 of a Commission on Population Policy represented the first concrete action in this field, and the title of its report was to reveal an alarmist attitude: *Will the Swiss die?* (Sterben die Schweizer aus?). Its content was much less alarmist however, its authors restricting their analysis to a description of the demographic trends and avoiding controversial interpretations, especially with regard to the admission and naturalization of immigrants. Only in the last chapter of the report was an explicit pro-natalist stance adopted. Arguing that a pro-natalist policy could result in positive results, and that state intervention could be justified, the report concluded by suggesting the increase of fertility to replacement level and the attainment of a stationary population (Blanc *et al.*, 1985; Henripin, 1985).

Several conclusions can be drawn from the previous review of population-related initiatives. First, although governments in most countries claimed to be relatively satisfied with their demographic situation, they nevertheless did not ignore the recent demographic trends and instead launched a series of initiatives in order to further examine the causes and consequences of this situation. Second, the scope of these initiatives tended to be large. Demographic trends were not seen from a narrow perspective, but instead more broadly in relation to various economic, social, and political factors. Third, despite the acknowledgement that the current demographic trends might require some adjustment measures, very few of the initiatives reviewed above suggested the adoption of pro-natalist interventions.

8.4   The pro- and anti-interventionist countries

The fact that pro-natalism found very few supporters among governments may in a sense be surprising considering the persistence of below-replacement fertility, and above all the fact that the new demographic situation had raised sufficient queries and concerns to lead to the setting up of major initiatives. The fact that a non-alarmist tone was adopted in most of the reports reviewed above, and that disagreement still persisted among scholars with regard to the consequences of fertility decline, may partly explain the unwillingness of most governments to endorse pro-natalist policies. In addition, the pro- or non-interventionist attitude of governments was also influenced by the perceived public versus private nature of fertility decisions, and the perceived cost and benefits of pro-natalist intervention.

The interventionist countries

France's attitude towards the demographic situation and the role of the government contrasts sharply with that of most other countries. First, contrary to other governments, the French one perceives a real need for pro-natalist intervention. As revealed in the United Nations Population Inquiry referred to in Section 8.2, France was among the very few countries to be dissatisfied with its demographic situation. Second, the French government moreover sees intervention in the demographic sphere as its responsibility. Contrary to other countries, removing obstacles to fertility is seen as the duty of the state: 'It is the duty of the Government to eliminate obstacles to an increase in fertility, while concurrently protecting the right of couples to determine their own family size' (United Nations, 1989a: 13). Third, the French government does not perceive pro-natalist intervention as an infringement of individuals' freedom of choice, but instead as an enhancement of this freedom inasmuch as such interventions may help individuals to fulfil their fertility expectations. Fourth, in contrast to most other governments, the French one strongly believes in the potentially positive effect of pro-natalist measures. And finally, despite the high cost of pro-natalist measures, the government sees this expenditure as completely justified as an insurance against depopulation.

The gap between France and most other countries is therefore enormous. In fact such an endorsement of pro-natalist intervention is shared only by Greece and Luxembourg. Greece, as seen in Chapter 7, had already endorsed pro-natalist interventions through the adoption of a population policy in 1971 — that is, at a time when fertility was still well above replacement level. This early concern was recently revived in view of the steep decline in fertility to unprecedented low levels (1.4 children per woman in 1990). In fact, the demographic situation even led to a major pre-electoral debate in 1990 with all parties eventually including measures to reverse the demographic trends in their programmes (European Observatory on National Family Policies, 1991: 25). Similarly, in Luxembourg the government explicitly acknowledged the desirability of pro-natalist interventions. The endorsement by the government of the 1977 and 1991 reports referred to earlier was an indication of this willingness to intervene in order to increase fertility.

To these countries, one should add the case of Quebec, in view of its strong pro-natalist orientation which contrasts sharply with that of the Canadian government. The sharp decline in fertility from one of the highest in the industrialized world to one of the lowest (1.42 in 1987)[3], combined with a distinct linguistic situation, have raised considerable concern about the future of the French speaking population. Titles such as *Le choc démographique; Le déclin du Québec est-il inévitable?* (Mathews, 1984), and *Naitre ou ne pas être* (Henripin, 1989) have revealed the alarmist way in which the issue has been raised in scholarly circles. Among the wider public, the issue has also received attention, especially as a reaction to the often alarmist way the matter has been reported in the press. A series of newspaper articles entitled '*Un Québec sans enfant*' (Falardeau, 1988) illustrates well this widespread concern. At the government level, the debate was launched in 1985 with the publication of a report entitled *Etude de l'impact culturel, social et économique des tendances démographiques actuelles sur l'avenir du Québec comme société distincte* (Quebec, 1985). The term 'distinct society' encapsulates here the whole political context within which the political question has been raised: a fear of depopulation and cultural assimilation. This concern has led to the adoption of a comprehensive family policy, with the encouragement of increased fertility as one of its main objectives.

The non-interventionist countries

To these countries must be contrasted others which have explicitly or implicitly rejected the notion of pro-natalist intervention. There is first the case of the Nordic countries. Fertility decline and the population issue had attracted considerable attention in the 1930s and led to major governmental initiatives. This early interest in population issues faded away during the subsequent periods. Some population-related initiatives were launched in the 1980s but without any reference to the possible adoption of pro-natalist interventions.

In Sweden, interest in the population question was expressed in Parliament in the late 1970s when the government acknowledged that a population policy was under consideration (McIntosh, 1983: 154). Lack of consensus about the economic effects of below-replacement fertility, a political ideology which promoted freedom and equality, and a general lack of interest in the question among the public, seem

---

[3]Since then, fertility has increased steadily to reach 1.72 in 1990.

to have prevented the government from taking further action. In fact, the Swedish government made clear its position at the 1993 European Population Conference (referred to in Section 8.2), in stressing that it was aware that 'possible future imbalances of the population's age structure could lead to problems ... [but that] ... it was not contemplating the introduction of any specific demographic policies or targets' (United Nations and Council of Europe, 1994: 325).

In Denmark, a position of non-intervention was also expressed by the government at the 1993 European Population Conference, when it stated that it had adopted 'no policy aimed at influencing the size, the growth, or the structure of the population [and that] ... direct regulation of the size or the structure of the population is not considered a governmental task' (ibid. 133). Aware of the major demographic changes, the government nevertheless acknowledged that population ageing will require some 're-adjustment processes and new ways of thinking' (ibid.). The position of the Finnish government diverged slightly with that of the other Nordic countries. In the 1960s the Finnish government had adopted a pro-natalist stance in view of its unprecedented low level of fertility. This position tended to be maintained during subsequent years, although not forcefully. For example, in a study of the effects of fertility decline on labour force supply in 1983, it was argued that these effects could be partly accommodated through measures to reduce the obstacles between employment and parenthood (Fortier, 1988). At the 1993 European Population Conference, references to an active policy were again made by the government, which stated that 'there may be good grounds for attempting to influence population trends, given the fact that the capacity of the population to provide social security and the economic development of the country are dependent on population structure' (United Nations and Council of Europe, 1994: 147). On the other hand, no explicit pro-natalist policy has yet been adopted by the Finnish government.

The other group of countries which has not endorsed the pro-natalist option are Austria, Belgium, Germany, Italy, and Switzerland. In Austria, concern about the new demographic situation led to the holding of a meeting on the long-term consequences of population trends in 1988. Pro-natalist policies are however not on the agenda. The government is instead giving preference to measures targeted at the welfare of families and the reduction of income inequalities (ibid. 64). Confronted with a persistent low level of fertility, the Belgian government is also not considering the adoption of pro-natalist policies. References were made in 1993 to measures allowing 'families of a size sufficient to insure the replacement of generations' (ibid. 78). However, the measures suggested consisted of flexible solutions to adapt to the new population age structure, rather than of solutions to modify the demographic trends (ibid. 73–5).

In Germany, a reluctance to intervene on fertility trends also characterized the attitude of the government, despite its stated dissatisfaction towards its demographic situation. As revealed in its official statement to the European Population Conference in 1993, the German government may be willing to take some actions, but the term pro-natalism continues to be avoided: 'The changes in the number of inhabitants and in the age structure will have consequences in nearly all spheres of state and society and require measures to be taken in many political fields' (ibid. 163). No explicit references to pro-natalist interventions were made by the German government during this conference, although it was acknowledged that 'demographic side-effects [of family policy measures] deemed desirable may occur' (ibid. 167). Undeniably, memories of the Nazi population policy continues to prevent the German government from adopting an explicit pro-natalist stance. In Italy this reminiscence was explicitly referred to by the government at the 1993 European Population Conference. While indicating that measures were currently being considered to limit some of the undesirable effects of population ageing, the government also stressed its historical resistance to intervene in the field of population: 'Until a few years ago, Italian politics totally ignored population issues, partly because Italy's population was fairly stable and could therefore be managed routinely, and partly because Fascist population policies were still very vivid in the politicians' memories (and in public opinion), so that no collective or social value tended to be ascribed to demographic facts which were completely relegated to the private sphere' (ibid. 209).

Switzerland, despite the government's dissatisfaction towards the country's demographic situation, has also been hesitant to endorse an explicit pro-natalist stance. In fact, an opposite view was expressed in 1993 by the government when it insisted that it 'has not so far considered comprehensive action with regard to population in view of the expected population growth and changing age structure' (ibid. 331). Furthermore, it was stressed that 'in the government's view, measures aimed at having a direct influence on births cannot be reconciled with the rights of the individual and personal dignity' (ibid. 334).

Finally, a third group of countries have rejected pro-natalist intervention on the grounds that there is no need for it or that the population is already large enough. In the United Kingdom, the politicians' lack of concern about the demographic situation contrasts sharply with the prevailing attitude of their French neighbours. A legacy of Malthusian considerations seems to have inhibited government officials in Britain from paying much attention to the decline in fertility. The only exception was in 1988 when comments on the 'demographic bomb' were made in Parliament (Evans, 1988). Fertility decline, it was argued, was like a time bomb and would lead to serious labour shortages. Generally speaking, however, the demographic situation in Britain has not been the subject of much attention. Instead, it is the demographic situation in the less developed countries which has tended to attract more interest. The setting up of an All Party Parliamentary Group on Population and Development in 1979 reflected well this concern, especially in view of its emphasis on the causes and consequences of rapid, rather than low, population growth. One of the major activities of the Group was to host the conference in 1992 which led to the adoption of the European Agenda for Action on World Population (referred to in Section 8.2), which stressed the need for a reduction in population growth. This attitude of the British government towards the demographic question was restated at the European Population Conference in 1993. Not only was the government said to be unconcerned about its domestic fertility level, but it also believed that the ageing of the population was not a real problem. The social and economic issues that it raises 'will prove manageable' (United Nations and Council of Europe, 1994: 360). This position of no problem – no intervention, thus, diverged sharply from that of most other governments.

Similarly in Canada, after showing some interest in the population question, the government also adopted the no problem–no intervention position. Commenting on the report of the National Review of Demographic Trends (set up in 1987), and brushing aside the numerous social and economic implications that this report implicitly suggested, the Minister of National Health and Welfare in his official response instead insisted that the report dismissed 'the myth that Canada as a nation is facing a population crisis' (Canada, Health and Welfare, 1989). This position thus contrasts sharply with that adopted by the Quebec government. Finally, the other country to reject the need for a pro-natalist intervention is the Netherlands, although for other reasons. As mentioned earlier, since the 1970s the Dutch government has oscillated between fears of over-population and depopulation, between the need for intervention and the absence of such a need. In its statement to the European Population Conference in 1993, the Dutch government reverted to its original stance in stating that it would prefer the population to stabilize at a somewhat lower level than the prevailing figure of over 15 million (United Nations and Council of Europe, 1994: 242).

Undeniably, although countries in the industrialized world have experienced similar demographic changes since the 1970s, and although they have all expressed a certain degree of interest in these changes, their respective responses have varied widely. While an explicit pro-natalist stance has been adopted in France, Greece, Luxembourg, and Quebec, an explicit opposition to any population-related intervention, on a no-need ground, has been expressed in Canada and Britain. Between these two extremes, countries such as Finland and Germany have acknowledged that interventions to encourage fertility may be desirable, but have not yet implemented any concrete action, while countries such as Belgium, Denmark, and Sweden, have been unwilling to intervene on fertility matters.

8.5 Governmental actions in France and Quebec

France and Quebec are among the few cases in which an explicit pro-natalist stance has been adopted. This stance has also been accompanied by the adoption of a comprehensive policy. Some of the main features of this policy are highlighted below.

The French pro-natalist policy

The French government's attitude towards the population and family question differs fundamentally from that of other countries in its acknowledgement of the existence of a depopulation threat and the need for pro-natalist intervention. This position is not surprising considering the country's long tradition of pro-natalism. But what also distinguishes France's position from that of other countries is the strong belief in the potentially positive effect of pro-natalist measures on fertility. To back up this argument, the French government has regularly referred to the apparent gap between people's ideals and achievements with regard to family size.

For example, in a survey conducted in 1982, adults aged between 25 and 34 years old said that their ideal family size was 2.5 children (Bastide, Girard, and Roussel, 1982: 902). However, according to estimates, women from these cohorts will end up with only 2.1 children on average (Council of Europe, 1991). This gap between ideals and achievements has consequently been interpreted as an indication of the presence of obstacles to fertility. The following statements, from pro-natalist supporters and politicians, illustrate well this view:

Children born are less numerous than children desired . . . There is therefore a gap between desires and what the will dictates . . . The reasons for this gap are above all material . . . The desire for children is larger than the number of children born . . . This signifies that there are obstacles which prevent couples from having as many children as they would wish to . . . This is what I would call fertility-brakes . . . The objective is not to increase the total fertility rate or the cohort fertility like 20 years ago, but of allowing the expression of a new right . . . the possibility of having the number of children that parents desire. (a.t., Girard and Roussel, 1981)

Without discussing the validity of these assertions, it ought to be pointed out that the desires of individuals with regard to family size have been proved to be highly volatile and unreliable (Westoff and Ryder, 1977). This perceived gap between fertility desires and outcomes nevertheless provided the government with some of its arguments to justify the adoption of pro-natalist measures.

It was under the presidency of Giscard-d'Estaing that France experienced a major wave of pro-natalism from the mid-1970s. Throughout his mandate, Giscard-d'Estaing reiterated his pro-natalist orientation and the commitment of his government to 'strengthen family policy for pro-natalist reasons' (Macintosh, 1983: 122). The government was not the only actor to display a strong pro-natalist banner. Pronatalist supporters, such as Michel Debré, added much to the debate in emphasizing the dramatic aspect of the demographic situation, and the need for immediate pro-natalist intervention. Debré referred to the demographic situation as the 'death ante-chamber' (a.t., Debré, 1979), and made government intervention an utmost priority: 'Whether public opinion is convinced or not, the time has come to inform and act. It is the duty of the authorities and policy- makers. It is the future of France and the French people which is at stake' (a.t., Debré, 1975).

During this period even the public expressed a favourable attitude to pro-natalist interventions. Asked whether they supported the adoption of pro-natalist measures, 59 per cent of respondents at a survey carried out in 1978 replied that they supported such an action, as opposed to 29 per cent who disagreed (Girard and Roussel, 1979: 579–80). Encouraged by such public support, the government introduced in 1980–81 a series of measures intended to boost fertility. It was above all the third birth that this series of measures was targeting. If couples had a first and second child spontaneously, it was argued, they faced considerable financial difficulties with regard to the third one. It was consequently towards the third child that government support had to be targeted. This third child package included three main elements: (1) increase in the duration of paid maternity leave from 16 to 26 weeks for the third and subsequent children; (2) increase of the post-natal cash benefit from 260 per cent of the base wage to 717 per cent for the third and subsequent children; and (3) extension of the old-age pension credit to mothers of three children (since 1972 only mothers with four or more children had been entitled to pension credits). Despite this package and the repeated statements of government to support families, these measures did not match public and official expectations. According to McIntosh, they 'were met with dismay on both sides of the National Assembly and by commentators in the Press [since] the measures fell short of the global family policy that had been repeatedly promised since 1975' (1983: 130–31).

Since the change of the French presidency in 1981, concern about the demographic situation has been maintained. In fact, as commented in the press, 'the decline in fertility preoccupies Frenchmen much more than their European neighbours' (a.t., Herzlich, 1990). The willingness to promote the family for pronatalist reasons seems however to be partly fading. In particular, the newly elected government in 1981 questioned the social justification of the third-child policy. All children, it argued, should be entitled to the same state support. As a consequence, the differential post-natal allowance, which had been introduced by the previous government, was abolished and replaced by a uniform rate. Some preferential treatment for the third child nevertheless continued to exist, and was reinforced in 1985 with the introduction of a child-care allowance for mothers with three or more children.

The Quebec pro-natalist policy

The other place where explicit pro-natalist actions have been taken is in Quebec. From the 1980s, the Quebec government had been much concerned about the province's declining fertility. The policy conducted by France seems to have been a major source of inspiration. It was in 1981 that the government expressed for the first time its interest in the population question through the setting-up of an Inter-Ministerial Committee on the Family. After a series of subsequent initiatives, the government eventually published in 1987 a document stating the main orientations of its family policy. Acknowledging the demographic problem which was confronting Quebec society, it stressed the need for a strong family policy as a potential remedy to the demographic birth deficit:

The family policy has its own aims, and, denatality problem or not, we need to adopt such a policy. But, if the family, family responsibilities and interest in children are favoured and supported by society and the State, we are justified in thinking that this could have an impact on birth rates. In this respect, the family policy may become part of a population policy, especially if it reduces the constraints associated with child-rearing that parents face and which can be felt like a social penalty rather than as a social contribution. (a.t., Quebec, Ministry of Health and Social Services, 1987: 7)

Among the recommendations included in this document, two are worth mentioning: one concerning the setting-up of a Family Council, the other asking all ministers to 'think family', that is, to assess the impact of their interventions on families. This latter recommendation turned out to be more symbolic than concrete as a systematic assessment would have required the adoption of appropriate evaluation instruments. Nevertheless, through this statement the government explicitly acknowledged the importance that it attached to families. The recommendation concerning the Family Council was more concrete. Set up in 1987, it was given the mandate of advising the government on all questions of family interest. The next action in this field was then taken in 1989 through the adoption of a first plan for the family. The plan covered a wide range of sectors and measures including financial support to families, housing, education, child care, ethnic minorities, family law, and benefits to large families. In particular, a lump sum of 3,000 dollars (Canadian)[4] was introduced for the birth of a third child in the government's 1988-9 budget (500 dollars for the first and second). During the subsequent years, this baby-bonus was increased. In 1992, it stood at 8,000 dollars (Canadian) for a third and subsequent child. Although no pro-natalist objective was stated in this plan, it nevertheless acknowledged the government's desire to better support families and welcome children so as to 'encourage and help families' (a.t., Quebec, 1989: preface). In 1992, a second family plan was adopted, and further strengthened the government's commitment to support families. With regard to fertility-related policies, the actions taken by the French and Quebec governments were unique. Although similar measures were introduced by governments in other countries, their objective was confined to the improvement of the standard of living of families, without any direct reference to pro-natalist objectives.

8.6 Conclusion

In a way which recalls the 1930s concern about population decline, the persistence of unprecedented low fertility levels through the 1970s and 1980s raised major concerns in most industrialized countries. The numerous demographically-related initiatives launched during this period reflected the increasing awareness and attention devoted to the population issue. Two main factors tended to dominate the agenda: (i) the economic impact of fertility decline, for example on labour supply; and (ii) the social and economic impact of population ageing, especially on the financing and provision of pensions and health care. While in the 1960s, declining fertility caused concern in a limited number of countries, in the post-1975 period anxiety spread gradually to most countries. But, despite this common concern, there were major differences in the extent to which alarm about the population issue was raised across countries. In particular, a sharp contrast existed between, on the one hand, governments in countries such as France, Greece, Luxembourg, and Quebec, which perceived the recent demographic trends as undesirable, and which considered that it was a state duty to intervene in order to increase fertility, and on the other governments in countries such as the United Kingdom, which saw no problem with the current demographic situation, or any need or justification for intervention.

The gap between the pro-natalist / pro-interventionist countries and the non-interventionist ones was therefore wide. Divergence in the perceived consequences of depopulation, and above all, in the legitimacy of state intervention (from a moral and social point of view) was at the core of this split among countries. Between

[4] In 1987, the exchange rate was 1.23 Canadian dollar for 1.00 US dollar.

these two extremes, governments in other countries have tended to acknowledge the existence of a population problem, especially a population ageing one, but have been unwilling to adopt a pro-natalist stance — instead opting for a pro-family one. Thus, if countries have not largely differed in terms of the issues raised since 1975, they clearly have done so in terms of the ways that these issues have been perceived, and the ways governments have perceived their role in this matter.

9

THE FAMILY AS A POLITICAL ISSUE

The decline in family size is only one aspect of the deep transformation which the family has undergone since the 1960s. Increases in divorce, lone-parenthood, birth outside wedlock, pre-marital cohabitation, and in the proportion of economically active mothers, have changed the reality of families. The traditional breadwinner and housewife model is no longer dominant, and has been joined by a constellation of other models of families. For governments, these transformations have represented a major challenge. New legislation had to be adopted with regard to working mothers, lone-parents, and non-married cohabitants, and new measures had to be introduced in order to better support the new families.

The ways in which this challenge has been addressed by governments varied greatly across countries. While some countries have quickly adapted their policies to the new family types, others have maintained their support for a more traditional family. Moreover, while some countries have endorsed full responsibility in the provision of support for families, some have adopted a more limited approach.

9.1 The transformations of the family

In contrast to the immediate post-war period when the traditional family was highly praised and experienced renewed support, the last three decades have witnessed deep transformations of the family. Fertility, marriages, cohabitation, divorce, and the participation of women in the labour force, have all been on the increase and have changed the dynamics of family formation and dissolution. If the 1960-75 period witnessed the onset of some of these transformations, the period from 1975 witnessed their deepening and extension to all countries. These demographic changes are important for they have challenged the existing systems of state support for families.

With regard to marriages, the post-1975 trend has confirmed the earlier one: fewer young people are getting married, but they tend also to marry at an older age. While in the period 1960-75 this trend was mainly confined to the Nordic countries, it has now been observed in all countries. While in 1975, total period first marriage rates[1] below 75 per cent were observed in only few countries (e.g. Denmark, Finland, Sweden, Switzerland), by 1990 a completely reversed situation

---

[1] The total period first marriage rate is the sum of age specific first marriage rates observed during a given year. Like its fertility equivalent (the total period fertility rate) it is highly sensitive to changes in the timing of events —here in the timing of entry into first marriage.

had taken place. Marriage rates above 75 per cent were then being observed only in Portugal.[2] Even in Greece, Italy, and Spain, they have declined below 75 per cent. This change is significant for although such low values partly reflect a delay in the age at first marriage, they also reflect a deep change in the attitude towards marriage. The post-war universality of marriage has undeniably disappeared. In parallel to this change, a strong increase in non-marital cohabitation has been observed. For example, while in 1980 in Britain only 3 per cent of women aged 18–49 were cohabiting, this was the case of 8 per cent of them in 1988 (Coleman and Salt, 1992: 188). For a majority of young people, cohabitation however still represents a prelude to marriage rather than a permanent alternative to it. In Britain, among women married in 1980–84, 26 per cent had cohabited before marriage (ibid. 187). In Sweden, where the highest level of cohabitation is observed, nearly all marriages are preceded by a period of cohabitation (Hall, 1993).

If marriage has become less popular, it has also become increasingly unstable. The 1960–75 period witnessed a strong increase in the divorce rate which deepened during the subsequent period (at least in some countries). In 1990, more than one third of marriages could be expected to be dissolved by divorce in several countries, including Austria, Canada, Denmark, Finland, Luxembourg, Norway, Sweden, Switzerland, the United Kingdom, and the United States. Even in countries such as Greece, Italy, and Portugal, where divorce rates are still relatively low, significant increases have been observed since 1975. The percentage of children born out of wedlock has also increased substantially. If in the early 1970s, levels above 15 per cent were observed in only Sweden, by 1990 levels above 25 per cent were observed in several other countries (e.g. Denmark, Finland, France, New Zealand, Norway, Sweden, United Kingdom, United States). Only in Belgium, Greece, Italy, Japan, Spain and Switzerland were less than 10 per cent of children born out of wedlock in 1990. As a result of the increasing trend in divorces and children born out of wedlock, the percentage of lone-parent families has also increased. In Britain, for example, the percentage of lone-parents among families with dependent children has increased from 8 per cent in 1971 to 14 per cent in 1986 (Coleman and Salt, 1992: 228).

Finally, the earlier trend towards the increasing participation of women in the labour force has also persisted. While the cross-national average (based on 22 countries) in the participation rate of women aged 15–64 was 47 per cent in 1975, it had reached 59 per cent in 1990. Even in traditionally low-level participation countries, a strong increase has been observed, for example in the Netherlands, Portugal, and Spain. It is however when data are broken down by number and age of children that the increase becomes most remarkable. For example, while the participation of women with 1, 2, 3, or more children in England and Wales was respectively 50 per cent, 46 per cent, and 44 per cent in 1973, the corresponding figures for 1990 were 66 per cent, 65 per cent, and 50 per cent. For women with at least 1 pre-school child, the participation in the labour force increased

---

[2] Data for Ireland, Japan, Luxembourg, New Zealand, and the United States are missing. Persistent high marriage rates may still be observed in some of these countries.

from 25 per cent in 1973 to 36 per cent in 1988.[3] Britain in fact belongs to a group of countries for which the participation of women in the labour force is still limited when pre-school children are present. This is not the case in some other countries, e.g. Sweden. Thus, while the 1960–75 increase was mostly confined to women with limited family responsibilities (i.e. no dependent children, or no pre-school children), the post-1975 increase has spread to women with pre-school children. In this respect, strong inter-country differences remain. If it can be argued that the increase in the participation of women in the labour force has forced governments to modify their support to working mothers, it is also likely that the nature and extent of government support has also influenced the level of women's participation in the labour force.[4]

From the above figures, it is apparent that the post-war traditional and stable family has undergone major transformations, which have considerably deepened since 1975. It is also apparent that, although the magnitude of the changes has varied across countries, the general trends have been observed in all countries. Even in southern Europe where the family had until recently appeared as partly immune to deep transformations, major changes have been taking place since 1975. Despite these changes, major inter-country differences persist with the Nordic countries at one end of the spectrum with their high prevalence of non-traditional families, and the southern European countries at the other end where the transformations undergone by the family have still been limited, although on the increase.

9.2 The family on the political agenda

To say that the family has received utmost priority since 1975 would obviously overstate the attention which has been devoted to family issues by governments. However, it is evident that family issues have received increasing attention, and moreover, that the support of families has emerged as a major political winner. Even in countries such as Britain and the United States where governments have maintained their policy of limited support for families, they have been anxious to state that they cared about the family. Statements such as 'Our government must never impede nor work against the . . . family' by ex-President Carter in the United States in 1979 (Steiner, 1981: 6), or 'We are the party of the family' by Mrs Thatcher in Britain in 1977 (Henwood and Wicks, 1988: 7), illustrate well the importance attached to the family.

At the international level, two main actors have contributed to the increasing visibility of the family as a political issue since the mid-1970s: the European Community and the United Nations. At the European Community level, one of the first initiatives was the adoption by the European Parliament of a resolution stressing the need to: 'identify and take into account those aspects of Community

---

[3] It should be noted that a large proportion of economically active women with children in Britain hold part-time rather than full-time jobs. For women with a pre-school child, 25 per cent were working part-time in 1988 as compared to only 11 per cent working full-time.

[4] This two-way effect between policies and demographic changes will be further discussed in Chapter 11.

economic, social and cultural policy which relate to the family . . . encourage the adoption by the Member States of policies that take account of the multiple needs of the family and where appropriate, harmonize these policies at Community level' (European Community, 1983). Through this resolution the Parliament emphasized the political dimension of family issues, and more precisely its European dimension. In the same resolution, it also called on the European Commission to draw up an action programme 'to promote the launching of family policies in the Member States' (ibid.). If, so far, the term 'family policy' had been very infrequently used in political circles, with this resolution it was to enter the political vocabulary of the European Community and its Member States.

Following this first initiative, the Parliament proposed the setting up of an Observatory on National Family Policies, which was to be one of the concrete outcomes of the increasing interest of the Community in the family. Composed of independent experts from each Member State, the Observatory was set up in 1989 and was given the task of monitoring the development in family policy in each of the Member States and producing an annual report. In August 1989, the Commission took a further step by issuing a communication which identified five sectors which would require regular concerted action at the Community level (Commission of the European Community, 1989a):

1. The inclusion and consideration of the family dimension in the establishment of appropriate Community policies.
2. Evaluation of the impact of other policies on the family.
3. The reconciliation between professional life, family life and the sharing of family responsibilities.
4. Adoption of measures to protect certain categories of family, notably single parent and large families.
5. The special protection of the most deprived families.

Although these sectors have not been enshrined in formal directives (at the time of writing), they signal the intention of the Commission to increase its actions in the field of family policy.

The other theme which received attention at the European Community level was that of family poverty. This concern for the societies' poorest led to the launch in 1975 of the first Poverty Programme, or Pilot Schemes to Combat Poverty, which was modelled on the Irish initiative of 1973. Based on a series of regional projects, it revealed, among other things, the high incidence of poverty among one-parent families (Room, 1990: 87). This first programme was then followed by a second one (1985–89) and a third one (1989–94), all paying great attention to the issue of family poverty and highlighting the related inadequacies in the national systems of cash transfers.

At the United Nations level, the family and children have also received considerable attention in recent years. The United Nations first adopted a Declaration on the Rights of the Child in 1924, and again in 1959. In 1989 a new Convention on the Rights of the Child was adopted. With respect to social security and social policy, the convention acknowledges the right of the child to appropriate health

care facilities and education, and to an adequate standard of living, particularly
with regard to nutrition, clothing, and housing (articles 24, 27, 28). Moreover, it
acknowledges the right of children of working parents to child-care services and
facilities. More generally, the convention recognizes the importance of the family
and the right to public support: 'the family, as the fundamental group of society
and the natural environment for the growth and well-being of all its members and
particularly children, should be afforded the necessary protection and assistance
so that it can fully assume its responsibility within the community' (UNICEF, 1990).

The other major initiative of the United Nations in the field of family issues
was the declaration of 1994 as the International Year of the Family. Again, this
initiative has had a considerable impact at the country level, especially through the
setting up of national committees to promote and prepare the International Year.
The message carried by the United Nations re-emphasized the importance of the
family and its right to protection: 'the family constitutes the basic unit of society
and therefore warrants special attention' (United Nations, 1991: 8). Through the
activities surrounding the International Year, the United Nations aimed at increasing
public and private awareness of family issues, and the need to better support
families.

At the national level, initiatives launched by governments since 1975 have revealed an increasing interest in family issues. Some of these initiatives are reported
in Table 9.1. The Australian report on families published in 1986 as part of the
government's Social Security Review, and the New Zealander report on families
published by the Social Advisory Council in 1984, are two examples of such initiatives. In Austria and in Germany, the publication of reports on the family (following
the first reports published in the 1960s) reflected the interest of governments in
family issues with the question of how to better support families central to them.
In addition, these reports have also covered special themes such as the situation of
children with difficulties (in the third German report) and the situation of elderly
members in families (in the fourth German report).

In Italy and Portugal, the governments' initiatives took the form of commissions
on the family, respectively in 1981 and 1982. Through these initiatives, governments
have been concerned to find ways of further supporting families and preventing
their further weakening. The family, it is argued, still constitutes a fundamental
pillar of society, but institutions have to be adapted to better reflect its new needs
and realities.

In France and Luxembourg initiatives related to families have been launched
since 1975. In contrast to the other countries, these initiatives have tended to place
a considerable weight on fertility decline and the pro-natalist issue. But here also,
the issue of how to better support families has been central. In France, the family
was given special attention in 1975 in the report of the Groupe de prospective
du VII Plan sur la famille. In this report, the authors noted that the nature of the
relationship between the family and the state had considerably changed.

Table 9.1 *Family-related governmental initiatives, since 1975*

Country	Start-up year	Title of initiative
Australia	1986	Report on Families' Situation and Trends
	1986	Report on Income Support for Families
Austria	1979	Second Report on the Family
	1990	Third Report on the Family
Belgium	1988	Agreement on Family Policy
Canada	1984	Task Force on Child Care
	1987	Special Committee on Child Care
	1978	Senate Report on Child Benefit
Denmark	1976	Commission on Childhood
	1980	Commission on Family Policy
	1981	Commission on Youth
	1988	Committee on Childhood
	1988	Report on Child Policy
Finland	1980	Report on the Welfare of Families
	1983	Committee on Parenthood and Employment (Working Time)
France	1975	Report of the Prospective Group on the Family
	1985	High Council on Population and the Family
	1985	Report on the Family Policy
	1990	Governmental Plan for the Family
Germany	1975	Second Report on the Family
	1979	Third Report on the Family
	1986	Fourth Report on the Family
Greece	1983	First Plan on Social Policy
	1988	Second Plan on Social Policy
Ireland	1980	Report on Family Income Support
	1980	Task Force on Child Care
	1990	Working Group on Child Care Facilities
	1991	Programme for Economic and Social Progress (including child care services)
Italy	1981	Commission on the Family
	1982	Report on Family and Income
	1985	Commission on Poverty
Japan	1992	Study on Fertility Trends and Family Policy
Luxembourg	1977	Study on the Family
	1991	Report on Population and Family Benefits
New Zealand	1984	Social Advisory Council Report on Families

Table 9.1 *(Cont.)*

Country	Start-up year	Title of initiative
	1986	Royal Commission on Social Policy
Norway	1977	Report on Children
	1981	Commissioner for Children
Portugal	1980	State Department for the Family
	1982	Commission on the Family
Quebec	1988	First Governmental Plan of Action on Family
	1992	Second Governmental Plan of Action on Family
Spain	1988	Ministry of Social Affairs (with special responsibility for family policy)
Sweden	1975	Family Assistance Commission
	1979	Commission on the Economic Situation of Families
Switzerland	1978	Report on the Situation of the Family
	1982	Report on Family Policy
United Kingdom	1975	Children's Act
	1980	Child Care Act
	1981	All Party Parliamentary Group for Children
	1986	Children and Young Persons Act
	1989	Children's Act
	1991	Child Support Act
United States	1980	White House Conference on Families
	1992	Commission on Urban Families
European	1975	First European Poverty Programme
Communities	1985	Second European Poverty Programme
	1989	Third European Poverty Programme
	1989	Observatory on National Family Policies
United Nations	1979	International Year of the Child
	1989	Convention on the Rights of the Child

More specifically, it had resulted in an increasing invasion of the public sector into family life and in the shrinking of the functions of the family. The neutrality of the state towards family structure, and its non-interference into private family life, was consequently recommended (Laroque, 1985: 28–9). The family was then given further visibility in 1985 through the setting up of a High Council on Population and the Family. This new Council had a strong pro-natalist orientation. Mandated to report to the President on the demographic problems and their consequences, it was also asked to examine questions related to families.

In Luxembourg, particular attention was given to family issues in 1977 with the setting up of a commission on the family. The objective of the study was twofold: on the one hand it aimed at analysing the social structure of Luxembourg, and on the other, at describing its modes of reproduction and family composition. The report, entitled *Familles et structures sociales au Luxembourg*, included discussion of trends in family formation and dissolution, and in female labour force participation. In addition, it included the results of a survey of public attitudes on family-related topics such as marriage, the impact of birth on family life, and contraception. No policy recommendations were formulated in this report (Fortier, 1988). Attention was also devoted to family issues in the 1977 and 1991 reports on population referred to in the previous chapter. In fact, over the past decades, the Luxembourg government has regularly reiterated its interest in family issues, its pro-natalist orientation, and its desire to strengthen its support for families. For instance, in a statement made in 1989, the government reaffirmed its commitment to families by saying that: '[the family] represents a priority concern for the Government ... By means of a global, coordinated approach, it intends to continue a creative policy for promoting the family' (European Observatory on National Family Policies, 1990: 9). In 1992, the government again referred to the global character of family policy, and made further promises of improved state support for the family (European Observatory on National Family Policies, 1992: i. 30).

In Switzerland, the family question was first addressed in a report on families in 1978, and subsequently given more visibility with the setting up of a working group on the family in 1979. The report of the group endorsed a pro-family approach in calling for the adoption of measures to better reconcile employment and family responsibilities, a more active housing policy, and the development of counselling and education services for parents. In addition, the reform of family benefits to better support families with children was also recommended (Switzerland, Office Fédérale des assurances sociales, 1982). Some of these recommendations appeared also in the report of the 1984 Commission of Population which was referred to in Chapter 8. As in Luxembourg and France, the family policy in Switzerland has thus been explicitly linked with pro-natalist issues. However, as of 1994, no explicit and comprehensive pro-natalist policy has been formulated and adopted.

Finally, the other country where family issues have been addressed through government initiatives is the United States, with the 1980 White House Conference on the Family and the 1992 Commission on Urban Families. The first of these initiatives was launched by President Carter following repeated promises concerning the holding of such a conference. Initially promised for shortly after the election, the conference had to be postponed several times owing to organizational difficulties. The change of its name from the 'Conference on the Family' to the 'Conference on Families', reflected one of the numerous difficulties which confronted the President and the conference organizers. There was no longer one single family type but instead a plurality of family types. The White House Conference had to reflect this new reality. The conference eventually took place in the summer of 1980, and was marked by much disagreement and dissatisfaction among the different actors involved. An apparent lack of consensus about the role of the government was stressed by several people: 'despite the feeling that the family values are eroding, and that action needs to be taken to help families, diverse viewpoints about family life may prevent the emergence of sufficient consensus about the role of govern-ment' (Antler, 1978: 21). This interest of the American government in families, and concern about their instability were again stressed in 1992 in the address of President Bush announcing the setting-up of a Commission on America's Urban Families. In his address, the President underlined the numerous difficulties con-fronted by families, in addition to identifying the problems of the cities as one of the major causes of the dissolution of the family (The Family, 1992: 3).

Despite the wide gap that exists between research-type initiatives like those reviewed above and the actual formulation and implementation of policies, these initiatives are nevertheless significant for at least two reasons. First, they underline the fact that the transformations undergone by the family in recent decades have not passed unnoticed but have conversely received significant attention by gov-ernments. And second, they also underline the fact that this concern about family issues has not been limited to a small number of countries but has instead been widely shared across countries.

9.3 Specific initiatives towards families

Working parents

The issue of working parents had attracted considerable attention in the Nordic countries in the 1960s and early 1970s. Since 1975, the issue has continued to receive attention in these countries. For example, the Finnish Committee on Work-ing Time in 1983 devoted a large part of its work to ways of better reconciling parenthood and employment. Similarly, the Swedish Family Assistance Committee in 1975 devoted attention to the issue of working parents by recommending the extension of the duration of the maternity and parental leave, and the introduction of the right to reduce hours of work for parents with children under the age of 3. Drawing attention to the long hours that many children spent in day nurseries, the Committee felt that both parents and children would benefit from shorter working hours (Liljestrom, 1978: 44–5).

Since 1975 the issue of working parents has been raised by other governments, especially from the standpoint of child-care facilities. In Canada, for example, the issue has been addressed by the 1984 Task Force on Child Care, and the 1987 Special Committee on Child Care. While the former proposed the development of a publicly funded child-care system, the latter proposed a 700 million dollar child-care package which would include a refundable child-care tax credit and subsidies to parents (Canada, Ministry of Supply and Services, 1989). In Ireland, the child-care issue was addressed by the Working Group on Child Care Facilities in 1990. The initiative was set up under the auspices of the Department of Labour and was followed by concrete measures (see Section 10.3). The child-care issue has also been addressed as part of larger initiatives such as the New Zealand Royal Commission on Social Policy (in 1986). Moreover, the Portuguese government launched in 1991 its programme entitled 'Strengthening Solidarity and Improving Quality of Life' which outlined a series of strategies including some to better conciliate family life and employment (European Observatory on National Family

Policies, 1992: i.). Similarly, in Japan in its 1991 New National Action Plan Towards the Year 2000, and its 1992 Five Year Plan, the government has emphasized the objective of bringing greater equality between men and women, and introducing more facilities and support for working mothers (Hayashi, 1993). Rather than being confined to the Nordic countries the issue of working parents has therefore been raised in a wider range of countries.

Countries have differed widely however in the extent to which they consider supporting parents as a government responsibility. While governments in the Nordic countries have tended to adopt a supportive policy in providing working parents with extensive leave and provision for child-care, governments in countries such as the United Kingdom have been opposed to the endorsement of such a public responsibility. For example, ex-Prime Minister Thatcher in Britain has been formally opposed to the adoption of a national child-care policy on the grounds that it may be detrimental to the development of children (Pienaar, 1990). Similarly, in Ireland the government has been opposed to taking full responsibility in the provision of child-care facilities. References to the development of child-care facilities have been included in the government's 1991 programme of economic and social development. But, rather than taking full responsibility in the provision of these facilities, the government has instead expressed its desire to encourage employers to develop such facilities (European Observatory on National Family Policies, 1991: 36). Support for families, in this case the provision of child-care facilities, is not seen entirely as a state responsibility, but also as the responsibility of individuals and of private employers.

On the other hand, even in countries where governments have adopted an apparently more supportive attitude towards working parents, the objectives and nature of this support have varied. For example, in contrast to the Nordic sex-equality objective, the policy conducted by the German government has been to support a more traditional sex role. As pointed out by Hantrais (1994), the German tax system, the limited provision of day nurseries for children under the age of 3, and the existence of extensive child-care leave, have all favoured a traditional housewife and male breadwinner model.

Low-income families

The issue of poverty among families is another theme which has attracted considerable attention since 1975. As seen earlier, this theme was addressed by the European Community through its Poverty Programmes. The Finnish report on the welfare of families (in 1980), the Italian report on family and income (in 1982), and the Swedish Commission on the economic situation of families (in 1979), are further examples of related initiatives. In addition, a series of other initiatives has examined the adequacies of the existing systems of income support for families. This includes the 1986 Australian Report on Income Support for Families, the 1987 Canadian Special Report on Child Benefit, the 1980 Irish Report on Family Income Support, and the 1991 Luxembourg Report on Family Benefits. Divergent stances are apparent from these reports. For example, while the Australian report recommended the maintainance of universal family allowances (Brownlee, 1990), the

Canadian report concluded that child benefits would be most useful if directed to families with lower incomes, rather than being paid to all families (Canada, Standing Senate Committee on Social Affairs, Science and Technology, 1987). In fact, the issue of targeted versus universal benefits has been discussed widely since 1975. In the context of tight government budgets and high levels of unemployment and poverty, it has been argued in several circles that money would be better spent by targeting benefits at families in greatest need.

In the United States the whole issue of family poverty and income support has been raised from a completely different angle. Already in the 1960s the American government was concerned about the perceived work disincentives inherent in benefits such as the AFDC. This concern, along with the issue of lone-parents, received considerable attention again in the 1980s. The publication of Murray's book, *Losing Ground*, in 1984, added much to the debate in stressing the unintended and undesirable effects of welfare benefits, including the disincentive to take up employment. As in the 1960s under the Nixon administration, the government was not indifferent to these arguments, and introduced in the late 1980s a series of reforms of welfare benefits, including a reinforcement of their workfare elements. For example, the 1988 Family Support Act adopted by the Reagan administration included educational and training programmes for mothers receiving AFDC benefits, and aimed at increasing their employability.

In Britain the link between poverty, welfare benefit, and work disincentive has also attracted attention as part of the general debate about the underclass. But while the Conservative government has regularly referred to the introduction of workfare benefits, as of 1994, it has not taken any concrete action.

Lone-parent families

In view of their increasing prevalence and their high level of poverty, lone-parent families have received considerable attention from governments since 1975. But again, while most countries have adopted a particularly supportive attitude towards lone-parents, in the United States and Britain a different attitude has prevailed. Welfare benefits, it was argued in some circles, were encouraging husbands to desert their wives and pregnant mothers to remain unmarried. In order words, they were partly responsible for the increase in lone-parent families. In Britain, the issue led to fierce debates in Parliament in the early 1990s with the Conservative government being accused of blaming lone-mothers for intentional welfare dependency (Waterhouse, 1993). In contrast to other countries where the increase in lone-parent families has been perceived as requiring further state support, in Britain and the United States it has instead been perceived as a social phenomenon requiring severe reforms of the existing welfare benefits.

Children's rights and situation

Following the adoption by the United Nations of the Convention on the Rights of the Child in 1989 (see Section 9.2), the theme of children's rights has received considerable attention at the national level. In this field, Norway emerged as a front runner in the protection of children's rights with its report on children in 1977, and above all with its appointment of a children's commissioner (or Ombudsman) in 1981. This last initiative constituted a major innovation in the policy of governments towards families as it gave children a voice and a representative to protect their interests. With this appointment, the Norwegian government acknowledged the need to give special protection to children:

Children constitute a weak and vulnerable group within the population. Official goodwill is not always sufficient to ensure that the needs and rights of children are properly protected, nor do they have much chance of winning when the interests of children conflict with the interests of well organized or stronger groups. Children and groups working with and for children — in the Commissioner — have an independent, public spokesperson, which is one way of protecting the interests and needs of children and young people ... The Commissioner shall promote the interests of children in the private as well as public sectors. (Norway, Ministry of Foreign Affairs, 1990)

More specifically, the mandate of the children's commissioner is to protect and represent children's interests, to ensure that legislation relating to the protection of children is observed, and to propose measures which can strengthen children's safety, and solve or prevent conflicts between children and society (ibid.).

In Denmark, children, as a political theme, have also been the target of government intervention. In fact, not less than fourteen committees on children's issues have been active since the 1980s. The report on child policy, published in 1988, has been one of the concrete outcomes of these committees. In particular, the report stressed the need to enhance the cultural environment of the child, and to improve the provision and quality of child-care establishments (European Observatory on National Family Policies, 1990: 50). Much of the discussion and action in this field has been centred on pre-school age children, thus giving a special orientation to the family question. A focus on young children has also characterized the approach of the Dutch government in recent years. One concrete action in this field has been the request by the Minister of Health, Welfare and Cultural Affairs to the Netherlands Family Council in 1991 to report on policies related to young children. Concern about children, especially children of working parents, vulnerable groups, and cultural minorities seem to have been the main motive behind this request. In particular, the government has mandated the Family Council to formulate proposals which would give support to 'child upbringing, the quality and level of child care centres, and vulnerable groups of families of Dutch or foreign origin' (European Observatory on National Family Policies, 1992: i. 33).

Another country where children's issues have attracted a considerable interest is Britain. The British government has a long history of intervention in the field of protection of children, through a series of Acts concerned with the well-being of children in difficulties or need (e.g. maltreated, delinquents). In recent years, a series of other Acts in the same tradition has been adopted, including the Children's Act 1975, the Child Care Act 1980, the Children and Young Persons Act 1986, and the Children's Act 1989. This last Act was once again mainly addressed at children in need, and attempted to strike a balance between the interests, rights, and duties of parents, children and the wider community. As commented by Eekelaar and Dingwall, 'Most of it [the 1989 Act] is concerned with the conditions under which the state should intervene in the relationship between parents and their children, and therefore concerns public law' (1990: 19). Through these interventions, and their emphases on children in need, the British government has therefore been giving a special orientation to its policies of the family — an orientation which gives primacy to self-reliance and restricts state intervention in the case of family dysfunctions. This orientation was furthermore reflected in the setting up of an All Party Parliamentary Group for Children in 1981. Although the mandate of the group was broad, its work has tended to focus on specific categories of children, for example, on those whose opportunities in life are restricted by very low income, and those with special educational needs, or with emotional and behaviourial difficulties. This orientation places Britain in a distinct category of countries.

If governments in all countries have been paying attention to family issues since the mid-1970s, not all have been willing to support them through publicly funded measures. For example, the British and American governments have perceived the increase in lone-parent families as a social malaise and have partly put the blame on welfare benefits which, it is argued, unintentionally encourage lone-parenthood. In other countries, on the other hand, a more supportive attitude has been adopted towards lone-parents — as a category of families requiring special protection. A similar split has been observed towards working parents. While not being opposed to working mothers, the American and British governments have not seen it as their responsibility to support the provision of facilities for this group of citizens. In contrast, governments in the Nordic countries have seen the support of working mothers as their responsibility, especially with the view of achieving greater equality between men and women. These inter- country differences have contributed to give very distinct orientations to the politics of the family.

9.4 A policy for the family

Although all countries since the turn of the century have introduced measures to support families, in very few cases have these measures been part of a coherent and comprehensive policy. In most cases, state support for families has taken the form of an amalgam of cash and in-kind benefits. The major exception here is France through the adoption of its Family Code in 1939 which for the first time brought support for the family under a single umbrella. Its implementation, however, was spread across several ministries and departments and, thus, lacked harmonization. In the other countries, it is only from the mid-1970s, that the concept of family policy experienced growing popularity among policy-makers. Not only had additional support to be given to families, but the amalgam of measures aimed at supporting families also needed reforms to bring in more coherence and harmonization. But, while such interest for the formulation of a comprehensive and coherent family policy was expressed by several governments, it was followed in most cases by limited results.

Until the mid-1970s the term 'family policy' had been little used. Its use became more prevalent thereafter, partly influenced by initiatives taken by the European Community (see Section 9.2). At the national level, the term family policy has been used in several initiatives in recent years, for example in the Danish Commission on Family Policy in 1980, and the Swiss Report on Family Policy in 1982. The decision of the Spanish government in 1988 to give to the Ministry of Social Affairs special responsibility for family policy also illustrates this increasing use of the term. The agreement on family policy by the Belgian government in 1988 provides yet another example. Through this agreement, the government aimed at implementing a global policy which would eliminate all elements that could hinder the family's development (European Observatory on National Family Policies, 1990: 9). Similar objectives or desires were also expressed by other governments. For example, the Royal Commission on Social Policy in New Zealand in 1986 recommended the development of a family policy. When asked what needed to be done to make the country a more fair and just society, the Commission replied that 'one of the critical steps in that direction would be to ensure that New Zealand develops a family policy or at least a coherent stance on family matters' (New Zealand, Royal Commission on Social Policy, 1988: iv. 603). But severe budget constraints have prevented the government from taking concrete steps in that direction.

In southern European countries, where the recent transformations undergone by the family have raised concerns, governments have launched several actions in relation to family policy. In Portugal, the orientations of a future family policy were laid down by the State Department for the family in 1980. A family policy had to: (i) be prepared, analysed, and integrated in a global framework; (ii) be given a promotion objective (i.e. to promote family values); and (iii) stress the participation and involvement of several social actors (Nazareth, 1989: 226). This orientation was then given a higher profile through the setting up of a Commission on the Family in 1982 which emphasized the key words 'involvement, competence, and solidarity'. Together with the 1980 initiative, the commission marked a real turning point in Portuguese family politics. However, this development came to an abrupt end in 1983 with the abolition of the State Department for the Family, apparently due to difficulties related to the implementation and co-ordination of a global family policy.

In Greece the adoption of a family policy was also strongly favoured by the government. This was stressed for example in both the 1983 and 1988 government's reports on social policy which endorsed the need to develop a coherent and comprehensive family policy (European Observatory on National Family Policies, 1991: 25). In addition, the importance of the family as a social institution and the government's responsibility to support it, were highlighted in the country's constitution adopted in 1986. The new constitution acknowledged the family as 'the requisite foundation for the duration and enhancement of the Nation' and gave the state the responsibility of 'protecting childhood, motherhood, and marriage' (ibid. 24). Finally, in Italy, the government at the end of the 1980s also indicated that it was time to develop and implement an effective family policy. A bill on this matter, and another on family law, were presented to Parliament in 1991 (European Observatory on National Family Policies, 1992: i. 26). However, some observers have pointed out that only slow progress in this field has been made as a result of the inability of the central political- administrative system to promote a family policy. A more active role has therefore tended to be played by regional authorities

(Donati, 1989: 168-9).

Some of France's and Quebec's action in the field of family policy has already been discussed. In France, the publication of a report on family policy in 1985, and the adoption of a Plan for the Family in 1990, are two further examples of the active role taken by the government towards providing a coherent and comprehensive policy for families. In particular, the 1990 Plan was designed as a comprehensive programme to renew family policy (David and Starzec, 1991: 111). As pointed out by some observers, support for such a comprehensive family policy has however gradually weakened over the years (European Observatory on National Family Policies, 1991: 31). While a large-scale and global family policy is still under consideration, major obstacles, including unemployment, poverty, and the country's deficit, have apparently prevented further expansion and consolidation of the French family policy. Commenting on this recent development, the European Observatory on National Family Policies reported: 'If families have not formed the subject of any thorough renewal of policy in 1990, it is because the national interest has focused on the need to combat the financial deficit characteristic at the present time of the various social security schemes' (ibid.). On the other hand, in Quebec despite similar financial obstacles, the government has maintained its high support for its family policy, as reflected in its second Plan of Action on the Family (1992).

In the United States, the closest the country came to the concept of a family policy was in 1976 under Carter's administration. In the course of his presidential campaign Carter made a series of promises related to family issues, among which was a 'family impact statement'— the idea being to evaluate the consequences of governmental actions on families. The concept had originally been given visibility by Senator Mondale in 1974-75, and then through the setting-up of a Family Impact Seminar in 1976. The objective of the seminar was clear: 'to examine the political, administrative, and substantive feasibility of developing a process to produce family impact statements on selected public policies ' (Steiner, 1981: 30). The idea was appealing. However, over the following three years, the initial enthusiasm for the idea gradually faded. Practical and conceptual difficulties meant that by the seventh meeting of the seminar, thirteen of the twenty-one members sent their apologies (ibid.). If instituted, such a family impact statement would not have provided a coherent and comprehensive family policy such as that considered by some European governments. However, it would have introduced an instrument which could have monitored and assessed the action of various departments on families. Rather than a centrally implemented policy, it would have provided guidelines for all departments involved in family matters.

In the United Kingdom, the government has never come close to adopting a European-style family policy. The Children's Act 1989, focused mainly on children in need, reflecting the Conservative government's own view about a British- type family policy. Events in 1994 did however take an unexpected turn with the appointment of the Health Secretary as co-ordinator on family policy (Brown, 1994). Although the role given to the Secretary was essentially that of co-ordinator, and left the policy lead with individual departments, it nevertheless gave the Secretary the chance to influence some of the Department's agendas. More than symbolic, this action was highly significant. Not only was the term 'family policy' used for the first time in British politics, but this action also went against the restricted way the government had so far viewed its responsibility towards the family. The concrete realizations of this new co-ordinator remain to be seen. Her debut in March 1994 was promising however when she stated that more help with child care for working families was among her priorities. If formalized, this help would mark a complete departure from the policy of former Prime Minister Thatcher who was entirely opposed to the provision of public child-care facilities. During subsequent interviews in 1994 the Health Secretary reverted to a rhetoric emphasizing private responsibilities and non-governmental intervention. Although recognizing the importance of parenting, she stated that any action 'should not be government driven but achieved through improving the partnership with voluntary organizations' (Family Policy Studies Centre, 1994).

Beyond the cross-nationally shared interest in family issues and family policy, different objectives have been given to family policy among countries. While in countries such as France and Quebec family policy has been given a pro-natalist objective, in the Nordic countries it has been seen from a social policy point of view, as a way of bringing equality between men and women. While in southern European countries family policy has been seen as necessary to support new families, in the United States it is still seen as something falling outside government responsibility. If the transformations undergone by the family have led to significant policy initiatives, the specific governmental responses have obviously varied widely across countries.

9.5 Conclusion

In a way which recalled the 1930s fear of family decline, the deep transformations undergone by the family from the mid-1970s have put the family on the political agenda. Issues of divorce, lone-parenthood, female employment, and the rights of children, have been raised in most countries and have led to numerous initiatives. There has been consequently great similarity across countries in that all of them have seen the emergence of the family as a major political issue. Beyond this similarity, there have however been major differences across countries in the ways family issues have been addressed and in the degree of commitment of governments to support families. While governments in France and Luxembourg have explicitly linked fertility and family issues and have adopted an explicit pro-natalist attitude, governments in most other countries have focused solely on family issues, considering the fertility question outside areas of government responsibility. Moreover, while governments in countries such as Belgium have opted for a comprehensive support for families, others, such as the British and American governments, have restricted their intervention to families in greatest need, and relied more heavily on private and employers' provision of family benefits.

Obviously, these broad orientations and contrasts simplify a more complex reality. The fact that governments in most countries have not adopted an explicit, comprehensive, and coherent family policy means that actions of governments towards families have remained piecemeal. The overall commitment of governments to support families in the 1980s was undeniably higher than it was earlier this century — but not necessarily more coordinated and harmonized.

10

RECENT TRENDS IN STATE SUPPORT FOR FAMILIES

The period from 1975 was one of significant reorientation for systems of state support for families. There was, first, the need to adjust benefits to better support families. Families had undergone major transformations, and adjustments were required to meet their needs. On the other hand, there were budget constraints which were severely limiting the expansion of the system of state support for families. The whole welfare benefit system had grown unchecked, and there were now calls to restrain its growth. Thus, while the first factor was calling for an expansion in state support for families, the second was calling for stabilization or contraction.

The results of these two opposite forces are analysed in this chapter. The objective is to examine the trends in family benefits since 1975 and to look for discontinuities either in the form of cutbacks or expansion. In addition, attention is paid to differences across countries and to patterns of divergence or convergence.

10.1   Cash benefits for families

Family allowances

In contrast to the period up to the mid-1970s when family allowances were subject to major expansion, since then, trends in family allowances have been characterized by a mixture of expansion and reduction. On the expansion side, the changes introduced have increased the coverage and rates of the schemes, or introduced specific supplements. For example, there was an increase in the coverage of the scheme in Germany in 1975 (benefits extended to the first child), in Japan in 1986 (benefits extended to the second child), and the United Kingdom in 1977 (benefits extended to the first child). Increases in family allowance rates following the abolition of tax relief for dependent children were also seen in some other countries (e.g. Australia 1976, United Kingdom 1977). In some cases, age-related supplements (e.g. Austria 1981, Luxembourg 1976, Netherlands 1983) and supplements for second, third, or subsequent children (e.g. Greece 1980, Sweden 1982) were introduced. These expansionist reforms were driven by different motives. For example, the extension of the family allowance scheme to the first child in Germany and the United Kingdom was part of the post-war trend towards the gradual introduction of universal benefits for all children. As of 1990, only in France and Japan were first children still ineligible for family allowances. On the other hand, the increase in family allowance rates following the abolition of tax relief was driven by a concern for equity so as to provide all families with identical support (as seen in Chapter 5 tax allowance tends to be more profitable to high-income families). The introduction of age-related supplements or supplements for children beyond the first one were also driven by a concern for equity —to reflect the fact that older children or larger families represent a bigger economic cost. It should however be noted that in some countries the age-related supplement was introduced for very young children instead of older ones so as to reflect the high cost of young children, especially if child-care is needed.

On the reduction side, and moving away from the principle of universality, family allowance schemes have been made subject to a means test in eight countries since 1975, i.e. Australia (1988), Canada (1992), Denmark (1976), Germany (1983), Greece (1989), Italy, (1988) Japan (1978), and Spain (1991). In two cases, Denmark and Japan, this means-test was subsequently abolished, respectively in 1981 and 1985. The nature of the reform varied substantially, ranging from a complete withdrawal of the benefit for higher-income families (e.g. Spain, Australia, Canada), to reduced allowance rates for higher-income families (e.g. Greece, Germany, Italy). In Italy, the family allowance rates were moreover made variable according to family structure (i.e. single-parent families, two-parent families) and to family size.

Undeniably, the introduction of such means tests represented a major shift in the policies of governments towards families; a break away from the principle of universality. A necessity to reduce public spending and a desire to better support the lower-income families were given as reasons to justify this policy. In the context of severe budget constraints, it was argued that governments should target their support to families in greatest need, rather than giving financial support to all families, regardless of their need. Such a decision was not without opposition. In fact, proposals to abolish universal family allowances were strongly opposed in some countries on the grounds that not only had the state an obligation to support all families, but also that a universal allowance was the most efficient way of reaching families in need (in view of the low take-up rate usually associated with means-tested benefits). For example, in Britain, where child benefit is still paid to all families on a universal basis (at the time of writing), a series of discussions has surrounded the future of this benefit since the mid-1980s. In particular, the Thatcher government repeatedly made it clear that 'a universal payment to all mothers regardless of a family's means was wasteful' (Financial Times, 1990). Instead, it favoured a means-tested scheme so as to better support families in greatest need.

The idea was very controversial and instead of completely abolishing universal child benefits, the government decided in 1987 to freeze them and let inflation gradually erode their value. But once again, this decision proved to be very controversial. In 1990, following pressure both from the opposition parties and its own back-benchers, the Conservative government eventually yielded and, instead of abolishing the universal benefits, partly increased their value (Stephens, 1990). The future of child benefits has since continued to be the subject of severe controversy with some members of the government again pleading for their abolition.

and their replacement by a means-tested scheme. A similar trend was observed in Ireland with the decision by the government in 1989 to impose a means test on the previously universal child benefits. But, this raised so much opposition that it eventually forced the government to abandon the project (European Observatory on National Family Policies, 1991: 87).

In the United States, the discussion has focused on the AFDC scheme. Since its introduction in 1935, the AFDC has been subject to major reforms, including the addition of work incentives in the 1960s. During the Reagan era, further emphasis was placed on these work incentives. In particular, following the 1988 Family Support Act, eligibility to AFDC benefits has been linked to enrolment in work, education, or training programmes. This requirement applies to mothers with children over the age of 3 (although states have the possibility of extending this requirement to mothers with children over the age of 1). In addition, and in order to encourage further the take-up of paid employment, after 1989, earned income of $90 per month could be regarded as work expenses before earnings were offset against AFDC benefit. Furthermore, child care expenses of up to $175 per month ($200 for children aged 2 or younger) could be deducted from earnings. The amount received under the AFDC scheme however remained low, and moreover varied greatly across states. For example, in 1992, the maximum AFDC grant for a one-parent family with two children —subject to a means test— varied between more than $600 per month in Alaska, California, Connecticut, Hawaii, New York, and Vermont, and less than $200 per month in Alabama, Louisiana, Mississippi, Tennessee, Texas, and Puerto Rico.

Levels of family allowances

Despite the changes of policy referred to above, the value of family allowances varied little between 1975 and 1990. As seen in Table 10.1, the allowances in 1990 were on average only slightly higher than in 1975.

From a value of 4.9 per cent in 1975, the average family allowances for twenty-one countries reached 5.0 per cent in 1990 (the United States is excluded). During this period, in eight cases, the value of the allowances decreased (Canada, Germany, Greece, Italy, Netherlands, New Zealand, Portugal, and Spain), while the largest increases were observed in Australia, Norway, and the United Kingdom. In some cases the apparent increase in family allowance rate followed the abolition of tax relief and its replacement by higher family allowances rates (e.g. Australia, United Kingdom). As of 1990, the highest levels were found in Austria, Belgium, Norway, and Luxembourg, and the lowest ones in Italy, Japan, and Spain.

The inter-country differences are obviously wide, the gap between the highest and the lowest value being 11 percentage points in 1990 (Austria versus Spain). This gap moreover tended to increase over time, being only 9 percentage points in 1975 (Belgium versus Australia). Since 1975, the values of family allowances therefore tended to slightly diverge across countries rather than to converge. When family allowances are expressed in dollars, values varied in 1990 between 186 dollars per month (in Austria) and 5 dollars (in Spain) (see Figure 10.1). In fact, the lowest value was observed in Italy where the recently imposed means-test denied families

Table 10.1 *Family allowances for a family with two children, 1975–1990*

Country	Allowances as a percentage of the average male wages in manufacturing			
	1975	1980	1985	1990
Australia	1.0	3.3	3.2	3.4
Austria	8.5	13.0	12.0	11.3
Belgium	10.4	9.8	11.0	10.4
Canada	4.5	2.8	2.8	2.4
Denmark	4.4	3.4	2.8	5.2
Finland	4.8	5.4	6.0	6.2
France	5.5	5.2	7.4	7.1
Germany	6.7	4.9	5.0	4.9
Greece	3.8	6.8	3.9	3.2
Ireland	2.7	2.5	2.9	3.0
Italy	5.9	4.6	2.3	0.0
Japan	—	—	—	0.6
Luxembourg	6.0	7.2	7.4	8.3
Netherlands	7.6	8.6	7.5	7.4
New Zealand	5.4	5.3	3.2	2.1
Norway	3.4	6.4	7.6	9.1
Portugal	7.5	3.8	3.4	4.9
Spain	2.6	1.0	0.5	0.3
Sweden	5.1	6.6	7.7	7.2
Switzerland	4.6	3.8	4.8	4.7
United Kingdom	2.7	8.9	8.8	6.3
United States	—	—	—	—

Australia: Means-test has been imposed on family allowances since 1988. Workers with earnings equal to the average male wage in manufacturing fall below this means-test, and are therefore entitled to the full family allowance rates. France: the rates are expressed as a percentage of a base wage. For the second child, they were equal to 22%, 23%, 32%, 32% in respectively 1975, 1980, 1985, and 1990. Germany: Lower family allowance rates have been introduced for high-income families since 1983. The rates indicated here correspond to the high ones. Italy: Means-test has been imposed on family allowance since 1988. Workers with earnings equal to the average male wage in manufacturing are no longer eligible to allowances. Japan: Family allowances rates varied between a minimum and maximum rates between 1978 and 1985. The minimum rates are used here. The scheme in force from 1972 to 1985 covered only the third and subsequent children. From 1986, the second child became also eligible. Switzerland: The rates used here correspond to those paid under the Federal scheme. Higher rates are available under some cantonal schemes. United States: Only means-tested benefits are available.

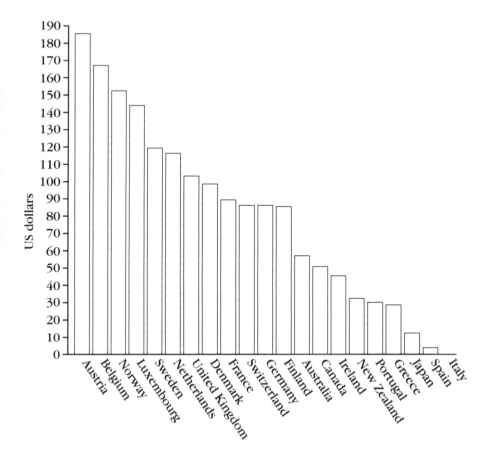

Fig. 10.1 *Family allowances to a two-child family, 1990*

Note: Monthly value of family allowances calculated on the basis of parity purchasing power indices (value in 1990 US dollars).

with an average income (ie equivalent to the average manufacturing wage) from eligibility to family allowances.

This inter-country ranking is interesting because contrary to what might be expected, the United Kingdom did not appear at the bottom of the distribution, despite its emphasis on limited state support. On the other hand, France did not appear at the top of the inter-country ranking, despite its explicit pro-natalist policy and the government's commitment to support families. What instead distinguished France was the modulation of family allowances according to the birth-order of the child. A larger allowance was paid for third and subsequent children than for the second child (no allowance was paid to the first child). In 1990, 592 French Francs were paid monthly for the second child, and 758 for the third one. A similar situation was observed in Quebec (data not shown in Figure 10.1) where, as of 1990, the allowance paid for the third child represented 2.5 times that of the second child, and nearly four times that of the first one. The difference was even more pronounced for birth grants. In 1990, 6,000 Canadian dollars were paid at the birth of the third and subsequent children, as compared to 1,000 dollars for the second child and 500 dollars for first one. Pro-natalist objectives justified such emphasis on the third child. [1]

Tax relief for dependent children

Indirect support, through the taxation system, continued to represent a major form of support for families in some countries. As seen in Chapter 6, tax allowances were abolished in several countries in the early 1970s and replaced by tax credit or higher family allowances because of their unfairness towards low-income families. Similar changes also took place in several countries from the mid-1970s (see Table 10.2).

As a result, while in 1975 tax allowances were still found in nearly half the countries, it was the case in only six of them in 1990 (Belgium, Finland, Germany, Japan, Switzerland, United States). On the other hand, by 1990 seven countries were providing families with a tax credit for children (Belgium, Canada, Greece, Italy, Norway, Portugal, Spain), and eight were not providing any form of tax relief (Australia, Austria, Denmark, Ireland, Netherlands, New Zealand, Sweden, and the United Kingdom). France and Luxembourg represented a special case in providing families with a family quotient tax system. [2]

The legislation in this field is complex. In Table 10.3, state support received by families through both family allowance and tax relief is compared using an index based on the disposable income of families (i.e. amount available after taxes, social security contributions, and cash transfers). The index expresses the supplementary disposable income of a one-earner two-child family, as compared to that of a single worker. Both families are assumed to have earnings equal to the average male wage in manufacturing. As of 1990, this index represented 17.4 per cent on average for all twenty-two countries, compared with 14.6 per cent in 1975. The inter-country difference is again wide. While in 1990, the disposable income of the two-child family exceeded by more than 25 per cent that of the single worker in Belgium, Denmark, Luxembourg, and Norway, a difference of less than 10 per cent was observed in Japan, New Zealand, Spain and the United States (see Figure 10.2).

[1] It should be noted that such a strong modulation by birth-order in family allowances is not necessarily associated with pro-natalist preoccupation, but may also be justified by a limited commitment of governments to support families, or simply be a reflection of the fact that two or three children are more expensive than only one.

[2] Under the family quotient, the taxable income and marginal tax rate are determined by the size and the composition of the family. In France each adult is considered as one share and each child as half a share (the third child is considered as one full share). The marginal tax rate is a function of the income divided by the total number of shares in the family (Grima, 1984).

Table 10.2 *Tax relief for dependent children, 1975-1990*

Country	Type of relief			
	1975	1980	1985	1990
Australia	C	—	A	—
Austria	C	—	—	—
Belgium	AC	AC	AC	AC
Canada	A	A	A	C
Denmark	—	—	—	—
Finland	AC	AC	A	A
France	Q	Q	Q	Q
Germany	A	A	A	A
Greece	na	na	C	C
Ireland	A	A	A	—
Italy	C	C	C	C
Japan	A	A	A	A
Luxembourg	Q	Q	Q	Q
Netherlands	A	A	A	—
New Zealand	—	C	C	—
Norway	—	C	C	C
Portugal	na	A	A	C
Spain	na	C	C	C
Sweden	—	—	—	—
Switzerland	A	A	A	A
United Kingdom	A	—	—	—
United States	A	A	A	A

Key: — = No scheme in force. na = Data not available. A = Tax allowances. C = Tax credit. Q = Family quotient.
Sources: Wennemo (1992).

Throughout the 1975–90 period, Austria, Belgium, and Luxembourg remained at the top of the distribution. On the other hand, France saw its position decline from second place in 1975 to ninth one in 1990. Again, the trend was more one of divergence than convergence. One point which is important to stress is the fact that the previous figures refer to a one-earner family. The index consequently captured the transfers provided for both children and the dependent wife. A different ranking would have appeared if only transfers to children had been taken into consideration.[3]

[3]Unfortunately, the OECD does not publish data for two-earner families. A recent study by Shaver and Bradshaw (1993) however sheds some light on this topic.

Table 10.3 *Index of disposable income for a two-child family, 1975–1990*

Country	1975	1980	1985	1990
Australia	13.7	11.7	10.8	10.7
Austria	23.0	21.1	24.5	23.6
Belgium	21.1	26.1	27.2	39.1
Canada	12.5	13.9	16.1	15.0
Denmark	15.6	15.4	19.3	26.3
Finland	21.5	16.0	17.6	20.8
France	23.5	21.6	19.2	19.2
Germany	15.9	19.6	18.4	21.2
Greece	2.4	12.0	21.4	23.2
Ireland	16.5	17.9	21.4	17.1
Italy	12.6	12.1	12.2	14.5
Japan	5.9	6.1	7.1	7.3
Luxembourg	26.4	30.1	32.9	34.1
Netherlands	15.8	14.9	17.4	12.3
New Zealand	9.9	13.6	17.2	2.5
Norway	14.8	23.0	23.8	25.7
Portugal	9.2	6.0	5.5	11.9
Spain	5.6	6.1	6.3	6.5
Sweden	16.9	16.6	17.0	15.0
Switzerland	10.5	11.6	13.8	14.1
United Kingdom	14.4	15.2	18.6	12.7
United States	13.6	12.4	10.7	9.7

Note: The index corresponds to the supplementary income available to a two-child family (with one earner) as compared to a single worker. It is calculated on the basis of the disposable income, i.e. income after taxes, social security contributions, and cash transfers. Earnings are equal to the average male wages in manufacturing.

Means-tested benefits

Since 1975 additional cash benefits schemes targeted at low-income families or lone-parent families have been introduced. For example, the French and Luxembourg governments introduced a minimum guaranteed income scheme, respectively in 1988 and 1986, while the British government replaced the former Family Income Supplement (introduced in 1971) by a new Family Credit (in 1988). The new scheme continued to be aimed at families in employment with low income. Families out of work or working only part-time were eligible to the means-tested Income Support (which replaced from 1988 the post-war Supplementary Benefit). In 1992, Family Credit was further reformed in order to reduce potential work disincentives in making eligible families working at least 16 hours a week (as compared to 24

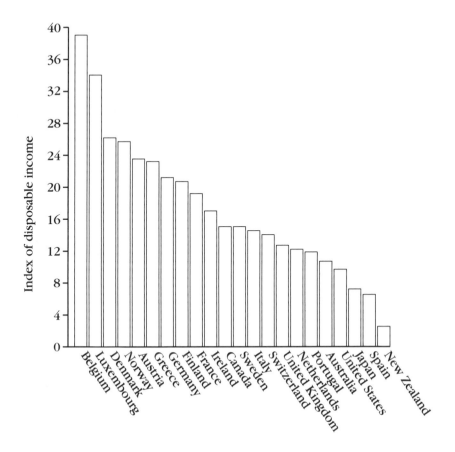

Fig. 10.2 *Cash transfers to families, 1990*

Note: The index represents the additional disposable income of a two-child family as a percentage of the disposable income of a single worker.

hours before the reform).[4]

With regard to support to lone-parent families, the Swedish and Danish governments had introduced already in the 1960s advance maintenance payment schemes. From 1975, governments in Belgium and Luxembourg adopted similar schemes, thus taking full responsibility for the support of lone-parent families. In contrast, in the United Kingdom, Australia, the United States, and Ireland, a more limited public responsibility was endorsed, restricting the government's role to the enforcement

[4] Through this reform, it is hoped that more parents will be inclined to accept employment, even if this were to be only 16 to 24 hours a week. Before the reform, such part-time work would not make them eligible to Family Credit.

of maintenance allowance payments by the liable parent. Rather than advancing the payment, the government acted only as an intermediate in enforcing the maintenance obligation of the liable parent. In the United Kingdom, the new scheme was introduced in 1991 as part of the Child Support Act.

In Australia and the United States a similar 'limited- public- responsibility' approach was adopted by the government. For example, the Australian Child Support Act of 1988, which established the Child Support Agency, reinforced the maintenance obligation of the non-custodial parent (Harrison, 1992). Similarly, in the United States, the private nature of child-support obligation was emphasized by the government through legislation, starting with federal legislation to enforce the collection of child support payment in 1950 (Garfinkel, 1992b: 209). Further legislation in 1984 (Child Support Enforcement Amendment) and 1988 (Family Support Act) reinforced this policy orientation (Garfinkel, 1992a: 26).

In terms of financial support, reforms brought about since 1975 by governments tilted further the balance towards greater selectivity. Family allowances were made subject to a means test in nearly one third of countries, tax relief schemes were further reformed to make them more equitable to low-income families, and new benefits targeted at families in greatest need were introduced. In the context of tight governmental budgets, these reforms have been seen as ways to contain or reduce state expenditure. Beyond this general trend, an increasing divergence across countries was observed. While the gap in the levels of family allowances between the most and least generous countries widened, further divergence was also observed between countries which took full responsibility in the support of families, through the provision of a minimum guaranteed income, and others which restricted their role to minimal support.

10.2 Maternity and parental leave benefits

With the increase in female labour force participation since the 1960s, maternity and parental leave benefits became an important form of state support for families. Initially restricted to the period immediately before and after delivery, the duration of the maternity leave was substantially extended. A range of other work-related benefits was also introduced including specific benefits for fathers, new extended periods of leave for child-care, greater part-time job opportunities, and more flexibility in the working schedules.

In this field, it is important to mention the ILO Convention on Workers with Family Responsibilities (no. 156). As seen in Chapter 6, the ILO had adopted its first Recommendation on Female Workers with Family Responsibilities in 1965. The 1981 convention went a step further in extending the coverage of this recommendation to all workers (men and women). The new convention included a series of measures aimed at improving the working conditions of parents, and at allowing them to reconcile more easily employment and family responsibilities. Furthermore, through this Convention the ILO was making explicit three main principles: (i) the responsibility of governments and employers towards working parents; (ii) the equality between men and women in child-caring and child-rearing responsibilities; and (iii) the enlargement of provision beyond the strict maternity leave — thus, establishing new standards with regard to workers with family responsibilities.

Maternity leave schemes

Already in the late 1960s and early 1970s, major improvements had been brought to the maternity leave schemes. With further increases in women's participation in the labour force, and especially mothers with young children, there were renewed calls for additional improvements to these schemes. The trends since 1975 with regard to the duration of the leave and maternity pay are reported in Table 10.4.

In contrast to family allowances, which stagnated in the 1975–90 period, maternity leave schemes were significantly upgraded in most countries. In terms of duration, maternity leave increased from a cross-national average (18 countries) of 15.5 weeks in 1975 to 22.1 weeks in 1990.[5] The strongest increases were observed among Nordic countries. Over the period 1975 to 1990, maternity leave was extended by 14 weeks in Denmark, 18 weeks in Finland, 10 weeks in Norway, and 35 weeks in Sweden. Sweden, with this increase, was obviously maintaining the leading position it had acquired in the 1960s. In the other countries, the increase has been more modest, of 2 to 4 weeks. This has been the case in Austria (4 weeks), France (2 weeks), Greece (3 weeks), Ireland (2 weeks), Japan (2 weeks), Luxembourg (4 weeks), Netherlands (4 weeks), and Spain (4 weeks). The particular case of France should be noted here. Although the duration of the maternity leave scheme was increased by only 2 weeks for the first and second birth, it was increased by 12 weeks for the third birth, bringing it to a total of 26 weeks. As said before, this emphasis on third births was part of the government pro-natalist policy. On the other hand, the duration of maternity leave was not subject to any increase during the 1975–90 period in Austria, Belgium, Canada, Germany, Italy, and the United Kingdom.

With regard to maternity pay, major increases were also observed in most countries. It was especially the case in Finland and Norway where reforms brought the value of maternity benefits more in line with those paid in the most generous countries. In Belgium, Ireland, and the United Kingdom, increases were also introduced, although in the last case, covering only a small fraction of women (to qualify for the higher cash benefits, women needed to have worked with the same employer for 5 years — as of 1990). When both the duration of the leave and maternity pay are combined in an index of maternity leave (see Figure 10.3), Canada, Greece, Ireland, Japan, and the United Kingdom appear at the lower end of the inter-country ranking in 1990, and Sweden and Finland at the upper end.

The case of Britain deserves some further comments. As pointed out earlier, the British scheme was very restrictive in terms of its eligibility criteria. In fact, according to a study carried out in 1988–89 among women in employment while pregnant, as many as 20 per cent did not receive any form of maternity pay (McRae, 1991). Following the adoption of a new directive on maternity leave by the Eu-

---

[5] The average excludes Australia, New Zealand, Switzerland, and the United States.

Table 10.4 *Maternity leave benefits, 1975–1990*

Country	Maternity Benefits							
	1975		1980		1985		1990	
	Duration in weeks	Pay %	Duration in weeks	Pay %	Duration in weeks	Pay %	Duration in weeks	Pay %
Austria	12	100	16	100	16	100	16	100
Belgium	14	60	14	80	14	80	14	80
Canada	15	67	15	60	15	60	15	60
Denmark	14	90	18	90	28	90	28	90
Finland	35	39	47	39	52	80	53	80
France	14	90	16	90	16	84	16	84
Germany	14	100	14	100	14	100	14	100
Greece	12	50	12	50	12	50	15	50
Ireland	12	65	12	65	14	70	14	70
Italy	20	80	20	80	20	80	20	80
Japan	12	60	12	60	14	60	14	60
Lux.	12	100	16	100	16	100	16	100
Neth.	12	100	12	100	12	100	16	100
Norway	12	30	18	100	18	100	35	80
Portugal	9	100	13	100	13	100	13	100
Spain	12	75	14	75	14	75	16	75
Sweden	30	90	52	70	52	70	65	75
Switz.	8	100	8	100	8	100	8	100
UK	18	30	18	30	18	30	18	45

Notes: Benefits expressed as a percentage of regular earnings. Australia, New Zealand, and the United States are excluded because of the absence of national maternity leave scheme. Belgium: From 1975 to 1989, benefits paid at 60% for the first 30 days, and at 80% thereafter. From 1989, benefits paid at 80% for first 4 months, 75% for months 5 to 14, and 75% for the last month. Finland: Until 1982, maternity benefits paid at a daily rate equal to 0.15% of yearly income (ie equivalent to 39% of daily earnings). Duration of the leave extended from 174 working days in 1975, to 234 in 1980, 258 in 1985, and 263 in 1990. France: Since 1981, the paid leave is of 26 weeks for the third and subsequent children. Ireland: Until 1981 flat rate benefits were paid (equal to 25% of the average female wage in manufacturing). They were supplemented by earnings-related benefits equal to 40%. From 1981, benefits equal to 80% of earnings (70% from 1984) were paid for women intending to work after the leave. For those not intending to return, flat rate benefits were paid. Norway: Between 1970 and 1977, a combination of flat rate benefits and earnings-related benefits were paid. They represented around 30% of the average female wage in manufacturing. In 1990, mothers were entitled to 28 weeks of leave at 100% of salary or to 35 weeks at 80% of salary. Portugal: Leave extended from 60 to 90 days in 1976. Sweden: In 1980 and 1985, benefits equal to 90% of earnings paid for the first 9 months, and flat rate benefits (representing about 10% of the average female wage in manufacturing) paid for the other 3 months. Overall, this represents benefits equal to 70% of earnings for the whole period. For 1990, the equivalence is 75%. Switzerland: The compulsory leave is 8 weeks. Maternity benefits are paid for between 3 to 8 weeks at full wage according to collective agreement. Mothers insured under a health insurance scheme are entitled to sick pay for a total of 10 weeks. United Kingdom: Until 1987 flat rate benefits were paid. They represented around 30% of the average of female wage in manufacturing. From 1987, women with at least five years employment with the same employer became entitled to benefits equal to 90% for 6 weeks, followed by flat rate benefits for 12 weeks. Overall, this represents benefits equal to 45% of earnings for the whole period.

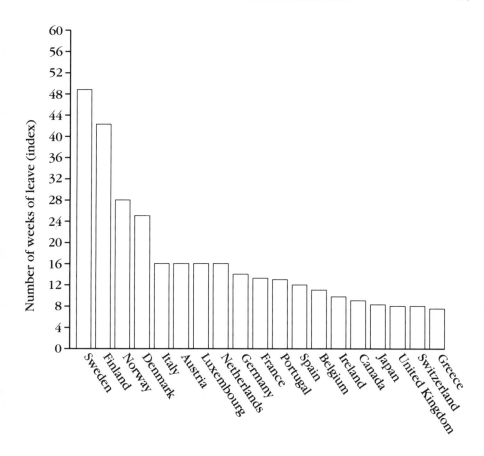

Fig. 10.3 *Maternity leave schemes, 1990*

Notes: The index used represents the number of weeks fully compensated for. It is obtained by multiplying the number of weeks of leave by the percentage of salary received during this period, (e.g. 14 weeks x 100% = 14). Australia, New Zealand, and the United States are excluded from this graph. See text for details about the provision of maternity leave in these countries.

ropean Community in 1992, this scheme had to be reformed. According to that directive, a minimum of 14 weeks of paid leave had to be provided during which benefits at least equivalent to sick pay had to be paid. Furthermore, the qualifying period could not exceed one year (European Observatory on National Family Policies, 1994: 34). As a result, the British government introduced new legislation. The Trade Union Reform and Employment Act 1992 gave the right to 14 weeks maternity leave to all pregnant employees, regardless of their length of service or hours of work. Their pay during that leave was regulated by a law adopted in 1994 which stipulated that any woman who had been continuously employed in the same job for 26 weeks was entitled to 6 weeks pay at 90 per cent of her regular earnings, and 12 weeks at flat rate benefits corresponding to the highest rate of Statutory Sick Pay.

The cases of Australia, New Zealand, Switzerland, and the United States also require some further comments. In Australia, although no national scheme was in force (as of 1994), a major development came in 1978 through a test case brought to the Conciliation and Arbitration Commission. The decision of the Commission that leave should be guaranteed subsequently led to the inclusion of provision for maternity leave in most federal and state awards. The leave consisted of an unbroken period up to 52 weeks (unpaid leave), including 6 weeks compulsory leave immediately after childbirth (ILO, 1988). However, these provisions did not cover all female workers. New South Wales was in fact the only state to have adopted legislation providing maternity leave entitlements for all working women not covered by federal awards (ibid.).

In New Zealand, until 1980, women were not covered by any national scheme, the responsibility of providing maternity leave being instead left to private employers. In 1980, however, the government adopted new legislation, the Maternity Leave and Employment Protection Act, which granted women the right to unpaid leave of 6 months associated with childbirth. The Parental Leave and Employment Protection Act 1987 then extended further the previous legislation, by increasing the duration of the optional leave to a total of 12 months, and by introducing a 14-week maternity leave, and a 2-week paternity leave. Leave remained unpaid however, thus still leaving room for private initiatives. Provision in this field seemed limited. For instance, Law (1982) reported that of the 900 collective agreements and awards reviewed and registered between 1978 and 1981, only a third contained maternity leave provision.

The other case which requires special explanation is that of Switzerland. Although the Federal Constitution stated that the government would introduce a maternity insurance, no such provision was made. The law only provided for an 8-week leave following delivery, with a compulsory 3-week sickness benefit. Mothers covered under a health insurance scheme were further entitled to sickness benefits for a total of 16 weeks (increased from 10 weeks in 1981). More extensive provisions were provided in some cantonal and private schemes. The situation was the subject of much dissatisfaction and several proposals were made for the adoption of a more comprehensive scheme at the national level. In particular, a proposal tabled in Parliament in 1980 stipulated a 16-week maternity leave with full wage compensation. The proposal was however turned down by the Federal Council (Switzerland, Office Fédérale des assurances sociales, 1982: 137–8).

In the United States, provision for maternity leave was provided in thirty states as of 1990. In twelve of them the provision applied only to state employees. In most cases, the leave was unpaid, with the exception of California, Hawaii, New Jersey, New York, and Rhode Island, where temporary disability insurance provided women with limited cash benefits (United States, Department of Labor,

1990).[6] Overall, estimates put at 60 per cent the fraction of the work force covered by paid or unpaid leave laws (maternity or parental leave, and leave for family illness) (ibid.). For several Americans, such a situation was clearly unsatisfactory, and pressure to introduce a national scheme came from various governmental and non-governmental circles. For example, an Advisory Committee on Infant Care Leave, convened at Yale University in 1983, recommended that:

Policies should be initiated to allow employees a leave of absence for a period of time sufficient to care for their newborn or newly-adopted infants. Such a leave should provide income replacement, benefit continuation, and job protection. The leave should be available for a minimum of six months, and it should include partial income replacement (75 per cent of salary) for three months, up to a realistic maximum benefit, sufficient to assure adequate basic resources for the families who need them most. Benefit continuation and job protection should be available for the entire six-month leave period. (Zigler and Frank, 1988: 344-5)

The government did not entirely endorse this recommendation, but tabled in 1985 legislation that would provide for job-protected parental, family, and personal disability leave. A modified bill was eventually adopted by Congress, but vetoed by President Bush in 1991, and again in 1992, on the grounds that it was not the government's responsibility to regulate fringe benefits. In early 1992, on the other hand, the Family and Medical Leave Act was passed by Congress and signed into law by President Clinton. This legislation provided public and private employees in firms with 50 or more workers with the right to take up to 12 weeks leave each year, to care for a new-born child, a newly adopted child, or one just entering foster care, to care for a seriously ill child, spouse or parent, or to care for an employee's own serious health condition.

Child-care leave

The other form of benefit which has been the target of major reforms since 1975 is the extended leave for child-care. As of 1975, only Austria and Italy had introduced such leave. Over the next few years, they were joined by a dozen more countries (see Table 10.5). In most cases, the leave remained unpaid, but in Belgium, Canada, Finland, France, Germany, and Luxembourg, cash benefits were also paid during the leave. In Belgium, the child-care leave was part of the interruption of professional career scheme which had been introduced in 1985.

According to this scheme, workers employed in the same enterprise for at least 12 months could request total interruption of their professional career for 6 to 12 months, or half-time interruption from 6 months to 5 years. The interruption of career could be requested for many reasons, including education and child-care. Flat-rate benefits were paid during this period (ILO, 1988).

---

[6] Federal legislation however gave some protection to pregnant women at work. The Pregnancy Disability Act 1978 was designed to protect pregnant women and new mothers from job discrimination or dismissal (Wisensale, 1994: 128). The Pregnancy Discrimination Act 1980 made women affected by pregnancy or childbirth eligible to the same treatment as other workers, including the receipt of fringe benefits (Trzcinski and Alpert, 1994: 541).

Table 10.5 *Child-care leave scheme, 1990*

Type of scheme	Country	Duration in months	Year of introduction
Paid optional leave	Finland	36	1980
	France	36	1977, 1985
	Austria	24	1956
	Germany	18	1979
	Luxembourg	12	1988
	Belgium*	12	1985
	Italy	12	1950, 1973
	Canada	6	1990
Unpaid optional leave	Spain	36	1980
	Portugal	24	1985
	Sweden*	18	1979
	Norway	12	1978
	Australia	12	1990
	United Kingdom	10	1976
	Greece*	6	1984
	Netherlands*	6	1990
	Ireland	3.5	1981

Notes: The duration of the leave (in months) includes the period covered by the paid maternity leave, with the exception of the countries marked by an asterisk (*). Austria: The initial child-care leave was for a period of 6 months. It was extended to 12 months in 1960 and to 24 months in 1990. Belgium: The leave is part of the 'Interruption of Occupational Career' scheme. Its duration varies between 6 months to 5 years. Finland: The initial scheme covered only parents with at least two young children. It was extended to all parents with a child under the age of 3 in 1989. France: In 1977 an unpaid leave of 24 months was introduced. It was extended until the child's third birthday in 1987. A child-care allowance was introduced in 1985 for women with three or more children. Germany: In 1979 a 6-month child-care leave was introduced. It was extended to 10 months in 1986, 12 months in 1988, 15 months in 1989, and 18 months in 1990. In 1993 the leave was extended to 3 years. Greece: Each parent is entitled to a non-transferable 3-month unpaid leave. Italy: Since 1950 women are entitled to a one-year unpaid leave. Since 1973, 6 of these months are paid at a rate representing 30% of usual wages. Luxembourg: In 1991 the scheme was extended to 24 months. In 1992, it was extended to 4 years for families with three or more children. Netherlands: A 6-month parental leave was introduced in 1990. It is not transferable and allows each parent to reduce his/her hours of work down to 20 hours per week. Sweden: The leave is independent from the paid parental leave. United Kingdom: A 29-week leave with a right to reinstatement was introduced in 1976.

In 1991, restrictions were imposed on this scheme, reducing the amount of cash benefit paid after the first year, or at the second and subsequent breaks (European Observatory on National Family Policies, 1994: 42).

In Canada, the parental leave introduced in 1990 allowed for 10 weeks leave (which can be shared between parents) during which the parent on leave received unemployment benefits (60 per cent of regular earnings). This brought to 25 weeks the total number of weeks it was possible to take on maternity leave and parental leave. In Finland, cash benefits were initially restricted to families with 3 or more children. In 1989, they were extended to all families with children. In France, a first unpaid child-care leave of 2 years was introduced in 1977 and covered women in companies with 100 and more employees. In 1985, cash benefits were introduced, but were restricted to families with 3 or more children. In Germany, a child-care leave of 6 months was first introduced in 1979. The leave was then gradually increased to 18 months in 1990, and to 36 months in 1993. During this leave, and from 1986, cash benefits were paid to all women for the first 6 months, and were subject to an income-test thereafter. Finally, in Luxembourg, the child-care allowance introduced in 1988 covered women not in paid employment or with very small earnings. Initially paid until the child's first birthday, it was extended to a second year in 1991. In 1992, the government extended the duration of the child care leave allowance from 2 to 4 years for families with 3 or more children.

In the other countries, the child-care leave was unpaid. In Sweden, the leave was regulated by the Child Care Leave Act adopted in 1978 which gave parents the right to leave of absence until the child was 18 months old. This was part of employment legislation and was distinct from the maternity and parental leave scheme described earlier. In Australia, the parental leave introduced in 1990 allowed for a leave of up to 1 year. In the Netherlands, the Parental Leave Act adopted in 1991 gave the right to parents with pre-school age children (below the age of 4) to part-time work — at least 20 hours per week — for a maximum of 6 months. In Greece, the leave for child-care may be up to 3 months for each parent (non-transferable) and may be taken until the child reached 30 months. Initially of restricted coverage, the leave was extended in 1988 to cover the private sector (only firms which employ over 100 people) as well as public sector employees.

From 1990, two other countries introduced similar schemes, Denmark and Japan. In Denmark, the 1992 Child Care Leave Act granted parents the right to between 13 and 36 weeks of leave — upon agreement between employer and employee. The parent on leave received 80 per cent of the maximum amount of unemployment benefit (European Observatory on National Family Policies, 1994: 42). In Japan, the 1-year parental leave was introduced in 1992. It was unpaid but the law asked employers to make efforts to provide suitable conditions for child-rearing.

Finally, mention should be made of the 1992 Child Care Recommendation of the European Community which recommended the introduction of special leave for employed parents, and the provision of child-care services while parents were working. Attempts to turn this Recommendation into a Directive however were blocked by the British government. As originally drafted, the Directive would have allowed parents to take up to 3 months to care for children aged 2 and under. The British government however clearly stated that it could not support such a Directive, considering the too great burdens that it would impose on employers (Family Policy Studies Centre, 1993). Further attempts by the European Commission to recast the parental leave in September 1994 were vetoed by Britain on the grounds that 'plans to give fathers of new-born or adopted children the right to three months unpaid leave would be immensely disruptive and destructive' (Gardner and Goodhart, 1994).

Relatively unknown until the mid-1970s, child-care leave has since received wide support. From a governmental point of view, it was a measure that could be presented as particularly 'family-friendly', and which did not involve any state expenditure if unpaid. Providing unpaid child-care leave may be a nuisance for employers who may have to find a suitable replacement for the worker on leave, but it did not in itself represent a cost, either for the employer or for the government. Child-care leave also tended to receive wide support from parents. For example, in a survey carried out by the European Community in 1989, more than 20 per cent of respondents said that the provision of parental leave should be given priority by the government.[7]

On the other hand, the provision of child-care leave (when unpaid and restricted to women) was criticized in some circles as a means of keeping women at home rather than providing them with more opportunities for equality. This criticism, for example, was made forcefully with regard to Germany — though, not fully justified as both mother and father are eligible to child-care leave. While the German government provided parents with one of the most extensive child-care leave systems, the fact that this leave was combined with a relatively low level of child-care facilities (see above) led critics to stress the traditional dimension of the policy in encouraging mothers to stay at home when their children were young.

10.3   Child-care facilities

As seen in Chapter 2, public child-care facilities were originally intended for the more disadvantaged classes, especially orphans and children from the working classes. From the 1960s onwards, and in view of the increase in female labour force participation, several actions were taken in order to extend the support of governments to all children of working parents. This support could take several forms, including direct and indirect subsidies, tax relief, the provision of public day care, pre-primary schooling, and after-school care. In view of this variety, inter-country comparison may be difficult to make. In Table 10.6, the provision for child-care is compared across countries by using an index expressing the percentage of below-school age children enroled in publicly funded child-care institutions. No distinction is made between full-time and part-time attendance. The inter-country differences are wide. While in 1988 in France and Belgium, more than 95 per cent

---

[7] The survey listed a series of measures and asked respondents to state what they thought should be the government's priorities to improve the life of families. 22% of respondents supported parental leave (Commission of the European Community, 1989b: Table A.38).

Table 10.6 *Public provision of child-care, 1988*

Country	Care as a percentage of children of given age groups	
	3 to school age	Under 3
Belgium	>95	20
France	>95	20
Italy[a]	>85	5
Denmark[c]	85	50
Sweden[b]	80	30
Greece	65	5
Germany[b]	65	5
Spain	65	na
Luxembourg[c]	55	<5
Netherlands	50	<5
Finland[b]	50	20
Norway[b]	50	10
United Kingdom	35	<5
Portugal	35	5
Japan[bd]	20	na
Canada[b]	15	<5
Australia[cd]	5	na

Notes: These figures include both part-time and full-time care, as well as subsidized family home-care, and pre-primary school institutions. [a]: 1986 figures. [b]: 1987 figures. [c]: 1989 figures. [d]: children aged 0–5. na: data not available.

Sources: Moss (1990), OECD (1991).

of the 3-to-school age children attended a day care institution, it was less than 15 per cent in Canada and Australia. By covering a wide range of institutions, this comparison may however be misleading. In particular, it should be noted that while in some countries day care was provided in the form of crêches, independently of the education system, in others, it was mainly provided as pre-primary schools. It was the case, for instance, in France, Belgium, and Italy where the high proportion of children enrolled in pre-primary institutions reflected belief in the benefits of early education rather than a will to support working mothers. On the other hand, in countries such as Sweden and Denmark, the extensive provision of child-care facilities was seen more as a mean of eliminating obstacles to female employment.

The provision of child-care facilities for children less than 3 years old was much more limited, being less than 20 per cent. The very high cost of infant care provision, along with the reluctance of parents to send their children at a very early age to day-care centres, seem to justify this situation. In terms of country-specific policies, a certain number of cases require further comments. In France, the government had from an early stage considered it a duty to provide child-care facilities. Thus, in contrast to most countries, already by the 1970s, the network of pre- primary schools and crêches was well developed. In 1970 there were already 28,000 places in collective crêches, and 4,000 in family crêches (CNAF, 1989: appendix). As mentioned before, the educational value of pre-primary education, rather than concern about working mothers, seemed to have provided the motive for this early governmental investment. From the 1970s, the provision of child-care facilities was extended further, especially as the result of some major initiatives. For example, in 1981 the administration council of the Caisse Nationale des Allocations Familiales (CNAF), gave number one priority to the policy of child-care services for young children. In 1984, the CNAF then launched the 'crêche-contract'. Based on agreement with other partners (e.g. private employers), the new scheme included grants to support the creation and functioning of new crêches. Between 1984 and 1993, 215 such contracts were signed, leading to the creation of 20,000 new places for children. In 1987, a similar scheme, the 'childhood-contract', was instituted and completed the overall policy of child-care services for children up to 6 years old.

In the Nordic countries, great importance was given to the development of child-care facilities. For example, between 1978 and 1987, the percentage of children aged 3-6 years old in day-care centres increased from 36 per cent to 56 per cent in Denmark, from 23 per cent to 32 per cent in Finland, from 23 per cent to 49 per cent in Norway, and from 48 per cent to 58 per cent in Sweden (excluding here children in home care). Despite this increase, the persistence of shortages led governments to further reinforce their support. For example, in 1985 the Swedish government adopted a resolution (Day Care for All Children) to the effect that day-care services should be available to all children aged $1\frac{1}{2}$-6 years by 1991, at the latest (Nasman, 1990). Budget constraints and the recent increase in fertility seem however to have prevented the attainment of this objective. In Finland, a similar plan was adopted by the government in 1990, which stipulated the right, as of 1995, to all children below the age of 7 of a place in a day-care centre. This plan furthermore gave families the choice between sending their children to the day-care centre or drawing a child-care allowance (Mikkola, 1991: 170).

In Quebec, the issue of child-care facilities received great attention from the 1970s. The objective of reducing the incompatibility between paid employment and parenthood, and more recently the objective of pro-natalism, have been the driving forces. The first concrete action had already been taken in 1974 with the adoption of the policy on child-care services (the 'Bacon Plan'). In 1978, a further policy was adopted which acknowledged (i) the right of parents to choose the type of care which corresponded best to their needs and aspirations; (ii) the necessity to diversify child-care types including family care and services for children of school age in order to provide parents with a real choice; and (iii) the principle of paying according to one's means, and the contribution of the State in the financing of child-care provision (Desjardins, 1991: 57). In order to better promote and monitor the development of child care, the government then created in 1979 the Office de services de garde à l'enfance. By that time, the expenditure on child-care had already strongly increased. While 1.2 million Canadian dollars had been spent in 1974–5, the expenditure reached 16.2 million in 1979–80 (ibid. 58).

In its first plan, adopted in 1983, the new Office stated its objective of doubling the number of places in day-care centres during the following five years, while also reducing regional disparities (ibid. 71). In fact, between 1981 and 1987, the number of places more than doubled, from 25,000 to 59,000. But this still left serious shortages, and in its second plan, adopted in 1986, the Office fixed at 50,000 the number of new places to be created before 1992. Budget constraints seem however to have restricted the actions of the government. In particular, the decision by the federal government in 1988 to withdraw its support from the development of child-care services, deprived the Quebec government of 48 million dollars (Quebec, Finance Ministry, 1989: 19). The Quebec government decided nevertheless to pursue its expansionist policy, and aimed at the provision of 130,000 places by 1993 (Quebec, Finance Ministry, 1988: 4).

In contrast to most other countries, governments in the United States and Britain were much more reluctant to take full responsibility for the provision of child-care services. The proposal for a national child development programme was vetoed by President Nixon in 1971. A second attempt, in 1975, then failed to achieve Congressional support. That same year, on the other hand, increasing funds were made available for child care for children of low-income working mothers or children in families with problems (as part of Title XX of the Social Security Act). Assistance for middle- and upper-income families came in during 1976 when the existing child-care tax deduction for low-income working families was transformed into a non-means-tested tax credit (Child and Dependent Care Tax Credit). This credit was subsequently increased for low-income families in 1986, under President Reagan. But, providing and subsidizing child-care was not, and is still not, seen as state responsibility. Conversely, and in an effort to encourage the provision of employer-sponsored child-care, the government introduced in 1981 the Dependent Care Assistance Plan, which provided employers with tax relief for the establishment of child care (Olmseat and Weikart, 1989: 376).

Despite these changes, discussion nevertheless continued about the exact role that government should play in the provision and financing of child care. In particular, the non-responsibility of the government in the provision of universal child-care facilities was reiterated under the Reagan administration, with preference being given to the provision of child-care for low-income families, and welfare beneficiaries (as part of the 1988 Family Support Act). Through this new Act, AFDC recipients who were engaged in state-approved education or training activity were made eligible for child care. The provision for child care was consequently part of the workfare ideology aiming at encouraging women to take up paid employment. If families purchased child care directly (instead of through state agencies), up to $175 a month for a child aged 2 and older, and $200 for a child under the age of 2, could be discounted against their earnings in the calculation of AFDC benefits. In addition, the new Act introduced a transitional child-care assistance aimed at families who lost eligibility to AFDC benefits due to increased income from work. This transitional assistance could last for up to 12 months. In 1990, an At-Risk

Child Care Program was authorized and provided funds for child-care services for low-income working families who would be at risk of becoming eligible for AFDC if child-care were not provided. Despite these provisions, the demand for day care still exceeded by far the supply. For example, among the 3–4 year old with working mothers in 1990, only half were cared for in day centres or by family day care. For the below 3 years old, this proportion was around 40 per cent.

In Britain, an opposition to state responsibility in the provision of child care, and to the development of a national child-care policy, also characterized the position of the Conservative government. For instance, former Prime Minister Thatcher explicitly stressed her opposition to any form of subsidized child-care facilities, arguing that it would 'swing the emphasis further towards discouraging mothers from staying at home' (Thatcher, 1993: 630) — a trend that she would strongly disapprove of. The shortage of child-care facilities could however not be ignored, and in 1991 in an effort to encourage employer-sponsored nurseries, the government introduced tax relief for employers providing work-place nurseries. The results were however limited. For example, in the Greater London metropolitan area, only sixty-two work-place nurseries were recorded, offering places to less than 2,000 children (Wood, 1991). The high cost of such nurseries seemed to be the main factor preventing more employers from providing similar facilities. A renewed call for employer-sponsored nurseries was then made in 1991 as part of the government's Opportunity 2000 programme which aimed at the promotion of women workers and the encouragement of employer-sponsored measures and services for families. Provision for child care was still very restricted, and the burden fell mostly on parents. The situation was not without strong opposition among the public and in Parliament. In particular, the Labour Party in its 1992 election campaign adopted a more interventionist attitude in promising a steady increase in nurseries and child care services (Financial Times, 1992). In fact, bowing to pressure the Conservative government announced in 1992 the development of up to 50,000 out-of-school places in the three years commencing April 1993 (European Observatory on National Family Policies, 1994: 51).

Debates have also recently re-emerged with regard to the value of pre-primary education and the role of the government as provider of such facilities. For example, while reports of both the National Commission on Education and the Royal Society of Arts in 1994 stressed the benefits of nursery education, the government has maintained its opposition to the introduction of universal nursery education (Judd and Crequer, 1994; and the Independent, 1994). Instead, the government has proposed a less expensive solution, that of granting parents the opportunity of sending their children to formal schooling from the age of 4. Budget constraints, and political opposition to greater state involvement in child-care type services seem to have prevented once again the British government from bringing additional support to families. A similar situation prevailed in Ireland with the government encouraging the development of employer-sponsored child-care facilities. In fact the Child Care Act 1991, rather than expanding state provision, only introduced measures for the supervision of pre-schools, playgroups, crêches, nurseries, some categories of child minders and other similar services for pre-school children. The responsibility of providing child-care facilities was still left to the private sector, but under government supervision — thus considerably restricting the role of the government.

A similar attitude prevailed in Australia where, following the initial government support for the provision of public day care (see Section 6.4), attempts were made to restrict access to subsidized child care and to define it as a service for families in need (Brennan, 1993: 13-4). In a similar vein, and after giving its initial support, the Canadian government withdrew its support for the provision of public day-care facilities. The 1988 Canadian Child Care Act, which was never adopted, would have committed the federal government to share both capital and operating expenditures up to a maximum of 4 billion dollars for a 7-year period (Canada, Ministry of Supply and Services, 1989).

It is obvious that the provision of child-care facilities varied widely across countries. These inter-country differences may be accounted for by different factors, including the level of participation of women in the labour force, as well as budget constraints. But above all, they tended to reflect differences in the perception of who should provide child-care facilities. While high-provision countries tended to acknowledge public responsibility in the provision of child-care facilities, low-provision countries tended instead to emphasize private responsibility. This dichotomy was referred to by the OECD (1991) as countries falling under the 'maximum public responsibility' model, and those falling under the 'maximum private responsibility' model. The Nordic countries, along with France and Belgium, belonged to this first category of countries, while the United Kingdom and the United States belonged to the second category.

10.4   Legislation on abortion and contraception

Following the significant reforms made to the legislation on contraception and abortion during the 1960-74 period, further liberalization was introduced from 1975. In Ireland, family planning services were legalized in 1979 through a law authorizing the sale of non-medical contraceptives to all adults aged 18 and over without a prescription (previously, contraceptives were available only to married couples with a prescription) (United Nations, 1987-90). The 1992 Health (Family Planning) Amendment eventually allowed for condoms to be sold in supermarkets, public bars and clubs to purchasers over the age of 17 years (European Observatory on National Family Policies, 1994: 77). Although some restrictions remained in access to contraceptives, these regulations constituted a remarkable step in a country still heavily influenced by the Catholic Church. In Spain, the use of contraception was legalized in 1978. In several countries, access to contraception was however still limited for teenagers and in some cases still required parental consent. It was for example the case in New Zealand where parental or medical permission was required for women under 16 years of age (United Nations, 1987-90).

With regard to abortion, six additional countries have authorized abortion on request since 1975: Canada (1988), France (1975), Greece (1986), Italy (1978), the Netherlands (1984), and Norway (1978) (see Table 10.7). In France, the liberalization of the legislation was initially intended for a period of 5 years. It was

Table 10.7 *Abortion legislation, 1990*

Reason for termination	Country	Year of introduction	Limit of pregnancy for authorization of termination
On request	Canada	1988	ns
	Greece	1986	12 weeks
	Netherlands[a]	1984	13 weeks
	Norway	1978	12 weeks
	Italy	1978	12 weeks
	France	1975	10 weeks
	Austria	1975	12 weeks
	Sweden	1974	18 weeks
	Denmark	1973	12 weeks
	United States	1973	12 weeks
Medical and socio-economic reasons	Luxembourg	1978	12 weeks
	Germany	1976	12 weeks
	Finland	1970	12 weeks
	Australia[b]	1969	ns
	United Kingdom[c]	1967	24 weeks
	Japan	1948	24 weeks
Other maternal health reasons	Spain	1985	12 weeks
	Portugal	1984	12 weeks
	New Zealand	1977	ns
	Switzerland	1937	ns
Prohibited	Belgium	1867	ns
	Ireland	1861	ns

Notes: ns = Not specified. [a]: Law adopted in 1981, in force in 1984. [b]: State of South Australia only. [c]: With the exception of Northern Ireland where abortion is authorized only for other maternal health reasons.

renewed in 1979, thus marking a definite end to the strict 1920 legislation (United Nations, 1989a: 37-8). In Canada the change in the law followed a decision from the Supreme Court in 1988 voiding the law allowing abortions in hospitals only and on medical grounds only (Henshaw, 1990). In practice, the law was however applied unevenly across the country according to the views of each individual abortion committee (United Nations, 1987-90).

Since 1975, further changes in the abortion legislation have also been brought in Germany (1976), Luxembourg (1978), New Zealand (1977), Portugal (1984), and Spain (1985). Abortion was still not permitted on request in these countries, but for more or less liberal reasons. In Belgium, where abortion was also prohibited, the legislation came close to liberalization in 1990 with a new Act which would have allowed women, distressed by their pregnancy, to request a doctor to terminate pregnancy, while making abortion still liable to punishment. The King however refused to ratify the act (European Observatory on National Family Policies, 1991: 16). In Germany, the law governing abortion was amended in 1974 to allow abortion on request in the first trimester. In 1975 this amendment was judged unconstitutional by the Constitutional Court. A more restrictive law, authorizing abortion on specific social and legal grounds, was adopted in 1976 (Kirk, 1981: 157). Following the country's reunification, and in view of a more liberal regulation in the former East Germany, Parliament eventually approved a liberal abortion law allowing women to have pregnancies terminated virtually without restriction during the first twelve weeks. The Federal Constitutional Court however did not allow parts of this new law to come into effect. The legislature was given a deadline to the end of 1994 for revised regulations (European Observatory on National Family Policies, 1994: 82).

In Portugal since 1984, abortion has been permitted but only on restricted grounds, i.e. to prevent danger of death or serious and irreversible effects on the health of the mother, when there are reliable reasons to presume that the child to be born will suffer incurably from disease or malformation, or when the pregnancy is due to rape (European Observatory on National Family Policies, 1992: ii. 181). In Spain since 1985, abortion has been permitted only in cases of rape, malformation of the foetus and danger to the mother's physical or mental health (United Nations, 1987–90). In 1991 some debates took place in Parliament on ways of possibly revising this legislation, but resulted in no clear position (European Observatory on National Family Policies, 1992: ii. 178). In Ireland, abortion continued to be illegal under the 1861 law. This prohibition was reiterated through the Eight Amendment to the Constitution Act in 1983 which acknowledges the right to life of the unborn child (ibid. 179). As a result of this prohibition, an increasing number of women underwent termination of pregnancy in England and Wales. The matter led to a major court case in 1992 when a 14-year old girl was given an injunction preventing her from travelling to England for the purpose of having an abortion. The injunction was eventually lifted by the Supreme Court on the grounds that there was a serious danger to the life of the mother should the pregnancy continue (ibid. 180). A national referendum followed resulting in a majority opposition to liberalization of abortion, but a majority support for the right to travel abroad for abortion, and the right to give and receive information on abortion services (Murdoch, 1992). The government then indicated its willingness to change the legislation to conform to the wishes of the electorate (European Observatory on National Family Policies, 1994: 86).

Finally, another country where the abortion issue led to fierce debates is the United States. In particular, the Supreme Court's decision in 1992 to uphold legal abortion and to give states new powers to restrict their abortion legislation, relaunched the whole debate on the issue (The Economist, 1992). The matter was made highly visible during the Republican Convention in 1992, placing President Bush under strong pressure to take a position on the issue (Cornwell, 1992). Since then President Clinton overturned some pieces of legislation introduced by his predecessors, especially a law banning federally financed clinics from offering abortion counselling (Usborne, 1993).

As a result of these changes, as of 1990, a total of ten countries were offering abortion on request. Although all countries acknowledged the principle of voluntary parenthood and freedom of access to contraception, major differences still persisted in the availability of contraception (especially for minors), and in the abortion legislation. In particular, in some predominantly Catholic countries, the issue was still subject to fierce controversy and only authorized on limited grounds.

10.5 Family benefit packages

One of the main objectives of this chapter has been to examine the differences across countries in the provision of support for families. With regard to the inter-country disparities in cash benefits, and limiting the comparison to the value of family allowances for a two-child family as of 1990, three groups of countries may be distinguished:

- The high support countries (with family allowances above 140 dollars per month): Austria, Belgium, Luxembourg, Norway.
- The medium support countries (with family allowances between 85 and 140 dollars per month): Denmark, Finland, France, Germany, Netherlands, Sweden, Switzerland, United Kingdom.
- The low support countries (with family allowances below 85 dollars per month): Australia, Canada, Greece, Ireland, Italy, Japan, New Zealand, Portugal, Spain, United States.

This classification is based on one form of cash benefits only, and does not reflect the overall state support for families. Neither does it reflect the possible variation in the inter-country ranking when other forms of cash benefits are taken into account, or when the analysis is conducted by type of families and income. As discussed in the introduction of this book, such variation was revealed by Bradshaw *et al.* (1993) in their studies of cash benefits for families in fifteen countries. It is however reassuring to see that the distribution suggested above broadly corresponds to the overall ranking obtained by these authors on the basis of a wider range of cash benefits.

When countries are compared on the basis of their maternity and parental leave schemes, a completely different story emerges. Limiting the comparison to the value of the maternity leave index (as reported in Figure 10.3), as of 1990, the following ranking is observed:

- High support countries (index above 25 weeks): Sweden, Finland, Denmark, Norway.
- Medium support countries (index between 10 and 25 weeks): Austria, Belgium, France, Germany, Italy, Luxembourg, Netherlands, Portugal, Spain.

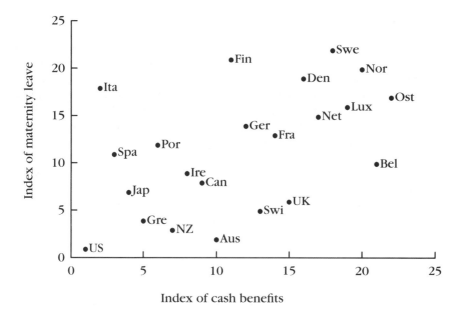

Fig. 10.4 *Support for families, 1990*

Aus: Australia; Ost: Austria; Bel: Belgium; Can: Canada; Den: Denmark; Fin: Finland; Fra: France; Ger: Germany; Gre: Greece; Ire: Ireland; Ita: Italy; Jap: Japan; Lux: Luxembourg; Net: Netherlands; NZ: New Zealand; Nor: Norway; Por: Portugal; Spa: Spain; Swe: Sweden; Swi: Switzerland; UK: United Kingdom; US: United States.

- Low support countries (index below 10 weeks): Australia, Canada, Greece, Ireland, Japan, New Zealand, Switzerland, United Kingdom, United States.

Obviously, there is not a perfect correspondence between support for families in the form of cash benefits, and support in the form of maternity leave. But, when the two indices are graphed against each other, some clusters of countries become distinguishable. In Figure 10.4, the countries are compared on the basis of their level of cash support (y-axis) and their level of support for working parents (x-axis). Only the ranking of countries is used here, i.e. a high value on the graph corresponds to a high ranking with regard to either family allowances or maternity leave. The graph obviously simplifies a much more complex reality but the emerging clusters of countries are undeniably meaningful.

(i) The first cluster comprises the four Nordic countries (Denmark, Finland, Norway, Sweden), and is characterized by a high ranking on the maternity leave index, and an average to high ranking on the cash benefit index. (ii) The second comprises the Continental European countries (excluding the Southern European countries), clustered around France, Germany, and the Netherlands. It is characterized by a high ranking on the cash benefit index, and an average one on the maternity leave index. It is thus diametrically opposed to the first group of countries. (iii) The third cluster comprises the Anglo-Saxon countries, grouped around Australia, Canada, Ireland, New Zealand, and further away the United Kingdom. It is characterized by an average ranking on the cash benefit index, and a low one on the maternity leave index. Japan also appears in this cluster. (iv) The fourth cluster comprises the Southern European countries (Italy, Portugal, Spain, with Greece further away), and is characterized by a low ranking on the cash benefit index, and an average one on the maternity leave index.

State support for families is obviously not limited to these two types of benefits, and a more comprehensive and statistically rigourous analysis would be needed in order to better map the actual degree of correlation between the various components of the families' benefit package, as well as the actual distances between countries. None the less, this simple graph suggests the existence of distinct approaches to state support for families.

10.6 Conclusion

At the beginning of this chapter, two factors were identified as exerting opposite pressure on family benefits: budget constraints, which have squeezed state support for families, and the transformations undergone by the family, which have called for improvements in state support for families. From this review of recent trends in state support for families, it has appeared that the influence of these two factors has been different according to the type of benefits and the country. In particular, it has been pointed out that while small increases were observed with regard to cash benefits, substantial upgrading has taken place with regard to maternity leave benefits. Budget constraints seem thus to have prevented the expansion of cash benefits while having less effect on maternity leave benefits. While the universality of cash benefits has been questioned, and preference given to means-tested benefits, the support for working mothers has conversely increased. Despite budget constraints, the issue of sex equality in the labour force seems thus to have justified the need for further upgrading of maternity leave schemes. It has to be acknowledged that the cost and financing of cash benefits and maternity leave benefits are very different, and it may not be surprising that budget constraints have had different effects on these two types of benefits. Thus, since the mid-1970s maternity leave benefits have been upgraded significantly in all countries, with the Nordic countries taking a clear lead. On the other hand, little progress has been recorded in countries such as the United States, Australia, and New Zealand, where the responsibility for providing maternity leave benefits is not considered as an entirely public responsibility. Large disparities were also seen with regard to the provision of child-care facilities. Although improvements were observed, the trend in the provision of child-care clearly reflected the struggle between budget constraints on the one hand, and on the other, the need for improved facilities following further increases in the participation of women in the labour force. Views about the private or public nature of the provision of child-care facilities have also conditioned the responses of governments.

Since 1975, the profile of family issues has been raised in all countries, and special attention has been devoted to low-income families and working parents. But behind this general trend, the disparities across countries in the provision of family benefits remained large, especially as a result of diverging views concerning the role of governments as welfare providers.

11

CONCLUSION

If the terms 'family policy' and 'family-friendly policy' nowadays appear regularly on the political agenda of governments, it is the result of a long development. From very restricted interventions limited to the most necessitous and vulnerable families, governmental support for families has been greatly expanded. While there are obvious inter-country variations in the ways governments have viewed families and their own role as welfare providers, the inter-country similarities in the development of family policy over time are also striking. Yet, in the literature on family policy, the development of family policy has rarely been studied from a comparative perspective. While some studies have compared governmental support for families at one point in time, others have examined the historical development within the framework of single-country analysis. This book therefore aimed at filling this gap by analysing the development of family policy from both a historical and cross-national perspective.

Another objective in this analysis is the assessment of the interplay between demographic changes on the one hand, and family policy on the other. If the nature of family policy itself has changed greatly during the past 100 years, families have also changed greatly. The argument here has been that these demographic changes have acted as major catalysts in the call for greater or reformed state support for families. While the decline in fertility and its consequences on population growth and population ageing have called for measures either to increase fertility or to adjust the economy and institutions to the new demographic situation, other family transformations such as the increase in lone-parenthood and the participation of women in the labour force have also called for specific governmental interventions. The cross-national analysis of this interplay between demographic changes and policy has revealed two main dimensions: one common to all countries, which underlined similarities in the development of family policy over time, and another specific to each country, or groups of countries, which revealed distinct models, or traditions, of family policy.

11.1 The general story

Over time, various themes and issues have captured political attention, and various reforms have been brought to the existing systems of state support for families. Some of the main landmarks in family policy development are summarized in Table 11.1.

Table 11.1 *Landmarks in family policy development*

Period	Development landmark
1. 1870–1929	First maternity leave schemes (paid and unpaid). Preventive welfare and health measures for mothers and children. Cash benefits for necessitous mothers, widows and orphans. Strict legislation prohibiting abortion and contraception.
2. 1930–1944	Cash benefits to workers with dependent children (either as cost-of-living bonus or family allowances). Explicit pronatalist policies (in some countries, i.e. France, Germany, Italy, Japan, Spain).
3. 1945–1959	Universal family allowances (in some countries of initial limited coverage, and gradually extended to all families and children). Upgrading of maternity leave schemes. Other benefits to families in the field of social security, housing, and health.
4. 1960–1974	Means-tested benefits for low-income families and specific benefits for lone-parent families. Reform of tax relief schemes for dependent children. Liberalization of legislation on contraception and abortion (in some countries).
5. 1975–	Further upgrading of maternity leave schemes. Other benefits for working parents. Comprehensive family policy (in some countries). Increase in publicly founded child-care institutions. Reform of family allowances and introduction of a means-test (in some countries). Liberalization of legislation on abortion (in some countries).

Period 1: 1879–1929: The first period extends from the end of the nineteenth century to 1929. It was a period marked by rapid urbanization and industrialization. A few families benefited greatly from this new situation, but for most of them it meant having to cope with small salaries, poor living conditions, and hazardous and unhealthy working environments. These changes in the socio-economic environment of families did not leave governments indifferent. High levels of poverty, and high levels of infant and child mortality became major preoccupations and were to

lead to the first interventions of governments to support families. In essence, these interventions were mostly of a preventive nature: protection of women at work through the introduction of the first maternity leave schemes, and protection of women and children through the setting-up of the first maternal and child welfare centres. Cash benefits for needy mothers and for widows and orphans were also introduced during this period, reflecting the very limited and selective character of these first forms of state support for families.

The other sector in which governments intervened during this early period was in the field of abortion and contraception. The decline in fertility after the 1870s and the apparent increasing willingness of women to limit family size led governments to adopt strict legislation prohibiting recourse to abortion and the sale, display, and advertising of contraceptives.

Period 2: 1930–1944: The second period covers the 1930s and early 1940s. It was a period marked by strong fertility decline and family transformations and was dominated by fears of population and family decline. For governments, which saw high fertility levels as a guarantee of military and political power, this new situation was particularly disturbing. Demographic projections published at that time, showing the likely decline of population in the near future, added to this concern. The increasing instability of families and the apparent weakening of paternal authority were equally disturbing as they threatened the most fundamental institution of society. In several countries this concern led to the launch of official commissions to study the problem and suggest countermeasures. For example, in Sweden the first Commission on Population was set up in 1935, while in France a Chief Committee on Population was appointed in 1939 in order to draw up the country's first comprehensive family policy.

It is in this context of fears of population and family decline that explicit pronatalist policies were adopted in France and Japan, as well as by Fascist governments in Germany, Italy, and Spain. Encouragement of fertility and marriage through birth bonuses, marriage loans, and other cash benefits were among the measures adopted by these governments (in addition to strict prohibition of abortion and contraception). In other countries, the concrete measures adopted by governments to better support families were still limited. Cash benefits to male workers with dependent children were introduced in some countries either as cost-of-living bonuses or family allowances. Mostly of a temporary nature, they were meant to better support families in a period characterized by high inflation.

Period 3. 1945–1959: The third period corresponds to the immediate post-war period and lasted until the end of the 1950s. With the return to peace, fertility had returned to high levels, and the family had been strongly revived and consolidated. Fears of population and family decline were no longer on the political agenda. Instead, during this period, governments were particularly active in strengthening and expanding their support for families. It was the golden age of the welfare state based on the principle of universality and support for all. Family allowances, which had been introduced at an early stage in some countries, were introduced in the rest on a universal basis. They were no longer seen as a temporary relief in time of economic recession, but were part of the new support provided by governments towards families. During this period, the mother and child relationship was strongly praised, and supported by policies which tended to encourage a traditional male-breadwinner family. Women, who had been particularly active in the labour force during the war, were therefore expected to return to a more traditional role immediately after the war. Measures to better protect pregnant women at work were enhanced, but the presence of the mother at home as child-carer was strongly encouraged above all.

Period 4. 1960-1974: The fourth period extended from the early 1960s to the mid-1970s, and witnessed major re-orientations in governments' family policies. There was first the issue of poverty. Brought to the forefront of the governments' agenda in earlier periods, it had disappeared in the immediate post-war period, as economic recovery and the expansion of the welfare state were believed to have eradicated the problem. This widespread view was challenged in the 1960s with the disclosure of new information showing that not only was poverty still present, but that it had become worse in recent times. Once again, governments were not to stay indifferent to this new situation, and a series of measures were taken to tackle it. If universality had dominated the immediate post-war welfare expansion, the rediscovery of poverty led to an era of greater selectivity and targeting of benefits. Means-tested benefits were introduced in order to better support low-income families, benefits specifically targeted at lone-parent families were introduced, as these families were judged to be more prone to poverty, and tax relief for dependent children was reformed so as not to penalize low-income families.

There was, secondly, the issue of women's equality and access to birth control. From the 1960s, demands for more equality in the labour market and more liberal access to means of birth-control seriously challenged the governments' policies. As a result, legislation on abortion and contraception, which had been tightened during the 1920s and 1930s, was partly relaxed, and measures were taken to ensure equality between men and women with regard to opportunities and treatment at work. There was, thirdly, the onset of significant family transformations. The baby-boom had come to a sudden halt in the mid-1960s, and families were again starting to show increasing signs of instability. This new situation initially raised concern only in a limited number of countries but gradually spread to other countries in the subsequent period.

Period 5. 1975 –: The fifth period runs from the mid-1970s onwards. The persistence of unprecedented low levels of fertility, the increasing entry of women into the labour market, and the diversification of family forms, forced governments to re-assess further their systems of support for families. Interventions took place at several levels, including further liberalization of legislation on abortion, improved support for working mothers, and further measures to tackle the problem of poverty among families with children. In addition, in view of unprecedented low levels of fertility, some countries once again raised the flag of pro-natalism and introduced measures to encourage families to have more children. The old issues of population and family decline were back on the agenda, but under a slightly different cover. While during the 1930s issues of pro-natalism, and military and political power dominated, it was under the cover of family-friendly policies that governments' interventions later took place. In very few cases was an explicit pro-natalist stance adopted. Instead the actions of governments were mainly driven by considerations related to the well-being of families and the reconciliation of work and parental responsibilities.

Clearly, what is today referred to as family policy is the result of a long development, starting with limited measures aimed at protecting mothers and children, to a more comprehensive package of cash and in-kind benefits aimed at all families. But behind this trend, there have been distinct country-specific variations in the ways population and family issues were raised, as well as in governments' responses.

11.2   Country-specific variants

These country-specific variants were found at two levels: in the attitudes of governments to population and family issues, some paying more attention to them than others, and in the type of policies adopted. From these variants, two main points emerge: first, that some of the inter-country differences observed today can be traced back to distant origins, and second, that some of the inter-country differences emerged at specific periods owing to specific circumstances. These cross-country variations are outlined below with references to the sub-periods distinguished in the previous section.

Period 1: 1870–1929. During this early period a sharp contrast appeared between France on the one hand, with its strong pro-natalist preoccupation, and Britain on the other where issues of overpopulation dominated the agenda. France's pro-natalism, although unique, can be linked to several factors including a precocious fertility decline, which was perceived as a real military handicap in a war-threatened period, as well as historical precedents. By contrast, Britain's preoccupation with over-population can be linked to reminiscences of Malthusian fears of an imbalance between population growth and food supply. Britain's higher level of urbanization and population density at the turn of the century may further explain the divergences in the attitudes of both countries to population growth.

Sharp divergences were also apparent with regard to policies. While the French government was introducing birth premiums and benefits for large families at a very early stage, in Britain, as in Australia, Canada, and the United States, more limited systems of cash benefits were introduced, restricted to widows and orphans. While in the former case the policy measures were motivated by pro-natalist consideration, in the latter they already reflected an attitude of limited state intervention, targeted at the most necessitous and deserving families. This contrast between France on the one hand, and Britain and the United States on the other, has been maintained over time.

Period 2: 1930–1944. In the second period, fears of population and family decline, which had so far been restricted to France, spread to many more countries. This was particularly the case in countries threatened or actively involved in the Second World War. In Britain, France, Japan, and the United States, as well as under the Fascist regimes of Germany, Italy, and Spain, significant initiatives were launched by governments either to study the demographic situation or to introduce countermeasures. A strong population growth was seen as essential in order to maintain military and political dominance. Under the Fascist regimes, this pro-natalist inclination was accompanied by strong eugenic principles and led to measures which were to be strongly disapproved of by the international community.

In terms of policy, divergences appeared between France and Japan on the one hand, which adopted an explicit pro-natalist policy, and Britain and the United States on the other, which opted for a non-interventionist policy. Sweden appeared in a third category, since the policy adopted aimed at encouraging higher fertility while at the same time making means of family limitation more accessible. In contrast with most countries where strict legislation prohibiting abortion and contraception was introduced, in Sweden and Denmark the policy adopted by the government followed a principle of voluntary parenthood and liberal access to means of family limitation.

Period 3: 1945-1959. The third period encompasses the immediate post-war period. With the return to high levels of fertility and the strengthening of the family, earlier fears of population and family decline were eliminated in most countries. It was particularly the case in Germany where the experience of the Nazi population policy led to censorship of demographic issues. Only from the 1970s was the population issue to re-emerge on the political agenda in Germany. There were however two countries where population issues continued to attract attention during this immediate post-war period: France and Japan. While in France the population issue was raised under the banner of pro-natalism, in Japan it was raised under the banner of anti-natalism. In France, high fertility was seen as essential in order to restore the power of the country, while in Japan, the devastated economy, along with the repatriation of a large number of nationals, led the government to believe that the rate of population growth had to be slowed down if economic recovery was to be achieved.

In terms of policy, this period witnessed considerable convergence in family benefit schemes. This was particularly apparent in the case of family allowances, which by 1959 had been introduced in all countries except Japan and the United States. In most countries this development was part of the emerging welfare state and followed the wartime destruction and suffering which had paved the way for a more active role for governments as welfare providers. In contrast, in the United States the experience of the war put further faith in the private sector and, so prevented the extension of family allowances beyond their existing means-tested form. A convergence was also to be observed during this period with regard to maternity leave schemes, which were significantly upgraded. The exceptions were Australia, Canada, New Zealand, Switzerland, and the United States, where the responsibility of protecting pregnant women at work and compensating them for the loss of earnings was not seen as a governmental responsibility. Although some measures were adopted eventually in these countries during the subsequent periods, a policy of non- or limited intervention continued to characterize the position of these governments on maternity leave benefits.

Period 4: 1960-1974. In the fourth period, population issues which had disappeared from the political agenda of most governments reappeared under two opposite banners. While fears of over-population were raised in countries such as Japan, the Netherlands, the United Kingdom, and the United States, fears of depopulation were raised in countries such as Belgium, France, Germany, and Greece. The initiatives launched by governments during this period consequently differed completely. While in the United States the Commission on Population Growth and the American Future assessed the impact of high population growth upon economic and environmental resources, in France the government was mandating the High Committee for the Population and the Family to study ways of increasing fertility.

In terms of policy, the divergences were not so sh~
population nor fear of depopulation led to sig~
one exception: the Nordic countrie~   ountries so far
in terms of state support for fa   ~es significantly improved
their systems of maternity   ~ous. Economic imperatives and the
need to draw women i~   ~ur force seem to have been behind these policy
developments. F~   ~, the Nordic countries were to take the lead with the
most g~   ~ leave schemes. While in the other countries the presence
of r   ~ne was still promoted by governments, in the Nordic countries,
e~   ~ally in Sweden and Finland, the presence of mothers in the labour force was
~ported by government.

Period 5: 1975-. The final period saw the emergence of further concern about population and family issues. In particular, all countries during this period launched initiatives related to population and the family. Beyond this similarity, strong divergences were however once again observed. For example, population issues attracted considerable attention in Italy, Portugal, and Spain in view of rapid demographic changes and the unprecedented low levels of fertility. In contrast, in Britain the decline in fertility was not perceived as a serious issue and instead the threat of world-wide overpopulation continued to attract more attention. On the other hand, the whole issue of lone-parenthood and the undesirable effects of welfare benefits attracted considerable attention in Britain and the United States. Welfare benefits, it was argued, were discouraging individuals from seeking work and were providing incentives to form lone-parent families. Thus, while other countries adopted measures specifically to support lone-parents, measures were taken in Britain and the United States to eliminate the presumed incentives to form lone-parent families, and to reinforce the financial liability of the non-custodial parent. Again, a policy of limited state intervention and maximum private responsibility characterized the action of these governments.

In all other countries, there has been a clear trend in this recent period towards better governmental support for families. Talk about family policy has been widespread, and there have been deliberate efforts to better support working parents, lone-parents, and low-income families. Some major inter-country differences have been noticeable, especially with regard to the degree of support of government, and the type of intervention. While an explicitly pro-natalist policy has been adopted in a few countries (e.g. France, Greece, Luxembourg), a pro-family policy aimed at promoting either equality between men and women (e.g. the Nordic countries), or a more traditional sex role pattern (e.g. Germany), was adopted elsewhere. Britain and the United States appear here in a fourth category in view of their non-interventionist policy.

Beyond common trends in family policy development, it therefore appears clear that significant inter-country differences have existed at one point or another. While the common trends may be partly explained by common demographic changes, the inter-country differences may instead be linked to specific demographic trends, and specific historical or political circumstances.

11.3 Interplay between demographic changes and policies

Demographic changes have acted over time as major catalysts in the development of family policies. By creating new needs (either at the macro or micro level), demographic changes have prompted governments to intervene. Decreasing fertility, the increasing prevalence of lone-parenthood, and participation of women in the labour force, are all examples of demographic changes which have in the past prompted government to intervene. Similarly, changes in the socio-economic environment of families, for example the greater prevalence of poverty at the turn of the century, or the rediscovery of poverty in the 1960s, have also prompted governments to intervene. From this, it follows that developments in family policy can be seen as responses to new needs emerging from demographic changes which in turn have acted as a major driving force in the development of the governments' family policy. Changes in the social, economic, and demographic environment of families, or more precisely, changes such as the decline in fertility, the rediscovery of poverty, and the increase in the participation of women in the labour force, have all created new welfare needs and led governments to extend and reform their system of state support for families. In other words, from a theoretical point of view it could be argued that the development of family policy may be best explained by a variant of the 'industrialization thesis', or more precisely by a needs-response.

Although this explanation is well supported by historical examples, it remains incomplete since it does not take into account instances when non-governmental actors have played a major role in the development of policies. This was for example the case with pro-natalist associations in France at the turn of the century, which campaigns undeniably exerted pressures on the government to take a more active pro-natalist stance, with women's groups in the pre-World War II period, which actions influenced the adoption of some of the maternity policies, or with other interest groups, such as the Child Poverty Action Group in Britain, which have prompted the government to intervene with specific family benefit measures. Through their calls for the introduction of specific measures, and through campaigns which increased the visibility of some issues, these non-governmental actors have contributed to the development of family policy and forced the emergence of population and family issues on the political agenda of governments. These examples do not necessarily reflect a genuine conflict of interest or battles of power, but reflect the existence of forces that might have been too strong to be ignored by governments.

In addition to evidence supporting the 'needs-response' explanation, there is also considerable evidence in support of the 'action-response' one. These two theses are in fact compatible. Non-governmental actors of the 'action-response' thesis themselves might have been prompted by demographic changes. They might have acted as information diffusers, increasing the visibility of demographic changes, and making more concrete the calls for improved or reformed state support for families. From this point of view, non-governmental actors may be seen as intermediaries in the interplay between demographic changes and policy. For example, the existence of active pro-natalist associations in France at the turn of the century was in itself a response to declining fertility. Through their activities and campaigns, these associations made the fertility issue more visible, and exerted more pressure on the government to intervene. Similarly, the Child Poverty Action Group in Britain was set up following the disclosure of information revealing the magnitude of the poverty problem, thus contributing to its increasing visibility.

Seen from a comparative perspective, these two theses help to further understand the existence of both similarities and dissimilarities across countries in the development of family policy. First, the fact that demographic trends have been similar across countries may explain why they have tended to initiate similar responses from governments. Secondly, the fact that these demographic trends have in some cases diverged across countries, either in their timing or in their magnitude, may explain the emergence of country-specific variations. Thirdly, the fact that non-governmental actors differed across countries, either in their nature or activities, may further add to the country-specific variations. To these explanations, one may add the existence of country-specific historical circumstances, ideologies, and political regimes, which may have further prompted dissimilar responses to similar demographic changes. Demographic changes may therefore have acted as major determinants of family policy development in prompting governments to respond — but to respond in a way which may have been shaped by the magnitude and timing of the demographic changes, and by a series of other country-specific factors, including the presence of non-governmental actors, as well as specific historical circumstances.

Although this is a plausible story, it still leaves as a grey area the reasons why governments did or did not respond, or devote attention to, population and family issues. At this level, a number of reasons may be suggested. First, a government may have acted out of welfare considerations. For example, the high prevalence of poverty among families with children, or the difficulties faced by working parents in trying to reconcile work and family responsibility, may be situations in which a government may legitimately want to intervene. For a government taking full responsibility in the protection of its citizens and in the provision of welfare, these two situations would clearly prompt it to intervene. Secondly, a government may have acted to please the electorate. For example, if the public strongly favours government intervention to further support working parents, or if some interest groups put pressure on the government to intervene in this field, it may decide to intervene in order to sustain its popularity. Thirdly, a government may have acted out of national pride or for reasons related to the protection of the nation. For example, in the context of strong linguistic cleavage, (e.g. French- speakers in Quebec) or strong ethnic diversity, (e.g. Luxembourg, Switzerland) a government may be more prone to intervene in order to protect the demographic survival of a linguistic minority or its native-born population. Fourthly, a government may have acted out of economic considerations, e.g. if it feared that the persistence of below-replacement fertility will have negative consequences on the economy, or that participation of women in the labour force will be needed in order to sustain economic growth. In both cases, a government may want to introduce specific measures because of economic considerations.

On the other hand, there may be reasons why a government may not have wanted to intervene in the family policy field. First, a government may not have wanted to intervene because it considered that it was not its duty to do so, for example, in the restoration of fertility above replacement level. This argument has been used, for example, by the British government, which considered population growth and fertility level beyond the area of government responsibility. Secondly, a government may not have wanted to intervene because of the fear that any intervention would interfere with the individual's rights and freedom. For example, the introduction of a pro-natalist policy may be seen as an infringement of the right of individuals to decide freely the number of children that they want. This argument has been used, for example, by the German government on the grounds that any pro-natalist policy would enter a sector which is entirely dominated by private freedom. Thirdly, a government may not have wanted to intervene because it saw no need to do so. For example, by denying the existence of a population crisis, the Canadian government has recently dismissed the need for any government intervention. Fourthly, a government may not have wanted to intervene because such an intervention would be too expensive. For example, the cost of measures to encourage higher fertility or to better support families financially may be prohibitive. Finally, a government may not have wanted to intervene because of fears of unintended and undesirable side effects. For example, British and American governments have been reluctant to expand welfare benefits further for fear that it may encourage welfare dependency and lone-parenthood.

If it is relatively easy to identify the main landmarks in family policy development and to highlight the main cross-national variants, it is obviously more difficult to explain the 'hows' and 'whys', where the 'hows' refer to the interplay between demographic changes and policies, and the potentially intermediate role of non-governmental social policy actors, and the 'whys' refer to a series of economic, social, and political considerations.

The other point to consider in this discussion of the interplay between demographic changes and policies is the potential effect of policies on demographic behaviour. Throughout this book, the emphasis has been put on the reverse relationship, from demography to policies. Yet there are also several instances when the possibility of policy-to-demography relationship was pointed out. Although a thorough discussion of this relationship would require a more extensive treatment, it is nevertheless worth underlining some of its aspects. The first thing to point out is the disagreement and uncertainty concerning the effect of policies on demographic behaviour. Some of France's pro-natalist activists and strong believers in the potentially positive effect of policies on fertility have been referred to in several chapters. In fact, throughout the history of its family policy, the French government's interventions have been motivated by pro-natalist objectives, and the government has tended to act in the belief it could influence fertility. The removal of fertility obstacles (mainly of a financial nature), it was believed, would result in higher fertility.

This belief in the potential of pro-natalist policies ought to be contrasted with the serious doubt expressed by other governments such as Britain. The fact that fertility in France and Britain has been following a similar trend since the mid-1960s, and this despite very different policies, has been used to disprove the French belief about the pro-natalist effect of their policies (The Economist, 1991). As seen in previous chapters, in most other countries disbelief about the effect of policies, or fear of interference in a sector considered essentially private, have tended to prevent governments from adopting explicit pro-natalist policies. But in Britain, as in the United States, this is only part of the story. For if the existence of a pro-natalist 'French- style' effect has been denied, belief in the existence of a 'Malthus-style' effect still persists. Welfare benefits, it is argued in some circles, can have an effect on fertility by encouraging the 'wrong' type of parents to have children. Poor parents and young mothers on welfare, it has been argued, may be inclined to have more children in order to be eligible for supplementary benefits.

Belief (or disbelief) in the potential effect of pro-natalist policies and in the potentially undesirable effect of other policies has thus been driving governmental action and policies. This assumed effect between policies and demographic behaviour is surprising, considering the limited and often questionable empirical evidence available to support this assumption. With regard to the effect of policies on fertility, a limited effect was suggested by Ekert (1986) and Blanchet and Ekert-Jaffé (1994) in their comparison of policies and fertility in respectively eight and eleven European countries. Cash benefits equivalent to those paid to families in France were found to account for a difference of 0.2 children per woman in the total fertility rate (Ekert, 1986: 344). On the other hand, Gauthier (1991) on the basis of a similar analysis (of twenty-two industrialized countries) found evidence of a much more limited effect. Increasing cash transfers to families by 25 per cent would increase the total fertility rate by only 0.02 children per woman. With regard to the effect of welfare on the incidence of lone-parenthood, empirical evidence was also very limited. For example, on the basis of British data, Ermisch (1991) estimated that a 10 per cent increase in welfare benefits would raise the percentage of women having a pre-marital birth by less than 2 percentage points.

If the analysis presented in this book provides some evidence of the effect of demographic changes on policies, limited evidence is available in the literature to substantiate the existence of any clear effect of policies on demographic behaviour.

11.4 Current models of family policy

The conclusions drawn in the previous chapters have pointed to the existence of strong differences among countries in terms of the governments' agenda and concern towards the demographic situation, but also in terms of the nature of governments' intervention and its corresponding level of support for families. While some governments have viewed in a more alarmist way the decline in fertility and the disappearance of the traditional male-breadwinner–housewife family, others have been much less alarmed and have put more faith in the societies' ability to adapt to the new demographic situation. And while some governments have opted for an explicitly interventionist policy aimed at encouraging fertility, or at promoting a traditional family structure, others have opted for a less interventionist approach, limited to cases of severe deprivation or dysfunction. What these differences suggest are the existence of different traditions, or models, of family policies. To conclude this analysis by suggesting models of family policy however represents a risky exercise: for models tend to ignore the dynamics of policies, and their continuities or discontinuities over time, as well as non-negligible differences among countries sharing a same model. On the other hand, such an exercise may be useful in further highlighting and summarizing the major similarities and dissimilarities observed across countries. Limiting the analysis to the most recent period, four main models of family policy may be distinguished:

1. *Pro-family/pro-natalist model*: for which the issue of a low fertility level is a main concern and is considered as requiring government intervention. Support for families is consequently seen as the responsibility of government, especially in relation to encouraging childbearing. Under this model, a great emphasis is placed on cash benefits and more particularly, towards the third child since financial obstacles are believed to be the main deterrent to the birth of a third child. This is especially the case in France and Quebec. In this model, relatively high levels of support are provided for maternity leave and child-care facilities. These measures are part of a general plan to reduce the obstacles to fertility, especially those between employment and family responsibilities. Working mothers are therefore not disapproved of, and conditions are created where being in employment is not an obstacle to childbearing. This pro-natalist orientation is combined with a relatively liberal legislation with regard to abortion. A principle of voluntary parenthood prevails so as to give all families the right to choose freely their family size, even though larger families are deemed more desirable.

2. *Pro-traditional model*: for which the preservation of the family is the main concern. Governments partly endorse the responsibility of supporting families, while at the same time encouraging a traditional male-breadwinner family. Under this model, a medium level of state support for families is provided. The government takes responsibility to support families, but a belief in the role of family, community, and charity support still dominates. Benefits for working

mothers are provided by government, but the persistence of some obstacles to women's employment (e.g. taxation) reflects a preference for a more traditional sex-role pattern. This preference is also reflected in the low provision of child-care, which does not give women the opportunity to combine employment and family responsibility easily. Instead, the government gives preference to extended leave for child-care, which allows mothers to stay at home with their young children while retaining job security. This model of family policy is characteristic of Germany. This policy is not attached to any pro-natalist objective, but is presented under the label of family-friendly policy. A certain degree of traditionalism also remains with regard to the abortion legislation, which is not as liberal as in other countries.

3. *Pro-egalitarian model*: for which the promotion of greater equality between men and women is the main objective. Governments take full responsibility in the support of families, especially working parents. This model stands in sharp contrast with the previous one. Instead of promoting a traditional family, the main concern has been the achievement of a more egalitarian sex-role model. For this, the government has taken full responsibility in creating conditions and opportunities to allow women to combine paid employment and family responsibilities more easily, and to allow fathers to take a larger role in child-caring. Legislation on parental leave, as opposed to maternal leave, has been one of the centre-pieces of this model. In addition, other benefits, such as leave to care for a sick child and extensive provision of child-care, have also been seen as ways of bringing equality between men and women. This set of measures and benefits is combined with a liberal legislation on abortion, thus following the principle of voluntary parenthood, which had been acknowledged at a very early stage in Denmark and Sweden.

4. *Pro-family but non-interventionist model*: for which responsibility to support families is taken by governments only for families in need. The participation of women in the labour force is not discouraged, but limited benefits are provided by the state to support them. Moreover, the traditional family continues to be highly praised. This model, thus, features a completely different attitude towards government's role as welfare provider. Belief in the self-sufficiency of families, and in the merit of a non-regulated market, has resulted in a system of state support for families with very low levels of support. Cash benefits have consequently been kept at a relatively low level, and preference has been expressed for targeted benefits. The argument is that targeted benefits better support families in real need. Provision with regard to maternity leave has also been kept at a very low level, the argument being that the government should not impose additional constraints and burdens on employers. The responsibility of providing such benefits is seen as being that of private employers (through collective agreements), and the state has kept its support in this field to a minimum. Similarly, provision for child-care has been seen as falling outside government responsibility. Informal arrangements and provision from employers have instead been encouraged. Governments adhering to this model of family policy (as in the United States and Britain) are not opposed to the participation

of women in the labour force, but they do not see the provision of support for working mothers as their responsibility. This approach to family policy is combined with a more or less liberal legislation on abortion.

These four models of family policy, as summarized in Table 11.2, are however found in their 'pure' form only in a limited number of countries. Instead, in most cases, a combination of models prevails. For example, while the relatively low levels of support provided to families in Australia would tend to suggest a non-interventionist model, the intention of some of the policies adopted recently by the government aims at bringing greater equality between men and women (e.g. the recent parental leave scheme), and would tend to suggest a pro-egalitarian model. The classification of countries suggested above consequently tends to place more weight on the outcome of policies, in terms of actual support, rather than on their strict intention.

Table 11.2 *State support for families and policy orientation*

Policy area	Type of policies			
	Pronatalist	Traditional	Egalitarian	Non-interventionist
Abortion	Liberal	Liberal$^-$	Liberal$^+$	Liberal$^{+/-}$
Cash benefits	High	Medium	Medium	Low
Maternity leave	Medium	Medium	High	Low
Child-care^a	Medium	Low	High	Low

Key: +/- = More or less liberal legislation. ^{a}: Provision for child-care facilities.

Nevertheless, the overlap between the above classification and that suggested in the recent welfare state literature is large. For example, our 'Nordic/pro-egalitarian' model, and our 'Anglo-Saxon/ non-interventionist' one, match Esping-Anderson's (1990) 'democratic' and 'liberal' models respectively, while our 'Continental/ traditional' model and our 'Continental/ pro-natalist' one approach Esping-Anderson's 'conservative' model'. And while in the above classification, Southern European countries were not singled out as a distinct case, the strict analysis of benefits' levels in Chapter 10 did place them in a separate category. In this case, the parallel would instead be with Liebfried's (1992) 'Latin Rim model'. The correspondence is however far from perfect as the above welfare state models do not reflect the government's attitude towards the population and family question, nor the objective behind its support for families, ie pro-natalist, pro-egalitarian, or pro-traditional.

11.5   The future of family policies

In view of the two opposite forces currently at play, with on the one hand budget deficits constraining governments to reduce their expenditure, and on the other, increasing demands for better support from working parents, lone-parents, and low-income families, two main questions arise: (i) Are we likely to see in the future a greater emphasis on family issues and willingness of governments to better support families? (ii) Are we likely to observe further convergence in the models of family policies?

Towards the century of the family?

In an article on the rights of children, Therborn (1993) argued that we have missed opportunities for making the twentieth century the 'century of the child'. On the other hand, and in view of the recent trends in family policy, one can legitimately ask whether we are likely to be heading towards the century of the family. Speculating about a whole century may be too adventurous. In the shorter term, several factors suggest that we are likely to see a persistence of family issues on the agenda of governments, at least for many years to come. First, despite recent increases in the total period fertility rate in some countries, a return to levels well above replacement is unlikely.[1] Anxieties concerning population ageing, potential labour force shortages, and population decline, are therefore likely to remain, thus maintaining a high profile on fertility issue. Secondly, the participation of women in the labour force is unlikely to experience a major reversal, thus keeping alive the issues of equality in the labour market and reconciliation between employment and parental responsibilities. As women continue to enter the labour market and to increase their level of attachment towards it, continued pressure will be exerted on governments and employers to adopt more parent-friendly policies. Thirdly, the high incidence of divorce and lone-parenthood is unlikely to disappear, thus further pressing governments to give special support to lone-parents and children of divorced parents.

Against this background, there are at least three factors which may restrict the intervention of governments and prevent them making the next decades those of the family. First, there are the budget constraints. The necessity to control public expenditure and to reduce countries' deficits will remain a major obstacle to further improvements in the level of state support for families. This is already apparent in several countries, including well-established welfare states such as Sweden. A greater involvement of employers in the support for families might be one way forward — as a way of reducing governments' financial burden, but also as a way of involving more partners in a more general type of support for families. A trend in this direction has already been observed in several countries, with the setting up of workplace nurseries and the adoption of career breaks or other flexible elements, to allow parents to combine employment and family responsibilities more easily. Secondly, there is the issue of population ageing. The increasing ratio of older people among the electorate, it has been argued, may have the tendency to shift the agenda of governments towards issues of the elderly rather than issues related to families with young children. For example, Preston (1984) has argued that the

---

[1] A note of caution is required since demographers have been renowned for failing to predict future demographic trends accurately. They saw neither the sudden reversal of fertility in the post-war period, nor its sudden halt in the mid-1960s. Whether they will fail to foresee another baby-boom is debatable.

increase in the number of elderly people in the United States has contributed to their improved well-being, while the decrease in the number of children has served to worsen their relative economic position. If so, a fierce battle in the allocation of resources between the elderly and children is likely to take place in the future, and may go against further improvements in state support for families. Thirdly, there is the non-interventionist and self-support ideology which is likely to continue to prevent further expansion of state support for families. While this argument may apply only to a limited number of countries, it will nevertheless remain a major obstacle to the adoption of a more comprehensive family policy in countries such as the United Kingdom and the United States.

In view of these varied elements, it is difficult to speculate about the exact future of family policy. What seems reasonable to suggest is that state support for families is likely to remain a major political issue during the next decades, but that budget constraints will severely limit government action. In particular, the issues of targeting of cash benefits, reconciliation between employment and family responsibilities, and employers' involvement are likely to characterize future trends in family policy. In addition, a trend towards better co-ordination between the different elements of state support for families is foreseeable.

Towards convergence in family policies?

Although governments are likely to face similar factors which may affect the future trends in family policy, their responses to these factors may continue to show significant differences. Differences in ideology, preference, and priority with regard to issues such as public responsibility, equity, equality, and cost containment are indeed likely to prevent considerable inter-country convergence in the systems of state support for families. Dissimilar institutional arrangements, historical precedents, differing attitudes to population and family issues, and dissimilar perception about the responsibility of the state as welfare provider are other factors which are likely to continue to give different orientations to the systems of state support for families. Having said that, a certain convergence is none the less possible within certain countries as a result of a strong political will. It is especially the case within the European Union where the objective of convergence in social policies and systems of welfare benefits has been recently adopted (European Parliament, 1992). The directive on the protection of pregnant workers and the recommendation on child care are two further initiatives which may bring convergence within the European Union. Difficulties in reaching agreement over the terms of these texts among member states may, however, prevent harmonization at very high standards, and may instead lead to the adoption of minimum common standards around which very distinct approaches to family policy are likely to persist.

REFERENCES

Abel-Smith, B. and Townsend, R. (1965), *The Poor and the Poorest*, (London: Bell).

Anderson, B. S. and Zinsser, J. P. (1988), *A History of their Own: Women in Europe from Prehistory to the Present*, vol. ii, (London: Penguin Books).

Antler, S. (1978), 'Family Policy and the Carter Administration', *Social Thought*, Fall 15–22.

Armitage, A. (1978), 'Canada', in (Kamerman and Kahn, 1978), 367–99.

Australia, Population Issues Committee (1991), *Population Issues and Australia's Future: Final Report*, (Melbourne: Government Printing Office).

Banting, K. G. (1979), *Poverty, Politics and Policy*, (London: Macmillan).

Bastide, H., Girard, A., and Roussel, L. (1982), 'Une enquête d'opinion sur la conjoncture démographique (janvier 1982)', *Population*, (4–5) 867–904.

Baude, A. (1979), 'Public Policy and Changing Family Patterns in Sweden, 1930–1977', in Lipman-Bluman, J. and Bernard, J., eds., *Sex Roles and Social Policy: A Complex Social Science Equation*, (London: Sage), 145–73.

Becker, G. S. (1981), *A Treatise on the Family*, (Harvard Mass.: Harvard University Press).

Berelson, B., ed. (1974), *Population Policies in Developed Countries*, (London: McGraw-Hill Inc.).

Berkowitz, E. D. (1991), *America's Welfare State: From Roosevelt to Reagan*, (Baltimore, Md.: John's Hopkins University Press).

Beveridge, W. et al. (1932), *Changes in Family Life*, (London: George Allen & Unwin).

Bishop, J. H. (1980), 'Jobs, Cash Transfers and Marital Instability: A Review and Synthesis of the Evidence', *The Journal of Human Resources*, 15(3) 301–35.

Blanc, O., Cuénoud, C., Diserens, M., Hang, M.-H., Heinzmann, H., Neury, J.-E., Schuler, M., and Traxler, J. (1985), *Les Suisses vont-ils disparaitre? La population de la Suisse: problèmes, perspectives et politiques*, (Berne: Editions Paul Haupt), Report of the Commission on Population Policy.

Blanchet, D. and Ekert-Jaffé, O. (1994), 'The Demographic Impact of Family Benefits: Evidence from a Micro-Model and from Macro-Data', in Ermisch, J. and Ogawa, N., eds., *The Family, the Market and the State in Ageing Societies*, (Oxford: Clarendon Press), 79–103.

Blom, I. (1991), 'Voluntary Motherhood 1900–1930: Theories and Politics of a Norwegian Feminist in an International Perspective', in (Bock and Thane, 1991), 21–39.

Bock, G. (1991), 'Antinatalism, Maternity and Paternity in National Socialist Racism', in (Bock and Thane, 1991), 233–55.

Bock, G. and Thane, P., eds. (1991), *Maternity and Gender Policies: Women and the Rise of the European Welfare States: 1880s–1950s*, (London: Routledge).

Booth, C. (1902), *Life and Labour of the People in London*, (London: Macmillan).

Borrie, W. D. (1974), 'Australia', in (Berelson, 1974), 270–93.

Borrie, W. D. and Spencer, G. (1965), *Australia's Population Structure and Growth*, (Melbourne: Committee for Economic Development of Australia).

Bourgeois-Pichat, J. (1974), 'France', in (Berelson, 1974), 545–91.

Bowlby, J. (1953), *Child Care and the Growth of Love*, (London: Penguin).

Bradshaw, J., Ditch, J., Holmes, H., and Whiteford, P. (1993), 'A Comparative Study of Child Support in Fifteen Countries', *Journal of European Social Policy*, 3(4) 255–71.

Bradshaw, J. and Piachaud, D. (1980), *Child Support in the European Community*, (London: Bedford Square Press).

Brennan, D. (1993), 'Australia', in (Cochran, 1993), 11–56.

Britain (1949), *Royal Commission on Population: Report*, (London: HMSO).

Britain (1967), *Plowden Report: Children and their Primary Schools*, (London: HMSO).

Britain (1974), *Report of the Committee on One-Parent Families (Finer Report)*, (London: HMSO).

British All-Party Parliamentary Group on Population and Development (1992), *European Agenda for Action on World Population*, (London: British All-Party Parliamentary Group on Population and Development), Report of the European Parliamentarians' Conference held in London, 31 Jan. - 1 Feb. 1992.

Brown, C. (1994), 'Bottomley to Target Child Care', *Independent*, 11 Mar.

Brownlee, H. (1990), 'Tax and Social Security Changes', *Family Matters*, Apr.(26).

Burgess, E. W. and Locke, H. J. (1945), *The Family: From Institution to Companionship*, (New York: American Book Company), 1st edition.

Buttafuoco, A. (1991), 'Motherhood as a Political Strategy: the Role of the Italian Women's Movement in the Creation of the Cassa Nazionale di Maternita', in (Bock and Thane, 1991), 178-95.

Canada, Health and Welfare (1989), 'Releases on Canada's Demographic Future Report', *News Release*.

Canada, Health and Welfare (1990), *Charting Canada's Future: A Report of the Demographic Review*, (Ottawa: Health and Welfare Canada).

Canada, Ministry of Supply and Services (1989), *Child Care in Canada*, no. 87-11E, (Ottawa: Ministry of Supply and Services).

Canada, Standing Senate Committee on Social Affairs, Science and Technology (1987), *Child Benefits: Proposals for a Guaranteed Family Supplement Scheme*, (Ottawa: Senate of Canada).

Carlson, A. (1990), *The Swedish Experiment in Family Politics: The Myrdals and the Interwar Population Crisis*, (London: Transaction Publishers).

Catholic University of Louvain (1977), *Rapport POLIWA: Etat démographique de la Wallonie et éléments pour une politique de population*, (Belgique: Département de démographie, Université Catholique de Louvain-la-Neuve).

Chafetz, J. S. and Dworkin, A. G. (1986), *Female Revolt: Women's Movements in World and Historical Perspective*, (Totowa: Rowman & Allanheld).

Charles, E. (1934), *The Menace of Underpopulation*, (London: Watts).

Chauvière, M. (1992), 'L'expert et les propagandistes. Alfred Sauvy et le Code de la Famille de 1939', *Population*, 47(6) 1441-51.

CNAF (Caisse nationale des allocations familiales) (1989), 'L'accueil des jeunes enfants: une priorité institutionnelle', *CAF Lettre*, (6).

Cochran, M., ed. (1993), *International Handbook of Child Care Policies and Programs*, (London: Greenwood Press).

Cohen, B. (1988), *Caring for Children: Services and Policies for Childcare and Equal Opportunities in the UK*, (London: Commission of the European Communities and Family Policy Study Centre).

Coleman, D. and Salt, J. (1992), *The British Population: Patterns, Trends and Processes*, (Oxford: Oxford University Press).

Commission of the European Communities (1989a), *Communication from the Commission on Family Policies*, vol. Aug., (Brussels: CEC).

Commission of the European Communities (1989b), *European Public Opinion on the Family and the Desire for Children*, no. 32, V/82/91-EN in Eurobarometer survey, (Brussels: CEC).

Commission of the European Communities (various years), *Comparative Tables of the Social Security Schemes in the Member States of the European Communities*, (Brussels: CEC).

Cornwell, R. (1992), 'Republican's Side-Step Abortion Fight', *Independent*, 18 Aug.

Council of Europe (1991), *Recent Demographic Developments in Europe 1991*, (Strasbourg: Council of Europe).

Council of Europe (1992), *Comparative Tables of the Social Security Schemes in the Member States not Members of the European Communities, in Australia and in Canada*, (Strasbourg: Council of Europe).

Council of Europe (various years), *Comparative Tables of the Social Security Schemes in the Member States not Members of the European Communities*, (Strasbourg: Council of Europe).

Cova, A. (1991), 'French Feminism and Maternity: Theories and Policies, 1890-1918', in (Bock and Thane, 1991), 119-37.

David, M.-G. and Starzec, C. (1991), 'France: A Diversity of Policy Options', in (Kamerman and Kahn, 1991), 81-114.

Debré, M. (1975), 'Un Favoritisme justifié', *Le Monde*, 15 July.

Debré, M. (1979), 'La France va craquer', *Le Monde*, 28 Mar.

del Campo, S. (1974), 'Spain', in (Berelson, 1974), 489–544.

Delhaxhe, A. (1989), 'Belgium', in (Olmstead and Weikart, 1989).

Dennett, J., James, J., Room, G., and Watson, P. (1982), *Europe Against Poverty: The European Poverty Programme, 1975–80*, (London: Bedford Square Press).

Derogny, J. (1956), *Des enfants malgré nous*, (Paris: Les éditions de minuit).

Desjardins, G. (1991), *Faire garder ses enfants au Québec ... une histoire toujours en marche*, (Québec: Les publications du Québec).

Djerassi, C. (1979), *The Politics of Contraception*, (New York: WW Norton & Cie).

Dumon, W., ed. (1989), *Family Policy in EEC-Countries*, (Belgium: Katholieke Universiteit Leuven).

Dumont, G., Chaunu, P., Legrand, J., and Sauvy, A., eds. (1979), *La France ridée*, (Paris: Librairie générale française).

Easterlin, R. A. (1987), *Birth and Fortune: The Impact of Numbers on Personal Welfare*, (Chicago: University of Chicago Press).

Eekelaar, J. and Dingwall, R. (1990), *The Reform of Child Care Law: A Practical Guide to the Children Act 1989*, (London: Tavistock/Routledge).

Ehrlich, P. (1968), *The Population Bomb*, (New York: Ballantine Books).

Ehrlich, P. and Ehrlich, A. (1990), *The Population Explosion*, (London: Hutchinson).

Ekert, O. (1986), 'Effets et limites des aides financières aux familles: une expérience et un modèle', *Population*, 41(2) 327–48.

Ermisch, J. F. (1991), *Lone Parenthood: An Economic Analysis*, (Cambridge: Cambridge University Press).

Esping-Anderson, G. (1990), *Three Worlds of Welfare Capitalism*, (Cambridge: Polity Press).

European Community (1983), 'Resolution on population policy', *Official Journal of the European Community*, (C184/117), 11 Nov.

European Community (1992), 'Council Recommendation on the Convergence of Social Protection Objectives and Policies', *Official Journal of the European Community*, (L245), 26 Aug.

European Observatory on National Family Policies (1990), *Families and Policies: Evolutions and Trends in 1988–1989 (Interim report)*, (Brussels: Commission of the European Communities).

European Observatory on National Family Policies (1991), *Families and Policies: Evolutions and Trends in 1989–1990*, (Brussels: Commission of the European Communities).

European Observatory on National Family Policies (1992), *National Family Policies in EC-Countries in 1991*, vol. i-ii, (Brussels: Commission of the European Communities).

European Observatory on National Family Policies (1994), *Trends and Developments in 1992: Technical Annex*, (Brussels: Commission of the European Communities).

Eurostat (various years), *Demographic Statistics*, (Luxembourg: European Communities).

Evans, P. (1988), 'Professions Worried over Fewer Young People', *The Times*, 5 Apr.

Falardeau, L. (1988), 'Un Québec sans enfants', *La Presse*, 10–17 Sep.

Family Policy Studies Centre (1993), 'No Right to Parental Leave', *Family Policy Bulletin*, Dec.

Family Policy Studies Centre (1994), 'Bottomley Promises Hands-Off Approach', *Family Policy Bulletin*, May.

Fédération des Familles de France (1989), *Histoire du mouvement familial*, (Paris: Fédération des Familles de France), Série Histoire et Institutions.

Ferrari, G. (1975), 'Italy', in (Kirk et al., 1975), 426–61.

Festy, P. (1979), *La fécondité des pays occidentaux de 1870 à 1970*, (Paris: Institut National d'Etudes Démographiques).

Financial Times (1990), 'Family Policy in Disarray', 24 Oct.

Financial Times (1991), 'The Vanishing Workers', 16 Dec.

Financial Times (1992), 'Election 1992: The Labour Manifesto', 19 March.

Fleming, S. (1986), 'Introduction', in *Eleanore Rathbone: Spokeswoman for a Movement*, (Bristol: Falling Wall Press).

Flora, P., ed. (1986-7), *Growth to Limits: The Western European Welfare States Since World War II*, (Berlin: De Gruyter), 4 vols.

Fortier, C. (1988), 'L'expérience d'autres gouvernements dans l'élaboration de projets similaires (rapport pour le Canadian Demographic Review)'.

Foster, K., Wilmot, A., and Dobbs, J. (1990), *General Household Survey, 1988*, (London: HMSO).

Frank, M. and Lipner, R. (1988), 'History of Maternity Leave in Europe and the United States', in Zigler, E. F. and Frank, M., eds., *The Parental Leave Crisis: Towards a National Policy*, (New Haven, Conn.: Yale University Press).

Frazer, D. (1984), *The Evolution of the British Welfare State: A History of Social Policy since the Industrial Revolution*, (London: Macmillan).

Gardner, D. and Goodhart, D. (1994), 'Portillo Uses Veto on EU Statutory Paternity Leave', *Financial Times*, 23 Sep.

Garfinkel, I. (1992a), *Assuring Child Support: An Extension of Social Security*, (New York: Russell Sage Foundation).

Garfinkel, I. (1992b), 'Child Support Trends in the US', in (Weitzman and Maclean, 1992), 205-18.

Garfinkel, I. and McLanahan, S. S. (1986), *Single Mothers and their Children: A New American Dilemma*, (Washington DC: The Urban Institute Press).

Gauthier, A. H. (1991), 'Family Policies in Comparative Perspective', Discussion paper No. 5, Nuffield College (Oxford).

Girard, A. and Roussel, L. (1979), 'Fécondité et conjoncture: Une enquête d'opinion sur la politique démographique', *Population*, (3) 567-88.

Girard, A. and Roussel, L. (1981), 'Dimension de la famille, fécondité et politique démographique. Nouvelles données dans les pays de la Communauté économique européenne et interprétation', *Population*, (6) 1005-34.

Glass, D. (1934), 'Divorce in England and Wales', *The Sociological Review*, 26(3) 288-308.

Glass, D. (1940), *Population Policies and Movements in Europe*, (Oxford: Clarendon Press). ↳ check

Glass, D., ed. (1953), *Introduction to Malthus*, (London: Watts).

Grima, M. (1984), 'Le quotient familial sous le feu des critiques', *Informations Sociales*, (4).

Hall, R. (1993), 'Family structures', in Noin, D. and Woods, R., eds., *The Changing Population of Europe*, (Oxford: Blackwell), 100-26.

Halsey, A. H., ed. (1972), *Educational Priority: EPA Problems and Priorities*, (London: HMSO).

Handler, J. F. (1973), *The Coercive Social Worker: British Lessons for American Social Services*, (Chicago: Rand McNally).

Hantrais, L. (1994), 'La fécondité en France et au Royaume-Uni: les effets possibles de la politique familiale', *Population*, (4) 987-1016.

Harrison, M. (1992), 'Child Maintenance in Australia: The New Era', in (Weitzman and Maclean, 1992).

Hayashi, K. (1994), 'Changing Environment for Birthgiving and Childcare in Japan', in *Low Fertility in East and Southeast Asia: Issues and Policies*, (Seoul: KIHASA (Korea Institute for Health and Social Affairs)).

Henripin, J. (1985), 'Notes de lecture', *Cahiers Québécois de Démographie*, 14(2) 295-97.

Henripin, J. (1989), *Naitre ou ne pas être*, (Montreal: Institut québécois de la recherche sur la culture).

Henripin, J. and Gauthier, H. (1974), 'Canada', in (Berelson, 1974), 403-26.

Henshaw, S. K. (1990), 'Induced Abortion: A World Review', *Family Planning Perspectives*, 22(2) 76-89.

Henwood, M. and Wicks, M. (1988), *Family Policy Position Statement*, (London: Association of County Councils).

Herzlich, G. (1990), 'L'obsession démographique', *Le Monde*, 17 May.

Hoem, J. M. (1993), 'Public Policy as a Fuel of Fertility: Effects of Policy Reform on the Pace of Childbearing in Sweden in the 1980s', *Acta Sociologica*, 36(1) 19-32.

Independent (1994), 'Part-Time Schooling from Age Three Urged', 18 Mar.

INED (1976), *Natalité et politique démographique*, no. 76 in Travaux et documents, (Paris: Institut National d'Etudes Démographiques).

International Labour Office (1924), *Family Allowances: The Remuneration of Labour According to Need*, (Geneva: ILO).

International Labour Office (1932), *Women's Work Under Labour Law; A Survey of Protective Legislation*, (London: P.S. King & Son, Ltd.).

International Labour Office (1933), *International Survey of Social Services*, (London: P.S. King & Son, Ltd.).

International Labour Office (1936), *International Survey of Social Services, 1933*, vol. i, ii, (London: P.S. King & Son, Ltd.).

International Labour Office (1939), *The Law and Women's Work: A Contribution to the Study of the Status of Women*, (London: P.S. King & Son, Ltd.).

International Labour Office (1946), *The War and Women's Employment. The Experience of the United Kingdom and the United States*, (Montreal: ILO).

International Labour Office (1949), *Conventions and Recommendations 1919-1949*, (Geneva: ILO).

International Labour Office (1963), *Women Workers in a Changing World*, vol. i, (Geneva: ILO).

International Labour Office (1964), *Women Workers in a Changing World*, vol. ii, (Geneva: ILO).

International Labour Office (1988), *Work and Family: The Child Care Challenge*, vol. 7 of *Conditions of Work Digest*, (Geneva: ILO).

International Labour Office (various years), *Yearbook of Labour Statistics*, (Geneva: ILO).

Jenson, J. (1980), 'Gender and Reproduction: Or Babies and the State', *Studies in Political Economy*, 20 9-45.

Johnson, S. P. (1987), *World Population and the United Nations: Challenge and Response*, (Cambridge: Cambridge University Press).

Jonsson, L. (1974), 'Sweden', in (Berelson, 1974), 113-48.

Jordan, B. (1991), 'Want', *Social Policy and Administration*, 25(1) 14-26.

Judd, J. and Crequer, N. (1994), 'Major Drops Nursery Places Pledge', *Independent*, 15 Mar.

Kahn, E. (1930), *Der internationale Geburtenstreik*.

Kaim-Caudle, P. R. (1976), 'Poverty in Australia', *Journal of Social Policy*, 5(4) 401-06.

Kaiser, R. B. (1987), *The Encyclical that Never Was: The Story of the Commission on Population, Family and Birth, 1964-66*, (London: Sheld & Ward).

Kamerman, S. and Kahn, A., eds. (1978), *Government and Families in Fourteen Countries*, (New York: Columbia University Press).

Kamerman, S. B. and Kahn, A. J. (1981), *Child Care, Family Benefits and Working Parents*, (New York: Columbia University Press).

Kamerman, S. B. and Kahn, A. J. (1982), 'Income Transfers, Work and the Economic Well-Being of Children: A Comparative Study', *International Social Security Review*, (3) 345-82.

Kamerman, S. B. and Kahn, A. J. (1987), *Child Care: Facing the Hard Choice*, (New York: Auburn House).

Kamerman, S. B. and Kahn, A. J., eds. (1991), *Child Care, Parental Leave, and the Under 3s. Policy Innovation in Europe*, (New York: Auburn House).

Kamerman, S. B., Kahn, A. J., and Kingston, P. (1983), *Maternity Policies and Working Women*, (New York: Columbia University Press).

King, A. (1973), 'Ideas, Institutions and Policies of Governments: A Comparative Analysis. Parts I and II.', *British Journal of Political Science*, (3) 291-313.

Kirk, M. (1981), *Demographic and Social Change in Europe 1975-2000*, (Liverpool: Liverpool University Press).

Kirk, M., Livi-Bacci, M., and Szabady, E., eds. (1975), *Law and Fertility in Europe*, (Belgium: IUSSP and Ordina Ed.).

Korpi, W. (1978), *Working Class in Welfare Capitalism*, (London: Routledge & Kegan Paul).

Krebs, E. and Schwarz, M. (1978), 'Austria', in (Kamerman and Kahn, 1978), 185-216.

Labour Gazette (1923), 'The Family Wage System Abroad', *Labour Gazette*, Mar.

L'Actualité (1990), 'Disparaitre', 1 Nov.

Land, H. and Parker, R. (1978), 'United Kingdom', in (Kamerman and Kahn, 1978), 331-66.

Langstead, O. and Sommer, D. (1993), 'Denmark', in (Cochran, 1993), 143-66.

Laroque, P. (1985), *La politique familiale en France depuis 1945*, (Paris: Commissariat général au Plan).

Law, M. (1982), 'Maternity Provisions in Awards and Agreements', *Labour and Employment Gazette*, Mar.

League of Nations (1919), *Report on the Employment of Women and Children and the Berne Convention of 1906*, (London: Harrison & Sons).

League of Nations (1924), 'Charter of Child Welfare', *League of Nations Monthly Summary*, Sept.

Leaper, R. (1991), 'Introduction to the Beveridge Report', *Social Policy and Administration*, 25(1) 3–13.

Leeuw, F. L. (1986), 'On The Acceptability and Feasibility of Pronatalist Population Policy in the Netherlands', *European Journal of Population*, (2) 307–34.

Lewis, J. (1980), *The Politics of Motherhood: Child and Maternal Welfare in England, 1900–1979*, (London: Croom Helm).

Lewis, J. (1991), 'Models of Equality for Women: The Case of State Support for Children in Twentieth-Century Britain', in (Bock and Thane, 1991), 73–92.

Lewis, J. (1992), *Women in Britain since 1945: Women, Family, Work and the State in the Post-War Years*, (Oxford: Blackwell).

Lewis, J., ed. (1993), *Women and Social Policies in Europe: Work, Family and the State*, (Aldershot: Edward Elgar).

Leybourne, G. G. (1934), 'An Estimate of the Future Population of Great Britain', *The Sociological Review*, 26(2) 130–8.

Liebfried, S. (1992), 'Towards a European Welfare State? On Integrating Poverty Regimes into the European Community', in Ferge, Z. and Kolberg, J. E., eds., *Social Policy in a Changing Europe*, (Frankfurt: Campus Verlag).

Liljestrom, R. (1978), 'Sweden', in (Kamerman and Kahn, 1978), 19–48.

Lindgren, J. (1978), 'Finland', in (Kamerman and Kahn, 1978), 270–94.

Livi-Bacci, M. (1974), 'Italy', in (Berelson, 1974), 647–78.

Lohle-Tart, L. (1974), 'Belgium', in (Berelson, 1974), 193–224.

Louros, N. C., Danezis, J., and Trichopoulos, D. (1974), 'Greece', in (Berelson, 1974), 171–92.

MacNicol, J. (1992), 'Welfare, Wages, and the Family: Child Endowment in Comparative Perspective, 1900–50', in Cooter, R., ed., *In the Name of the Child: Health and Welfare, 1880–1940*, (London: Routledge).

Mathews, G. (1984), *Le choc démographique: Le déclin du Québec est-il inévitable?*, (Montreal: Boréal Express).

McIntosh, C. A. (1983), *Population Policy in Western Europe: Responses to Low Fertility in France, Sweden and West Germany*, (New York: M. E. Sharpe).

McLaren, A. (1990), *A History of Contraception: From Antiquity to the Present Day*, (Oxford: Blackwell).

McRae, S. (1991), *Maternity Rights in Britain: The PSI Report on the Experience of Women and Employers*, (London: Policy Studies Institute).

Meadows, D. H., Meadows, D. L., and Randers, J. (1992), *Beyond the Limits: Global Collapse or a Sustainable Future*, (London: Earthscan).

Meadows, D. H., Meadows, D. L., Randers, J., and Behrens III, W. W. (1972), *The Limits to Growth*, (London: Pan Books).

Mearns, A. (1883), *The Bitter Cry of Outcast London*, (London: James Clarke).

Mikkola, M. (1991), 'Finland: Supporting Parental Choice', in (Kamerman and Kahn, 1991), 145–70.

Moors, H. and Palomba, R., eds. (1991), *People, Policy and Perspectives*, (Italy: Consiglio Nazionale dell Ricerche).

Moss, P. (1990), *Childcare in the European Communities 1985–1990*, (Brussels: Commission of the European Communities).

Moynihan, D. (1965), *The Negro Family: The Case for National Action*, (Washington DC: US Department of Labor).

Muramatsu, M. and Kuroda, T. (1974), 'Japan', in (Berelson, 1974), 704–30.

Murdoch, A. (1992), 'Both Sides Claim Victory in Abortion Vote', *Independent*, 28 Nov.

Murphy, M. (1993), 'The Contraceptive Pill and Women's Employment as Factors in Fertility Changes in Britain 1968-80: A Challenge to the Conventional View', *Population Studies*, 47(2) 221-44.

Murray, C. (1984), *Losing Grounds: American Social Policy, 1950-80*, (US: Basic Books).

Myrdal, A. (1939), 'A Programme for Family Security in Sweden', *International Labour Review*, 39(6) 723-63.

Myrdal, A. (1947), *Nation and Family: The Swedish Experiment in Democratic Family and Population Policy*, (London: Kegan Paul, Trench, Trubner & Co, Ltd.).

Myrdal, A. and Myrdal, G. (1934), *Crisis in the Population Question (Kris i Befolkningsfragan)*, (Stockholm: Albert Fonnier Forlag).

Nash, M. (1991), 'Pronatalism and Motherhood in Franco's Spain', in (Bock and Thane, 1991).

Nasman, E. (1990), 'Models of Demographic Policy: the Swedish Case'.

Neidhardt, F. (1978), 'West Germany', in (Kamerman and Kahn, 1978), 217-38.

New Zealand, Royal Commission on Social Policy (1988), *The Report, iv. Social Perspectives*, (Wellington: Government Printing Office).

Newman, G. (1906), *Infant Mortality: A Social Problem*.

Newsholme, A. (1889), *The Elements of Vital Statistics*, (London: Swan Sonnenschein & Co.).

Norvez, A. (1990), *De la naissance à l'école: santé, modes de garde et préscolarité de la France contemporaine*, (Paris: Institut National D'Etudes Démographiques et Les Presses de l'Université de France).

Norway, Ministry of Foreign Affairs (1990), *Commissioner for children in Norway*, vol. Feb., (Oslo: Ministry of Foreign Affairs), Norway Information.

OECD (1978), *The Tax/Benefit Position of Selected Income Groups, 1972-1976*, (Paris: OECD).

OECD (1979), *The Tax/Benefit Position of a Typical Worker in OECD Member Countries, 1978*, (Paris: OECD), Also issues in 1979-1983.

OECD (1980), *The Tax/Benefit Position of Selected Income Groups, 1974-1978*, (Paris: OECD).

OECD (1986), *The Tax/Benefit Position of Production Workers, 1979-1984*, (Paris: OECD), Also subsequent annual issues.

OECD (1991), 'Childcare in the OECD countries', *Employment Outlook*, Jul. 123-51.

OECD (1993), *National Accounts: Main Aggregates Vol.1. 1960-1991*, (Paris: OECD).

OECD (various years), *Labour Force Statistics*, (Paris: OECD).

Offen, K. (1991), 'Body Politics: Women, Work and the Politics of Motherhood in France, 1920-1950', in (Bock and Thane, 1991), 138-59.

Ogden, P. E. and Huss, M. M. (1982), 'Demography and Pronatalism in France in the Nineteenth and Twentieth Centuries', *Journal of Historical Geography*, 8(3) 283-98.

Ohlander, A. S. (1991), 'The Invisible Child? The Struggle for a Social Democratic Family Policy in Sweden, 1900-1960s', in (Bock and Thane, 1991), 60-72.

Olmstead, P. P. (1989), 'United States', in (Olmstead and Weikart, 1989).

Olmstead, P. P. and Weikart, D. P., eds. (1989), *How Nations Serve Young Children: Profile of Child Care and Education in 14 Countries*, (Ypsilanti, Mich.: The High Scope Press).

Patterson, J. J. (1981), *America's Struggle Against Poverty 1900-1980*, (Cambridge, Mass.: Harvard University Press).

Penn, H. and Riley, K. A. (1992), *Managing Services for the Under Fives*, (London: Longman).

Pestel, E. (1989), *Beyond the Limits to Growth: A Report to the Club of Rome*, (New York: Universe Books).

Pienaar, J. (1990), 'Thatcher Criticizes All-Day Nurseries', *Independent*, 18 May.

Piepponen, P. (1974), 'Finland', in (Berelson, 1974), 98-112.

Pistillo, F. (1989), 'Italy', in (Olmstead and Weikart, 1989).

Popenoe, D. (1988), *Disturbing the Nest: Family Change and Decline in Modern Societies*, (New York: Aldine de Gruyter).

Population and Development Review (1984), 'The European Parliament on the need for promoting population growth', *Population and Development Review*, 10(3) 569-70.

Population et Avenir (1985), 'Avoir beaucoup d'enfants en 1985 . . .', *Population et Avenir*, (574) 14-15.

Preston, S. H. (1984), 'Children and the Elderly: Divergent Paths for America's dependents', *Demography*, 21(4) 435-57.

Prost, A. (1984), 'L'évolution de la politique familiale en France de 1938 à 1981', *Le mouvement social*, (129) 7-28.

Québec (1985), *Etude de l'impact culturel, social et économique des tendances démographiques actuelles sur l'avenir du Québec comme société distincte*, (Quebec: Gouvernement du Québec et Commission de la Culture).

Québec (1989), *Familles en tête: plan d'action en matière de politique familiale 1989-1991*, (Quebec: Gouvernement du Québec).

Quebec, Finance Ministry (1988), *Budget 1988-1989: Discours sur le budget et renseignements supplémentaires*, (Quebec: Gouvernement du Québec).

Quebec, Finance Ministry (1989), *Budget 1989-1990: Discours sur le budget et renseignements supplémentaires*, (Quebec: Gouvernement du Québec).

Quebec, Ministry of Health and Social Services (1987), *La Politique familiale: Enoncé des orientations et de la dynamique administrative*, (Quebec: Gouvernement du Québec).

Questiaux, N. and Fournier, J. (1978), 'France', in (Kamerman and Kahn, 1978), 117-82.

Rathbone, E. (1924), *The Disinherited Family: A Plea for the Endowment of the Family*, (London: E. Arnold & Co.).

Rees, A. M. (1985), *T. H. Marshall's Social Policy in the Twentieth Century*, (London: Hutchinson).

Ringen, S. (1987), *The Possibility of Politics: A Study in the Political Economy of the Welfare State*, (Oxford: Clarendon Press).

Room, G., ed. (1990), *New Poverty in the European Community*, (London: Macmillan).

Rowntree, S. (1901), *Poverty: A Study of Town Life*, (London: Macmillan).

Saraceno, C. (1991), 'Redefining Maternity and Paternity: Gender, Pronatalism and Social Policies in Fascist Italy', in (Bock and Thane, 1991), 196-212.

Sardon, J.-P. (1990), *Cohort Fertility in Member States of the Council of Europe*, (Strasbourg: Council of Europe).

Sauvy, A. (1979), 'Les conséquences du vieillessement de la population', in (Dumont et al., 1979), 61-118.

Sauvy, A. and Hirsch, A. (1990), *La terre et les hommes: Le monde où il va, le monde d'où il vient*, (Paris: Economica-Unesco).

Schneider, S. K. (1982), 'The Sequential Development of Social Programs in Eighteen Welfare States', *Comparative Social Research*, 5 195-219.

Schubnell, H. (1974), 'West Germany', in (Berelson, 1974), 679-703.

Schubnell, H. and Rupp, S. (1975), 'Federal German Republic', in (Kirk et al., 1975), 298-333.

Seip, A.-L. and Ibsen, H. (1991), 'Family Welfare, Which Policy? Norway's Road to Child Allowances', in (Bock and Thane, 1991), 40-59.

Shaver, S. and Bradshaw, J. (1993), *The Recognition of Wifely Labour by Welfare States*, Discussion paper no. 44, Social Policy Research Centre, (Kensington: The University of New South Wales, Australia).

Silburn, R. (1991), 'Beveridge and the War-Time consensus', *Social Policy and Administration*, 25(1) 80-86.

Simons, J. (1974), 'Great Britain', in (Berelson, 1974), 592-646.

Smith, G. (1987). 'The Plowden Report Twenty Years on. Whatever Happened to Educational Priorities Areas (EPAs)?'. Mimeo.

Spengler, J. J. (1978), *Facing Zero Population Growth: Reactions and Interpretations, Past and Present*, (Durham, N.C.: Duke University Press).

Spengler, J. J. (1979), *France Faces Depopulation: Postlude Edition, 1936-1976*, (Durham, N.C.: Duke University Press).

Spiegelman, M. (1968), *Introduction to Demography*, (Cambridge, Mass.: Harvard University Press).

Steiner, G. Y. (1976), *The Children's Cause*, (Washington DC: Brookings Institution).

Steiner, G. Y. (1981), *The Futility of Family Policy*, (Washington DC: Brookings Institution).

Stephens, P. (1990), 'Partial Rise in Child Benefit Planned', *Financial Times*, 24 Oct.

Stoehr, I. (1991), 'Housework and Motherhood: Debates and Policies in the Women's Movement in Imperial Germany and the Weimar Republic', in (Bock and Thane, 1991).

Stopes, M. (1919), *A Letter to Working Mothers*, (Leatherhead: M. Stopes).

Sundstrom, M. (1991), 'Sweden: Supporting Work, Family and Gender Equality', in (Kamerman and Kahn, 1991), 171-200.

Switzerland, Office fédérale des assurances sociales (1982), *La Politique familiale en Suisse*, (Berne: Office fédérale des assurances sociales).

Symonds, R. and Carder, M. (1973), *The United Nations and the Population Question: 1945-1970*, (London: Chatto and Windus).

Teitelbaum, M. S. and Winter, J. M. (1985), *The Fear of Population Decline*, (London: Academic Press).

Thane, P. (1989), 'Old-age: Burden or Benefit?', in Joshi, H., ed., *The Changing Population of Britain*, (Oxford: Blackwell), 56-71.

Thane, P. (1991), 'Visions of Gender in the Making of the British Welfare State: The Case of Women in the British Labour Party and Social Policy, 1906-1945', in (Bock and Thane, 1991), 93-118.

Thatcher, M. (1993), *The Downing Street Years*, (London: HarperCollins).

The Economist (1991), 'The Missing Children', 3 Aug.

The Economist (1992), 'The High and Middle Ground', 4 Jul.

The Family (1992), 'Family Matters Declares President Bush', *The Family (Bulletin of the International Year of the Family)*, (1).

Therborn, G. (1993), 'The Rights of Children Since the Constitution of Modern Childhood. A Comparative Study of Western Nations', in Moreno, L., ed., *Social Exchange and Welfare Development*, (Madrid: Consejo Superior de Investigaciones Científicas), 67-122.

Tietze, C. and Henshaw, S. K. (1986), *Induced Abortion: A World Review*, (New York: The Allen Guttmacher Institute), 6th edition.

Tietze, W., Rossbach, H.-G., and Ufermann, K. (1989), 'Germany', in (Olmstead and Weikart, 1989).

Titmuss, R. (1943), *Birth, Poverty, and Wealth*, (London: Hamilton).

Tomlinson, R., Huss, M. M., and Ogden, P. E. (1985), 'France in Peril: the French Fear of Denatality', *History Today*, 3(5) 24-31.

Trzcinski, E. and Alpert, W. T. (1994), 'Pregnancy and Parental Leave benefits in the United States and Canada: Judicial Decisions and Legislation', *The Journal of Human Resources*, 29(2) 535-54.

Tschudi, P. (1985), 'Swiss Social Policy Since 1950', in Girod, R., de Laubier, P., and Gladstone, A., eds., *Social Policy in Western Europe and the USA, 1950-1980*, (London: Macmillan).

UNICEF (1990), *First Call for Children: World Summit for Children*, (Geneva: UNICEF).

United Nations (1948), *Yearbook 1948-1949*, (New York: United Nations).

United Nations (1959), *Yearbook 1959*, (New York: United Nations).

United Nations (1975), *Report of the United Nations World Population Conference, 1974*, (Geneva: United Nations).

United Nations (1984), *Population of Japan*, no. 21 in Country monograph, (Bangkok: United Nations, Economic and Social Commission for Asia and the Pacific).

United Nations (1987-1990b), *World Population Policies*, no. 102 in Population Studies, (New York: United Nations), 3 vols.

United Nations (1989a), *France*, no. 24 in Politique de population, (New York: United Nations).

United Nations (1989b), *Trends in Population Policies*, no. 114 in Population Studies, (New York: United Nations).

United Nations (1990a), *World Population Monitoring, 1989*, no. 113 in Population Studies, (New York: United Nations).

United Nations (1991), *1994 International Year of the Family*, (Vienna: United Nations).

United Nations (various years), *Demographic Yearbook*, (New York: United Nations).

United Nations and Council of Europe (1994), *European Population Conference, ii, Proceedings*, (Geneva: United Nations and Council of Europe).

United States (1972), *Population and the American Future: The Report of the United States Commission on Population Growth and the American Future*, (Washington DC: Government Printing Office).

United States, Children's Bureau (1913), *Baby-Saving Campaigns: A Preliminary Report on What American Cities Are Doing to Prevent Infant Mortality*, (Washington DC: Government Printing Office).

United States, Social Security Administration (1940), *An Outline of Foreign Social Insurance and Assistance Laws*, (Washington DC: US Social Security Administration).

United States, Social Security Administration (various years), *Social Security Programmes Throughout the World*, (Washington DC: US Social Security Administration).

Unites States, Department of Labor (1990), *State Maternity/Paternal Leave Laws*, (Washington DC: Women's Bureau), Facts on Working Women, No. 90-1.

Usborne, D. (1993), 'Clinton Move Reopens Abortion Battle', *Independent*, 25 Jan.

Van Praag, P. (1974), 'Netherlands', in (Berelson, 1974), 294-318.

Ve Henriksen, H. and Hotter, H. (1978), 'Norway', in (Kamerman and Kahn, 1978), 49-67.

Vedel-Petersen, J. (1978), 'Denmark', in (Kamerman and Kahn, 1978), 295-328.

Walsh, B. M. (1974), 'Ireland', in (Berelson, 1974), 8-41.

Waterhouse, R. (1993), 'Singling Out the One-Parent Families', *Independent*, 10 Nov.

Weitzman, L. J. and Maclean, M., eds. (1992), *Economic Consequences of Divorce: The International Perspective*, (Oxford: Clarendon Press).

Wennemo, I. (1992), 'The Development of Family Policy: A Comparison of Family Benefits and Tax Reductions for Families in 18 OECD Countries', *Acta Sociologica*, 35(3) 201-17.

Wennemo, I. (1994), *Sharing the Costs of Children: Studies on the Development of Family Support in the OECD Countries*, (Stockholm: Swedish Institute for Social Research).

Westoff, C. F. (1973), 'The Commission on Population Growth and the American Future. Its Origins, Operations and Aftermath', *Population Index*, 39(4) 491-503.

Westoff, C. F. (1974), 'United States', in (Berelson, 1974), 731-59.

Westoff, C. F. and Ryder, N. B. (1977), 'The Predictive Validity of Reproductive Intentions', *Demography*, 14(4) 431-53.

Wilenski, H. L. (1975), *The Welfare State and Equality: Structural and Ideological Roots of Public Expenditures*, (Berkeley, Calif.: University of California Press).

Wisensale, S. K. (1994), 'Family Leave Policy in the United States', *Social Policy and Administration*, 28(2) 128-38.

Wood, L. (1991), 'Criticism Over Nursery Provision', *Financial Times*, 28 Oct.

Wuermeling, F. J., Tiede, G., and Croll, M. (1958), 'Familienpolitik, Gesprach uber den Familienlohn mit Beitragen von Bundesminister', *Sozialer Fortschriff*, 7(5) 108-14.

Zigler, E. F. and Frank, M. (1988), *The Parental Leave Crisis: Towards a National Policy*, (New Haven, Conn.: Yale University Press).

Index of names

Index of subjects